Approaches to
Teaching Lafayette's
The Princess of Clèves

Aproaches to Teaching
World Literature
Joseph Gibaldi, series editor

For a complete listing of titles,
see the last pages of this book.

Approaches to Teaching Lafayette's *The Princess of Clèves*

Edited by

Faith E. Beasley

and

Katharine Ann Jensen

The Modern Language Association of America
New York   1998

For information about obtaining permission to reprint material from
MLA book publications, send your request by mail (see address below),
e-mail (permissions@mla.org), or fax (212 477-9863).

Library of Congress Cataloging-in-Publication Data

Approaches to teaching Lafayette's The Princess of Clèves / edited by
Faith E. Beasley and Katharine Ann Jensen.
p.   cm. — (Approaches to teaching world literature ; 61)
Includes bibliographical references and index.
ISBN 0-87352-745-3 (cloth). — ISBN 0-87352-746-1 (paper)
1. La Fayette, Madame de (Marie-Madeleine Pioche de La Vergne),
1634–1693.   Princesse de Clèves.   2. La Fayette, Madame de (Marie-Madeleine
Pioche de La Vergne), 1634–1693—Study and teaching.
I. Beasley, Faith Evelyn.   II. Jensen, Katharine Ann, 1957– .
III. Series.
PQ1805.L5A737   1998
843'.4—dc21   98-35540

ISSN 1059-1133

Cover illustration of the paperback edition: Drawing of Nemours spying on the princess
at Coulommiers, by Jules Garnier, engraved by A. Lamotte, from Lafayette,
The Princess of Clèves, trans. Thomas Sergeant Perry
(Boston: Little, 1891), vol. 2, front.

Published by The Modern Language Association of America
10 Astor Place, New York, New York 10003-6981

CONTENTS

PREFACE TO THE SERIES

In *The Art of Teaching* Gilbert Highet wrote, "Bad teaching wastes a great deal of effort, and spoils many lives which might have been full of energy and happiness." All too many teachers have failed in their work, Highet argued, simply "because they have not thought about it." We hope that the Approaches to Teaching World Literature series, sponsored by the Modern Language Association's Publications Committee, will not only improve the craft—as well as the art—of teaching but also encourage serious and continuing discussion of the aims and methods of teaching literature.

The principal objective of the series is to collect within each volume different points of view on teaching a specific literary work, a literary tradition, or a writer widely taught at the undergraduate level. The preparation of each volume begins with a wide-ranging survey of instructors, thus enabling us to include in the volume the philosophies and approaches, thoughts and methods of scores of experienced teachers. The result is a sourcebook of material, information, and ideas on teaching the subject of the volume to undergraduates.

The series is intended to serve nonspecialists as well as specialists, inexperienced as well as experienced teachers, graduate students who wish to learn effective ways of teaching as well as senior professors who wish to compare their own approaches with the approaches of colleagues in other schools. Of course, no volume in the series can ever substitute for erudition, intelligence, creativity, and sensitivity in teaching. We hope merely that each book will point readers in useful directions; at most each will offer only a first step in the long journey to successful teaching.

Joseph Gibaldi
Series Editor

PREFACE TO THE VOLUME

Ever since its publication in 1678, the novel *La Princesse de Clèves*,[1] by Marie-Madeleine Pioche de la Vergne, comtesse de Lafayette, has provoked discussion and controversy. In fact, no other French novel has a longer or more complex history of critical commentary. Lafayette's elusive heroine has been applauded as the consummate strong individual who charts her own course in a society that values conformity; she has also been dismissed as a weakling who is defeated by society and takes refuge in solitude. Lafayette's first critic sums up this contradiction, stating, "C'est une femme incompréhensible que la Princesse de Clèves. C'est la prude la plus coquette et la coquette la plus prude que l'on ait jamais vue" ("The Princesse de Clèves is an incomprehensible woman. She is the most coquettish prude and the most prudish coquette anyone has ever seen") (Valincour, *Lettres* 272–73). Twentieth-century students and even their professors may well have the same reaction to the princess and to the work as a whole: this novel can appear incomprehensible. On the surface the society Lafayette depicts has little in common with today's. The sixteenth-century French history she so meticulously incorporated into the fabric of her novel is a stumbling block for today's readers. The heroine finds love and then rejects it. Incomprehensible? Perhaps. But we find ourselves, as critics, teachers, and students, drawn to this novel of contradictions, controversy, and passion. And our reactions, like those of the centuries of readers before us, are often passionate.

In the 1980s and 1990s the popularity of Lafayette's masterpiece has increased dramatically, in large part because of the insights of feminist criticism and the development of women's studies. No longer confined to French departments and their courses on classicism, *La Princesse de Clèves* can now be found in a variety of classroom settings: in great works courses; in comparative literature courses on, for example, the development of the novel or on the relation between history and fiction; in women's studies courses on the female literary tradition; or in theme-oriented courses such as mother and daughter relations, as well as in every imaginable French course. Numerous English translations have been produced, reflecting the novel's incorporation into the overall college curriculum. The ways of teaching this classic novel are as varied as the scholarly debate around it. Students and faculty members can all agree that this timeless work constantly yields new interpretations and insights.

The present volume seeks to inspire and guide those who are approaching *La Princesse de Clèves* for the first time as well as to renew the interest of those who have been teaching the novel for years. The various approaches reflect current interests as reported in the MLA survey conducted for this volume. Most of the essays are informed by the American feminist scholarship that has renewed interest in *La Princesse de Clèves*, as well as by the rich tradition of French, American, and British scholarship on Lafayette and her work. Throughout the volume we have striven to describe the social context that formed and influenced Lafayette and her reading public. Our goal is to give colleagues, especially those who are not specialists in French literature or history, a sense of seventeenth-century France and show how the novel is a product of this milieu, for these are the keys to making the novel comprehensible and indeed enjoyable to students.

The introduction and part 1 of this book situate *La Princesse de Clèves* within the history of the novel in France and explain how the author incorporates history itself. Respondents to the MLA survey universally identified the historical aspects of Lafayette's novel as posing problems for students. We have attempted to address these problems in our introduction. Our introductory materials also include a guide through the maze of editions, background studies, and scholarly criticism of *La Princesse de Clèves*. While we have tried to give readers an in-depth view of what studies exist and where to find them, we do not pretend to provide a comprehensive review of all the criticism associated with the novel. As the bibliography at the end of the volume attests, that would be a herculean task, if it were indeed possible at all. Teachers can delve more thoroughly into various topics depending on their particular interests and course offerings. We have privileged criticism and studies in English and English translations of French works over those that exist only in French because the supposed public for this volume is English-speaking and not necessarily French-speaking.

Part 2 comprises the essays offering various approaches to the novel, and it is divided into three sections. In the first section the authors analyze specific aspects of the society depicted in Lafayette's novel, as well as the history of *La Princesse de Clèves*. Essays in the second section explore some of the primary themes in *La Princesse de Clèves*. The last section offers ways to teach the novel in specific settings such as in a class on masterworks in translation. Throughout the volume the authors use the French edition of *La Princesse de Clèves* most frequently ordered by colleagues, the Garnier-Flammarion edition. In 1996 Garnier-Flammarion published a new edition, edited and with an introduction by Jean Mesnard. All references in French refer to this edition. Terence Cave's translation, published by Oxford University Press in 1992, provides all the English translations of the text. Unless otherwise indicated, translations of other French texts are the authors' own. Throughout the volume, quotations and references to the French edition precede quotations and references to the English translation, which appear parenthetically.

We wish to thank the participants in the MLA survey, as well as our colleagues and students at Dartmouth College and Louisiana State University for their advice and encouragement and for serving as willing guinea pigs. We also give special thanks to Gervais Reed for the Undergraduate Study Guide and to

Anant Sundaram and John Protevi for technological and emotional support. It was a pleasure to work with James Poniewozik, our meticulous copyeditor. Joseph Gibaldi has been the perfect editor. We are deeply grateful to him for his endless patience and enthusiasm for this project.

Faith E. Beasley
Katharine Ann Jensen

NOTE

[1]Throughout the book we use the lower case for all titles of nobility with the exception of *Prince* and *Princess*. Because of MLA style regarding the capitalization of French-language titles, we have opted for this practice in order to retain the uppercase *P* in the title of Lafayette's novel. No distinction in rank should be inferred from this styling of the terms.

Introduction: *La Princesse de Clèves* and the History of the French Novel

In French literary histories *La Princesse de Clèves* is typically heralded as the "first" "modern" novel. This means that it analyzes the principal characters' thoughts and feelings instead of focusing on actions and heroic deeds. In other words, it is a psychological novel, not an adventure story. While anyone reading *La Princesse de Clèves* today for the first time could easily appreciate that this sober text, laden with historical details, is not an adventure story, the ways in which it is a psychological novel and, more specifically, the psychology of its characters (notably its heroine) are perhaps less clear and definitely *not* modern. It is also true, however, that certain of Lafayette's contemporaries themselves found the historical details to be encumbering and the princess's psychology—her motivations for confessing her love for another man to her husband and for refusing ultimately to marry Nemours—to be perplexing. The frustration that twentieth- and seventeenth-century readers of *La Princesse de Clèves* seem, somewhat uncannily, to share can be explained in large measure by the complex status of the novel in seventeenth-century France. Twentieth-century readers are often too far removed from the social, historical, and literary issues that informed the novel's development, while seventeenth-century readers were at times too deeply invested in these issues to appreciate how Lafayette positioned herself.

Throughout the seventeenth and much of the eighteenth centuries, the novel was a beleaguered genre in France. The serious, legitimate, and literary genres were derived from classical Greek and Roman models: tragedy, history, epic poetry, and moral or scholarly letters. While the novel's lack of a classical model made it suspect in the eyes of its detractors, its status as fiction—as a make-believe story—made it morally reprehensible. Fiction was seen as a lie; and it was thought that if readers of fiction took those lies for the truth, then nothing but moral degeneracy could result. If a novelist created a character who acted unconventionally, outside socially sanctioned limits, and who escaped punishment for this deviance, then readers might be tempted not only to condone but also to imitate this behavior, thus wreaking havoc in society. Clearly, then, detractors of the novel per se, like critics of any particular novel, were often ideologically motivated in their attacks on genre, form, style, and content (see May, *Le dilemme*).

The general charges of illegitimacy and immorality leveled at the genre had a great deal to do with the novel's association with women (see DeJean, *Tender Geographies*; Danahy, "Le roman"). More women wrote and published novels in the seventeenth and eighteenth centuries in France than in any previous or subsequent century until the twentieth. Many conservative thinkers believed that women were decidedly inferior to men; close to nature, women were prey to their passions, and their unexalted minds were occupied with frivolous concerns. Thus whatever they might write would "naturally" be marred, insignificant, and morally bankrupt. In addition, women's unprecedented literary productivity scandalized certain men who believed that only men should write and publish literature. These men, many of whom belonged or aspired to belong to the state-sponsored, all-male Académie Française (founded in 1634), whose task it was to establish the rules of French language and literature and thereby ensure cultural uniformity in the service of absolutism, had a vested interest in denigrating women's writing. Indeed, two members of the *académie*, Nicolas Boileau and Jean-Baptiste du Trousset de Valincour, were among the most ardent detractors of the novel genre.

While the Académie Française, under the auspices of its patrons — first Cardinal Richelieu and then Louis XIV — functioned as the official linguistic and literary governing body, feminocentric salons, or *ruelles* as they were known in the seventeenth century, constituted unofficial, yet highly influential, centers of linguistic and literary activity (see Lougee; DeJean, *Tender Geographies*; and Harth, *Cartesian Women*). Indeed, most novels of the period, as well as works in many other genres such as theater, poetry, and letters, were written, revised, and discussed in the salons. Presided over by women, such as the marquise de Rambouillet, Madeleine de Scudéry, Mme du Plessis-Guénegaud, and Mme de Sablé, salons were gatherings of the social and literary elite. Members of the Académie Française were as welcome as the major writers of the day. Unlike the eighteenth-century salons, each of these seventeenth-century gatherings was dominated by a woman. Lafayette had her own salon, was very active in salon life, and through it became connected to many intellectuals and writers of the period. In the salons, through highly codified, verbally sophisticated interactions and writings, men and women sought to re-create themselves in an ideal image of worldliness. They wrote poetry, letters, and novels individually and collaboratively, reading their own and others' work out loud and exchanging critical commentaries. By mid-century, such literary criticism was taken very seriously by most writers. The salons in fact constituted a new path of legitimization for authors (see Viala).

La Princesse de Clèves was most likely the result of a collaborative effort among salon habitués, probably Lafayette, Jean Regnault de Segrais (writer of prose fiction), and the duc de la Rochefoucauld (author of lapidary social criticisms published as the *Maximes*). Like many novels of the period, *La Princesse de Clèves* was published anonymously. Novelists chose anonymity when publishing their works for various reasons. First, since the literary establishment considered the novel a suspect genre, anonymity protected the novelist from direct critical attack. More important, the aristocratic ideals of seventeenth-century social life, whether court life or salon life, designated the labor, money, and notoriety associated with writing for publication as distinctly unrefined. Thus in the interest of maintaining class status, aristocratic authors, male as well as female, would often choose public anonymity.

Class concerns also intersected with gender issues on the matter of public anonymity. While it was seen to be beneath an aristocrat's dignity to publish, it was a worse infraction for a woman to publish her writing, because that violated not only good manners but also prescriptions for feminine morality and respectability. Women, then, frequently chose to publish their works either anonymously or under a man's name — as Lafayette did when she published her novel *Zaïde, Histoire espagnole* (1669–71) under Segrais's name. Lafayette's friend Scudéry used her brother George's name for many of her works. But Scudéry acknowledged authorship of her novels in her private correspondence and in the more private space of the salons. The question of authorial anonymity is thus very complex during this period. While many authors, male and female, refused to sign their publications, the public, inside and outside the salon, often knew the true author of a work. Boileau, among others, certainly knew who was responsible for some of the most popular works in the genre he so detested. He attacks Scudéry and her novels unremittingly in several of his works ("Satire X"; "Les héros de roman"; "L'art poétique") (see DeJean, "Lafayette's Ellipses"). Although Lafayette always denied her authorship of *La Princesse de Clèves*, Mme de Sévigné (a close friend of Lafayette's, a salon *habituée*, and a prolific letter writer) states in a letter that she suspects Lafayette and La Rochefoucauld of composing a novel together. In Lafayette's *Histoire de Madame Henriette d'Angleterre* (*The Secret History of Henrietta, Princess of England*), Henriette characterizes the narrator–memoir writer as someone who is known as a good writer. Lafayette's playing with anonymity is typical of many authors.

Over the century, the novel responded to shifts in taste and in mentalities in the salons and in the larger society as it waged an ongoing struggle for literary and moral legitimacy. During the first half of the century, in a modulation of the Renaissance's exuberant humanism and before Louis XIV took the throne and began to divest the nobles of effective political power, writers of most genres tended to express an optimistic belief in the power of the human mind and spirit to conquer external and internal obstacles. This form of the French novel is often referred to in English as romance, although in the seventeenth century pastoral novels such as Honoré d'Urfé's *L'Astrée* and Scudéry's *romans héroïques* were most frequently grouped together under the rubric of *roman*, or novel. Pastoral and heroic novels both featured multiple adventures and misfortunes through which characters proved their courage and spiritual nobility (see Coulet, "Le roman"; Kathleen Wine's essay in this volume). Patterned after the epic, one of the genres considered true literature, these early novels began in medias res and through several volumes of intricately woven plots and subplots recounted heroic acts of famous figures from ancient history. In trying to legitimate the genre, these authors sought to establish rules, adapted from Aristotle and Horace, that would both connect the novel to the literary epic and distinguish the two from each other. According to these guidelines, the novel was to be written in a less elevated style than the epic, to focus on love rather than war, include more episodes, and to concentrate on believable rather than on fantastic or magical events. Like the epic, the novel would respect the unities of place, time, and action (subordinating secondary plots to the principal plot) and depict the noble acts of highborn characters to serve a morally edifying purpose. Respect for the unities, however, meant that novelists often violated the principle of plausibility; for example, in order to adhere to the unity of place, writers overused chance or coincidence to bring various characters together. Moreover, in accordance with their own and readers' taste, novelists in the first half of the century anachronistically endowed their noble heroes and heroines of ancient times with seventeenth-century French virtues of worldliness and linguistic sophistication.

Scudéry, the salonnière, was one of the most prolific and popular writers of heroic novels. In her novels (*Ibrahim ou L'illustre Bassa*, 1641; *Artamène ou Le grand Cyrus*, 1649–53; *Clélie, Histoire romaine*, 1654–60), she foregrounds conversations among her characters against the backdrop of wars, abductions, and shipwrecks that characterize the French novel of the first half of the seventeenth century, simultaneously reflecting and shaping the verbal art of the salon. The preferred topic of conversation in her novels is love. The ideal that emerges from these conversations is a spiritual love that transcends carnal desire and that is in harmony with honor and reason. The focus on the characters' emotions and thoughts not only distinguishes Scudéry's novels, especially her last, *Clélie*, from others that present more action and less analysis but also reflects a shift in readers' and writers' interests. Scudéry changed the direction of the French novel. With the last volume of *Artamène ou Le grand Cyrus*, Scudéry offered "a new model for French prose fiction, feminocentric in content and oblique in narrative stance" (DeJean, *Tender Geographies* 48).

Somewhat after mid-century we also find an increased concern with understanding the human heart and mind. The optimistic belief in the human spirit and its heroic possibilities that characterized the first part of the period gave way to a more skeptical view. First, Louis XIV's reign (1661–1715) forced the aristocracy into an unaccustomed position of dependence as he erected a system of privilege based on merit rather than title. Whereas historically monarchs had shared power and favor with the nobles, Louis XIV arrogated to himself and his chosen ministers and favorites, often not of noble blood, all efficacious power. He in fact curtailed the power of the nobles, an action often attributed to the revolt against the crown by many of the nobles in the civil war known as the Fronde while he was a minor and his mother, Anne d'Autriche, was regent. Under absolutism, court life was closely monitored, and there was a pervasive sense of constricted liberty and curtailed possibility. In addition, the religious current of Jansenism, which insisted on the essential corruption of the human being because of original sin and on one's essential powerlessness to gain salvation, became increasingly popular. Jansenism and its secular offshoots envisioned the human heart and mind as ultimately unknowable. Thus writers and thinkers become interested in penetrating as far as possible the murky depths of the heart and in revealing the reality hidden beneath surface appearance.

This notion of ulterior motivations—what we would call the unconscious—intersects with a developing conception of history. History as it was traditionally understood recorded public acts (such as battles, treaties, and marriages) of great personages (such as kings, queens, and military heroes). (See Beasley, *Revising*, for a summary of the concept of history and history's relation to the novel during this period.) This officially sanctioned history was known as "general history." In contrast, another form of history, referred to as "particular history," developed in which the writer, often not an official historian, examined the underlying causes and motivations of an event. The primary practitioners of this form of history are female memorialists such as Montpensier, Mme de Motteville, and Lafayette herself in her *Histoire de Madame Henriette d'Angleterre*. This perspective on history is also related to the novel as it emerged after approximately 1660. Readers' tastes turned to shorter, more realistic fictions, called *nouvelles*, *nouvelles historiques*, or *histoires galantes* (see Godenne for a study of the *nouvelle* as a genre and its influence on the novel). The public demanded that these shorter fictions be above all *vraisemblable*, a complex concept that combines accepted societal notions of plausibility and propriety. To conform to this criterion novelists wove their fictions so closely into well-known historical events, principally those involving the sixteenth-century French court, that it became virtually impossible to tell the difference between history and fiction. The resulting fiction resembled the particular history offered by female memorialists. This reliance on history is not only a distinguishing characteristic of the genre but actually a requirement. (By contrast, we recall, heroic novels had used ancient history as a backdrop or anachronistically.) Authors of these new fictions were often called *historiens*, and their works *histoires*, thus playing on the ambiguity of the French term *H/histoire*, which means both *history* and *story*. Writers of the *nouvelle* typically researched a period thoroughly and then created fictional motivations to fill in the gaps of general history. Moreover, by turning their attention to the hidden intentions underneath historically verifiable facts, writers of *nouvelles* and proponents of particular history included women in their stories as prime characters in behind-the-scenes actions and intrigues. In contrast, general history, with its emphasis on military and diplomatic feats, focused exclusively on men as actors; women, when they figured at all, were objects of alliances among men. Writers of *nouvelles* thus rewrote history by providing insight through fictional creation into the inner recesses of events, as they used general history to establish the plausibility of their fictions and to legitimate the genre.

La Princesse de Clèves is a *nouvelle historique*; Lafayette uses historical sources very precisely to create her fiction and revises her sources to emphasize women's influence on history (see Beasley, "Lafayette," for a detailed analysis of Lafayette's use of history; what follows is a very brief summary of this analysis). The opening pages of *La Princesse de Clèves*, with their lengthy description of the court of Henri II, confounded certain seventeenth-century critics no less than they do today's readers. Although seventeenth-century readers expected the *nouvelle historique* to incorporate history in order to comply with the rule of *vraisemblance*, Lafayette presents a far longer and more complicated historical introduction than other *nouvelle* authors do. She features twenty-seven portraits of notable personages in Henri II's court, thereby allying herself with the portrait genre so popular in the salons. (Lafayette herself had contributed a portrait of Sévigné for Montpensier's compendium of such literary portraits, *Recueil des portraits et éloges*). Furthermore, because portraits accentuate personalities rather than actions, by using them for her historical medium, Lafayette privileges the interpersonal relations in court dynamics. The events she depicts concern love intrigues and marriages or plans for them — events in which women are often dominant. These amorous affairs are further linked to politics. In this way, Lafayette posits not only that political actions are inextricably bound up with interpersonal relations and individual personalities but also that the most imposing personalities are female. From the historical introduction, the history of *La Princesse de Clèves* is dominated by Diane de Poitiers, the king's mistress, and by female members of the court in general.

Indeed, Diane de Poitiers's story is the subject of one of the internal narratives, or "digressions." Along with the introductory portraits, Lafayette's presentation of five internal narratives (Mary Stuart, 84–85 [17–18]; Diane de Poitiers, 93–99 [26–31]; Mme de Tournon, 113–22 [42–51]; Anne Boleyn, 133–35 [60–63]; the vidame de Chartres, 149–57; 166 [75–81; 90]) has distressed and bemused critics since the novel's first appearance. All but one of these narratives, that of Mme de Tournon, are carefully grounded in history. Lafayette's contemporaries saw these narratives as digressions reminiscent of those in the heroic novel. But Lafayette's internal narratives, as subsequent analyses have shown, are very different from such narratives in earlier novels such as Scudéry's. They are all intricately related to the Princesse de Clèves's story (see Coulet, "Les romans"). The internal narratives thematically illustrate the dangerous realities underlying the supposedly calm exterior of court relations, in particular the perils of love. Since the princess hears each of the internal narratives, they compose part of her education, teaching her that past entanglements still affect present alliances and warning her that politics, passions, jealousies, and animosities form a complex web in which she could easily become ensnared. Specifically, the story of Mme de Tournon prepares the princess's confession to her husband of her love for another man, and the lost love letter that opens the vidame de Chartres's story precipitates the heroine's first and fateful experience of jealousy. Thus Lafayette uses history not only to render her fiction *vraisemblable*, thus conforming to the principal law of the genre, but also and foremost as a pedagogical tool for the princess.

Moreover, in three of the internal narratives, Lafayette rewrites her histori-cal sources, further distinguishing *La Princesse de Clèves* from the earlier forms of the novel, which simply inserted history as backdrop. In the Diane de Poitiers narrative, for example, Lafayette reworks the historical writings of Pierre de Brantôme (1537–1614), which present the king's mistress as primar-ily that, a woman emotionally bound to a man; what political power she has is entirely contingent upon him. By contrast, Lafayette privileges Diane's politi-cal strategies over her emotional bond to the king and frees Diane from the tra-ditional forms of female power identified by Brantôme — youth and beauty. Lafayette stresses that even though Diane is no longer young or beautiful, she continues to dominate the king absolutely despite infidelities on both parts. Contradicting the princess's mother's lessons about female virtue, marital fi-delity, and circumspect behavior in society, Diane de Poitiers exemplifies a woman's autonomy in love and a woman's political power. Mary Stuart, mean-while, integrates the princess into court life — thus exemplifying women's in-fluence on one another — and recounts her own history as well as that of Anne Boleyn, through which women are shown to be the motivating forces behind general history, though Boleyn is also the victim of a ruthless husband. Finally, Lafayette embellishes the historically verifiable story of the vidame de Chartres by portraying in detail his role as confidant to the queen, Catherine de Médicis. Whereas Lafayette's source, Le Laboureur (*Mémoires de Michel de Castelnau*, 1660), attributes the vidame's disgrace to the cardinal de Lorraine as well as to the queen, Lafayette unequivocally places in the queen's hands the political power that destroys the vidame. Moreover, the queen determines the condi-tions for the relationship in the beginning — conditions that the vidame is un-able to meet. Lafayette thus depicts Catherine de Médicis, like Diane de Poitiers, as a woman who determines her fate and those of the people around her.

Lafayette's depiction of empowered female figures from sixteenth-century French history relates to her fictional creation of an extraordinary heroine, one who deviates from the paradoxically intertwined marital and adulterous norms of the court. This deviation, as well as the "feminist" inflection Lafayette gave to her rewriting of history, understandably confounded seventeenth-century readers who expected or wanted to find in this *nouvelle* an unequivocal rein-scription of male dominance and privilege and a reflection of the accepted norms of female comportment.

Lafayette's interest in revising history neither began nor ended with *La Princesse de Clèves*. In 1665 Lafayette's friend Henriette d'Angleterre, wife of Louis XIV's brother, Philippe d'Orléans, asked Lafayette's help in writing her memoirs. Lafayette and Henriette d'Angleterre worked on the *Histoire de Madame Henriette d'Angleterre* from 1665 to 1670, when the princess sud-denly died. Years later, Lafayette added an account of the princess's death and a preface, and the manuscript was published posthumously in 1720. Another posthumous history was published in 1731, *Mémoires de la cour de France*

(*Memoirs of the Court of France*), which Lafayette composed during the 1680s. Her other works included the *nouvelles La Princesse de Montpensier* (*The Princess of Montpensier*), 1662; *Zaïde, Histoire espagnole* (*Zayde: A Spanish History*) 1669–71; and the posthumously published *La Comtesse de Tende*, 1724.

La Princesse de Clèves is not only fascinating as a text; it is also invaluable for enlightening a twentieth-century public about the complex intersections in the seventeenth century between literature and society, novels and ideology, primarily because of the intense debate that erupted on the novel's publication. (For a description and analysis of this debate, see Elizabeth C. Goldsmith's piece in this volume.) The princess's confession to her husband of her love for another man was publicly debated in *Le mercure galant*, a popular newspaper, as readers tried to explain this implausible act in a novel that had to be *vraisemblable*. Two lengthy critical texts appeared shortly after the publication of *La Princesse de Clèves*, Valincour's *Lettres à Madame la marquise de °°° sur le sujet de* La Princesse de Clèves and Charnes's response to Valincour, *Conversations sur la critique de* La Princesse de Clèves. The debate itself merits attention for the light it sheds on the seventeenth-century concept of literature and literature's function in society, society's expectations for authors, the forms and purposes of literary criticism, and the social norms governing comportment in the pages of literature and in society as a whole. We have found that students are fascinated by the texts of the quarrel, for these texts allow them to experience the novel as its first readers did. For this reason, we have included some notable passages from the quarrel and their translations in an appendix.

Part One

MATERIALS

Editions

French Editions

La Princesse de Clèves was first published anonymously in Paris by Claude Barbin in 1678. The novel has been republished many times throughout the centuries. We present only those modern editions that survey participants and contributors to the volume use and recommend.

Modern editions are based on the original publication, which is kept in the Bibliothèque Nationale in Paris. The edition that most survey participants use and that we recommend is the readily available, good-quality, and reasonably inexpensive paperback edition edited by Jean Mesnard and published by Garnier-Flammarion (Paris) in 1996. The edition contains a lengthy introduction by Mesnard, as well as appendixes containing a discussion of Lafayette's anonymity, seventeenth-century criticism of the novel, and a useful glossary of terms and characters.

In 1969 Integral Editions (Cambridge, Mass.) published a paperback edition of *La Princesse de Clèves* edited by Alain Seznec. Seznec provides an extremely useful introduction, situating Lafayette's novel within sixteenth- and seventeenth-century French history and culture. He also provides notes explaining terms and textual references such as *dauphin, Madame,* and *les reines.* This edition, which has obvious advantages for teaching, is out of print.

Larousse has published an abridged version of the novel in its series Nouveaux classiques Larousse avec documentation thématique. Some teachers find this version useful for undergraduate introductory courses; moreover, the thematic documentation, the vocabulary, and the "Guide de lecture" ("Reading Guide"), which provides detailed questions for textual analysis, can be very beneficial for students and teachers.

Christian Biet and Pierre Ronzeaud have done an edition combining *La Princesse de Clèves* and *La Princesse de Montpensier* in one volume for the Magnard series Textes et contextes. In addition to the text, the edition contains numerous excerpts from critical works inserted throughout to explain or interpret key moments such as the confession scene.

La Princesse de Clèves has appeared in collected works by Lafayette. These editions are useful for those who teach more than one work by Lafayette or who want to make her other works available to students for outside reading. The most readily available and inexpensive collection is the paperback edition La Princesse de Clèves *et autres romans,* edited by Bernard Pingaud and published by Gallimard (Folio series). The collection includes excerpts from the anonymously written *Triomphe de l'indifférence* and from Lafayette's *Zaïde* (sometimes spelled *Zayde*) and *Histoire de Madame Henriette d'Angleterre,* as well as the entire *Histoire de la Princesse de Montpensier, La Princesse de Clèves,* and *La comtesse de Tende.* In addition to a general biographical and literary preface, this edition offers an appendix ("Dossier") that provides Lafayette's biography and detailed information about the publication history, subject matter, and themes of each of the works.

Another excellent collection of Lafayette's novels (*La Princesse de Montpensier, Zaïde, La Princesse de Clèves*, and *La comtesse de Tende*) edited by Emile Magne, was published by Garnier in 1961 and reprinted in 1970. Alain Niderst provides an informative literary-historical and critical introduction and a chronological biography of Lafayette, followed by a bibliography of primary and secondary sources (the latter bibliography is now somewhat dated). The texts are carefully annotated to provide historical references and explanations.

The most recent collection of Lafayette's works is her *Œuvres complètes*, a hardcover volume edited by Roger Duchêne and published by François Bourin (1990). In addition to Lafayette's novels and historical memoirs, this edition includes her "portraits" and her correspondence. Duchêne provides excellent explanatory annotations and informative historical and critical prefaces to each work.

English Translations

Until 1978 the only English translation available in an affordable edition for classroom use was the 1950 translation by Nancy Mitford (Penguin Classics). In 1978 Leonard Tancock revised Mitford's translation for Penguin. Then in 1992 Penguin published an entirely new translation by Robin Buss, which is now the version available in the Penguin Classics series. Professors can choose among this translation and many others, the most widely used of which are Walter Cobb's (Meridian Classics, NAL, 1989), Terence Cave's (Oxford UP, 1992), and John D. Lyons's edited and revised translation of Thomas Sargent Perry's 1892 translation (Norton Critical Editions, 1994).

The translations and the presentations of the text vary greatly. (See Beasley's contribution to this volume for some specific differences.) Professors who are accustomed to the Mitford translation will be surprised by the newer editions. Mitford translated the novel very loosely, leaving out entire passages that she may have considered unnecessary for the plot and impediments to the reader's enjoyment. Sometimes she even added sentences to clarify Lafayette's text. While the Mitford translation may read easily, it is not Lafayette's novel. Tancock, in contrast, provided a very literal translation. Buss's principal purpose seems to be to make the text accessible to a twentieth-century English-speaking reader. The style and vocabulary thus occasionally lack some of the elegance and nuances found in some of the other translations. The notes consist of historical clarification and identifications of Lafayette's historical sources; there is no reference, either in the notes or in the introduction, to the complexities of specific terms. The introduction is a survey of some of the main themes in *La Princesse de Clèves*. Buss offers her own interpretations of the novel but does not situate them critically. In fact, she does not refer to any critical studies, and there is no bibliography. Instead of opening the text to interpretation, the introduction often closes discussion by positing Buss's views as the "correct" reading. For example, Buss states that the historical introduction that has elicited so much commentary "is neither purely decorative nor a history lesson, but a morality" (4), thus guiding the reader's interpretation perhaps more than a professor would like. Buss provides some explanation of French vocabulary, in particular the historically specific term *amant* (5–6). In general, while the translation is sound, the edition provides little supplementary information.

Many of the professors surveyed for this volume have been using Cobb's translation. Cobb seems to have a specific objective: to make the novel as easy to read as possible for the twentieth-century English-speaking public. While he is faithful to the content of the novel, his prose does not transmit the style of the French, and it eliminates many of the original's complex nuances. He divides sentences to make them shorter, uses simpler vocabulary than other translators do, and often seems more intent on getting the plot across as quickly as possible than on faithfully translating Lafayette's prose exactly. Cobb frequently opts for colloquial expressions and vocabulary. Apart from providing brief historical notes regarding events in the novel, he makes little effort to bridge the gap between the seventeenth century and the twentieth. Many of these notes are confusing and include gratuitous remarks that are curiously sexist. For example, in his explanation of the treaty of Cateau-Cambrésis, Cobb states that Lafayette, "with a woman's heart" (163), considers the marriage provisions as the important terms of the agreement. His descriptions of Catherine de Médicis focus on her appearance. He disputes Lafayette's claim that she was beautiful, stressing that the historian André Maurois notes that she was ugly. Cobb also states that Catherine "redeemed herself by presenting France with an abundance of royal progeny" (164). Cobb's notes are in striking contrast to Nancy K. Miller's excellent feminist introduction, in which she focuses on the princess's often extraordinary actions in the novel and the reception of this exceptional heroine by the public—both past and present. Miller underscores many of the novel's primary themes, such as maternal pedagogy, and prepares readers for Lafayette's universe. The bibliography at the end of the edition includes only the principal articles that informed the introduction and is not a general overview of studies of the novel.

Terence Cave has produced an outstanding translation that is as affordable as Buss's and Cobb's, and many scholars find it the best. Cave's elegant prose captures the essence of seventeenth-century French without being archaic. Because he remains faithful to the French and sensitive to all its nuances and connotations, including those that are historically specific, his text does not deny interpretations founded on rhetorical analyses of the French. One example of this preservation of seventeenth-century cultural and historical resonances is found in the passage in which the reine dauphine requests the princess to return the letter the vidame lost at the reine dauphine's "coucher." Cave retains *coucher*—"come to my *coucher* this evening to return it"—and adds a note explaining that this was "the last royal reception of the day" (70). He adds that Lafayette's choice of the term underscores how the reine dauphine is constantly exposed to the public eye. Other translations eliminate this reference. Cobb translates the reine dauphine as saying, "[B]ring it back to me this evening, to my bedroom" (71). Buss says, "Come to me this evening when I retire" (89), and Lyons similarly writes, "[C]ome to me this evening and bring it back to me" (49). In choosing *coucher* Cave maintains the specific French context and the complexities of the public and private spheres that are central to the novel as a whole.

Here and throughout, Cave notes particular vocabulary words that had certain connotations in the seventeenth century and might be misinterpreted by a twentieth-century audience. He also provides notes that explain Lafayette's many specific historical references. For those who like to compare with the French text, Cave, unlike other translators, respects Lafayette's paragraph divisions, making it simpler to find the equivalent passage in the French text. Cave's introduction provides an excellent and informative contextualization of the novel that is firmly grounded in both recent and classic studies, as evidenced by the extremely useful selected bibliography. Students and professors alike can learn a lot about the literary history of the novel, including the debates following its publication, and the overall cultural context of the seventeenth century that produced the novel. For the most part, Cave avoids imposing his own views, choosing instead to highlight particularities of the text and a variety of interpretations. The final section of the introduction is devoted to "language, style and the problems of translation" (xxvi). Cave gives English readers a sense of the complexity of Lafayette's prose and gives them insight into his translation of difficult terms such as *repos*. Here and throughout the introduction and the translation, Cave strives to re-create the experience seventeenth-century readers had when reading *La Princesse de Clèves*. There is an excellent chronology that places Lafayette's life and works in the context of seventeenth-century literary landmarks. In addition to the complete notes, there is a glossary of names that concisely identifies all the historical figures in and around events incorporated into the novel. This edition has the added advantage of including translations of Lafayette's first novel, *La Princesse de Montpensier*, and *La comtesse de Tende*, with explanatory notes.

The purpose of any Norton Critical Edition is to provide a text and a critical and historical apparatus with which to approach it. It is the supplementary materials that distinguish the edition edited by Lyons from the others and that constitute its principal merits. As Lyons explains in his preface, the translation was actually done by Thomas Sergeant Perry in 1892 and published later as part of the *Norton Anthology of World Literature*, with historical annotations by Patricia Meyer Spacks. Lyons has revised the translation by correcting some "infelicities of translation" and by "up-dating" the vocabulary but has kept Spacks's notes (vii). This translation is relatively good and fairly accurate, and it reads easily on the whole. Because of the effort to preserve the "old text" flavor,

however, some sentences seem archaic and awkward. The footnotes explain titles and historical events and personages, as well as some vocabulary. A short
introduction provides the novel's literary and cultural context. In the afterword,
Lyons continues in this vein, showing how *La Princesse de Clèves* is "a testimony to some of the major intellectual and cultural changes of the early modern period" (109), especially those regarding the concept of history and its use
in fiction. The afterword is followed by excerpts from contemporary reactions,
some of which Lyons translates for the first time. The excerpts include translations of passages from Valincour's and Charnes's contributions to the quarrel.
The selected examples of twentieth-century criticism illustrate a variety of critical perspectives on the novel. Regrettably Nancy K. Miller's ("Emphasis"),
Marianne Hirsch's, and Lyons's ("Narration") own frequently cited essays are
not included. The bibliography is extensive, and it complements the critical
texts. There is also a glossary of characters similar to the glossary in Cave.

The Instructor's Library

As the contributors to this collection composed their essays, most asked for re-
assurance. "This is supposed to be pedagogical, isn't it? I don't have to come up
with a new interpretation, do I?" they frequently wondered. One contributor
remarked that she was pleased she had finally been able to produce something
she liked. "I have had the worst case of 'anxiety of influence' ever for this project. Everyone I admire and all my friends have written something on *La
Princesse de Clèves*!" It is true that the amount of scholarship on this novel is
daunting. The bibliography at the end of this volume indicates the various
strains of criticism, but it is by no means exhaustive. Below we survey the principal topics to which critics have been drawn. The essays in the volume ex-
pound on these issues and describe more precisely the criticism related to each
subject.

Background Studies

To identify the innovations Lafayette brought to the genre of the *nouvelle historique,* it is important to understand the literary context of the mid–seventeenth century. Surveys such as Henri Coulet's *Le roman jusqu'à la révolution,*
Antoine Adam's *Histoire de la littérature française au XVIIe siècle,* and English
Showalter's *The Evolution of the French Novel, 1641–1782* provide excellent
analyses of the development of the genre. Roger Francillon's classic study
L'œuvre romanesque de Mme de Lafayette focuses specifically on Lafayette's
works within the literary context of her day, as does Pierre Malandain's concise
and useful *Madame de Lafayette:* La Princesse de Clèves. Francillon's work

demonstrates how *La Princesse de Clèves* fits within Lafayette's corpus. Micheline Cuénin's *Roman et société sous Louis XIV: Mme de Villedieu* is not simply an analysis of one of Lafayette's contemporaries, Villedieu. It is also a good presentation of the overall literary milieu. Two other critical works, Joan DeJean's *Tender Geographies: Women and the Origins of the Novel in France* and Faith E. Beasley's *Revising Memory: Women's Fiction and Memoirs in Seventeenth-Century France*, situate Lafayette and *La Princesse de Clèves* in the general literary and cultural context, especially with respect to women writers, and offer analyses of the trends of literary production during the ancien régime, primarily but not exclusively from a feminist perspective.

The distant and foreign culture depicted in *La Princesse de Clèves* often makes nonspecialists hesitant to teach the novel. There are, however, many fascinating studies that enlighten this enigmatic past. Court society and its conventions and beliefs are of course at the foundation of the novel. Norbert Elias's *La société de cour*, available in translation as *The Court Society*, provides useful keys to understanding this culture, in particular its use of etiquette. W. H. Lewis's *The Splendid Century* offers an overview, albeit at times somewhat oversimplified, of Louis XIV's reign, and it can be recommended to undergraduates. Erica Harth's *Ideology and Culture in Seventeenth-Century France* is a much more in-depth analysis of the workings of this celebrated century. Harth's work continues to be one of the most useful and comprehensive studies of the period. The social conventions and constructions of *honnêteté* are examined by Domna C. Stanton in her study *The Aristocrat as Art*. There are many studies by historians and literary critics in addition to DeJean's and Beasley's that highlight women's roles in politics, literature, and culture as a whole during this time. Dorothy Backer's *Precious Women* and Carolyn Lougee's *Le Paradis des Femmes: Women, Salons, and Social Stratification in Seventeenth-Century France* are ground-breaking works that delve into the world of the *précieuses* and the influential salons, although Backer's often mocking and satirical tone renders her work somewhat dated in the light of current historians' and literary critics' reevaluation of the salons and their importance. More recently, Elizabeth Goldsmith has analyzed the hallmark of the salon, conversation, in *Exclusive Conversations*, and Harth has focused on one important topic of conversation, Cartesian philosophy, in *Cartesian Women*. Ian Maclean's *Woman Triumphant: Feminism in French Literature, 1610–1652* remains a classic for the history of women during the first half of the century. Especially interesting is his discussion of marriage. Also useful is Natalie Zemon Davis and Arlette Farge's *Histoire des femmes en Occident*, volume 3, for the general position of women in France during the period. Harvard University Press has published an English translation of the series. For information specifically on Lafayette, one can still consult with profit and pleasure André Beaunier's works *La jeunesse de Mme de Lafayette* and *L'amie de la Rochefoucauld*. Some more-recent biographies of Lafayette include Roger Duchêne's biography, *Mme de La Fayette, la romancière aux cent bras*, Stirling Haig's

Mme de Lafayette in the Twayne series, Bernard Pingaud's *Mme de Lafayette par elle-même*, and Faith E. Beasley's entry on Lafayette in *French Women Writers: A Bio-bibliographical Source Book* ("Marie-Madeleine").

Critical Studies

When one turns to criticism devoted exclusively to *La Princesse de Clèves*, one discovers that almost every sentence has provoked some commentary. In fact, the novel's first critics, Valincour and Charnes, go through the work almost line by line. For winding through the maze of Lafayette criticism starting with these two seventeenth-century critics, Maurice Laugaa's *Lectures de Madame de Lafayette* is a gift. Laugaa provides a synthesized compendium of the seventeenth-century critical works for those who do not have time to read them in their entirety, and he extends his review beyond the seventeenth century to reveal the debates and interpretations sparked by the novel over a few hundred years. In "Lafayette's Ellipses: The Privileges of Anonymity" DeJean expands the discussion of the seventeenth-century quarrel and the novel's reception in general to address Lafayette's complex status as a female author and the narrative strategies Lafayette uses to subvert the expectations of her contemporaries. DeJean argues that Lafayette conceived of her anonymity as a powerful and liberating position. In *Public et littérature* Hélène Merlin offers a good overview of the novel's reception and shows how the quarrel reveals that the literary public was developing new ways of reading. She situates the quarrel in the context of other seventeenth-century literary debates, namely that surrounding *Le Cid* and the more general quarrel of the ancients and moderns. For those who want to delve into this fascinating literary milieu more deeply, Charles Williams's *Valincour* should be required reading. Through his study of Lafayette's primary critic, Williams depicts the various milieus that composed this complex society, in particular Louis XIV's court, the French Academy, the worldly milieu, and the more traditional military-oriented society of the noble courtiers. In the early 1990s three collections of essays on the novel appeared. The journal *Littératures classiques* devoted a supplement in 1990 to *La Princesse de Clèves* and *La Princesse de Montpensier*. In 1993 *Dix-septième siècle* published an issue on Mme de Lafayette in general (*Autour*). Both these volumes have interesting essays and reveal current trends in Lafayette scholarship. The collection *An Inimitable Example: The Case for* The Princesse de Clèves, edited by Patrick Henry, also has a number of interesting new essays.

The structure of the novel has elicited much critical commentary. Many critics have sought to explain Lafayette's seemingly outdated use of internal narratives, which are considered a hallmark of the heroic novel. J. W. Scott's " 'Digressions' of *The Princesse de Clèves*" shows how each narrative is intricately related to the main story, which is not true of such narratives in the heroic novel. In "Narration, Interpretation and Paradox: *La Princesse de Clèves*," Lyons also examines the internal narratives and their effect on the princess and shows how "the novel makes of its protagonist a figure in a struggle . . . between differing conceptions of the relationship between language and human conduct." He goes on to argue that the princess's role is "implicated in the generic transformation at the confluence of *nouvelle* and *roman*" (383), and he uses Lafayette's novel *Zaïde* to discuss this "generic transformation." In *"La Princesse de Clèves* et son unité," Marie-Odile Sweetser finds the unity of the disparate aspects of the novel in the creation of an individual, the princess, within a society that attempts to absorb her and make her conform to its expectations. Susan Tiefenbrun's *A Structural Stylistic Analysis of* La Princesse de Clèves offers a systematic study of the structure of the novel in general.

While the seventeenth-century debate reveals that Lafayette subverted some expectations, she also seemingly conformed to one rule of the genre when she composed *La Princesse de Clèves*, namely, that the work should be grounded in history in order to appear plausible—*vraisemblable*. Twentieth-century readers balk at this history in *La Princesse de Clèves*; thus many critical works are devoted to analyzing Lafayette's use and construction of history and to discussing the complex concept of *vraisemblance*. Henri Chamard and Gustave Rudler produced a series of articles that are still considered definitive, in which they identify Lafayette's historical sources. They place the sources alongside Lafayette's text, which allows one to see Lafayette's revisions as well as her often meticulous conformity to her sources. In *Order in the Court* Laurence Gregorio shows how history "takes on meaning, and generates meaning" in a variety of ways in the novel (111). Gregorio analyzes how history informs *vraisemblance*, thematic motif, and narrative technique and how Lafayette uses it to organize and structure the novel. In an interesting article, "L'écriture de l'histoire dans *La Princesse de Clèves*," Pierre Malandain situates Lafayette's novel in the context of the shift from an aristocratic to a bourgeois ideology that dictates individual and social behavior. In "A Tale of Two Henry's" Louise Horowitz offers a fascinating analysis of the historical context of the novel and the literary context of Corneille's *Le Cid* and Honoré d'Urfé's *L'Astrée* to explain the princess's refusal. Donna Kuizenga argues that the novel "offers a thoroughgoing examination of the impact of patriarchy's power on human relationships" (*"Princesse"* 76). Barbara Jones Guetti considers Lafayette's overall relation to the genre of history in her fictions and advances that Lafayette appropriates the official modes of discourse that silenced and delegitimized women. In *Revising Memory* Beasley discusses the connection between history and fiction during the period and argues that Lafayette revised the history she chose in order to advance an alternative notion of plausible (*vraisemblable*) female behavior for her protagonist. Beasley's argument concerning *vraisemblance* owes much to Gerard Genette's now-classic work, "Vraisemblance et motivation," which fortunately is available in English in the Norton Critical Edition. Genette shows how *vraisemblance* is defined by readers' expectations not only of plausibility but also of propriety. In "Emphasis Added" Miller extends this analysis to women's texts in general, and to *La Princesse de Clèves* in particular, to discuss the relationship among women, women writers, their plots, and *vraisemblance*. *Vraisemblance* is also the focus of Dalia Judovitz's far-reaching "The Aesthetics of Implausibility," in which Judovitz shows "how the novel's critique of language and its signifying capabilities transform novelistic reality and its representation of human conduct." In her view Lafayette offers a new aesthetics, in which the princess's "self-produced fiction . . . comes to dominate not only the world of the novel, but the real as well, since it announces a redefinition of the aesthetic norms of the period" (1038).

If *La Princesse de Clèves* is considered by many to be "the first psychological novel," it is due in large part to Lafayette's use of the narrator and her innovative interior monologues. Critics have long been drawn to the subject of narrative and authorial voice. Kuizenga's *Narrative Strategies in* La Princesse de Clèves provides an in-depth analysis of the novel focusing on Lafayette's use of perspective in her narrative strategy. Kuizenga offers careful readings in particular of the inscription of the reader and the roles of the narrator. Another study in this vein is DeJean's "Lafayette's Ellipses," in which the critic reveals how Lafayette's voice is inscribed in the text despite the veil of anonymity. In *L'œuvre romanesque de Mme de Lafayette* Francillon argues that Lafayette offers a new kind of narrator for the period, one who is both a psychologist and a memorialist. It is this complex narrative stance, in which a narrator reveals his or her intimate knowledge of the characters while maintaining the more traditional position of the omniscient *H/historien*, that marks Lafayette's text as original. In an equally classic study Jean Rousset argues that Lafayette's innovation lies in part in having the reader see events through the princess's eyes and not simply the narrator's (*Forme*).

When one turns from the novel's composition to its content, one becomes even more deluged by the tidal wave of Lafayette criticism. Critics from Valincour on have been compelled to analyze the actions of the princess, particularly the confession scene and her final rejection of Nemours, although scenes such as the reverie in front of Nemours's portrait, the princess's reaction to the lost letter and the rewriting of the letter by the princess and Nemours, and the stolen portrait have also provoked numerous analyses. The ending remains enigmatic. Some view the princess's retreat from society as a renunciation of passion and happiness, while others advance a more positive interpretation. The latter view, according to which the princess chooses to leave the court and Nemours in order to remain in control of her own emotions and story, is common among feminist critics. In "Emphasis Added" Miller is the first critic to argue that in *La Princesse de Clèves* Lafayette creates an alternative plot for women, thus challenging both literary and societal expectations for women's behavior. The concept of *vraisemblance* is also the focus of Inge Wimmers's analysis of the novel in *Poetics of Reading: Approaches to the Novel*. In "Aristocratic Ethos and

Ideological Codes" Ralph Albanese, Jr., argues that the princess's refusal of Nemours is "a profoundly class-oriented decision; she seeks to preserve intact a traditional class identity" (103).

The psychological nature of the text and the princess's extraordinary actions invite a psychoanalytic approach, such as Mitchell Greenberg's in *Subjectivity and Subjugation in Seventeenth-Century French Drama and Prose: The Family Romance of French Classicism*. Greenberg focuses on the construction of the princess's subjectivity and places Lafayette's work within the context of French classicism in general. Michel Butor accepts what almost seems to be a visionary invitation on Lafayette's part to do a psychoanalytic, specifically Freudian, analysis of the reverie scene, in which the princess dreamily winds ribbons around Nemours's cane. In her psychoanalytic reading Danielle Haase-Dubosc focuses on the confession scene to show how the princess's actions lead her to death.

Analyses of the princess's behavior have emphasized how the princess relates to her social milieu and how the novel is informed by Lafayette's seventeenth-century society. While most studies, in fact, deal at least tangentially with this overriding issue, some critics offer particularly focused analyses. For example, Christian Biet examines marriage in sixteenth- and seventeenth-century France, specifically how passionate love is rejected from the institution, to show the way that much of the plot of *La Princesse de Clèves* revolves around this question. Michael Danahy's work on the composition of the court in "Social, Sexual and Human Spaces in *La Princesse de Clèves*" is especially intriguing, in particular his analysis of the movements of men and women in various settings of the novel. In contrast to critics such as Beasley, who views Lafayette as highlighting female power, Danahy argues that men dominate Lafayette's construction of the court. He argues that the confession and refusal of Nemours arise from the princess's desire to "free herself from the abusive aspects of the monosexual spatial patterning that underlies the novel" (220). The current interest in women writers and women's issues has led many critics to focus on the female characters. For example, in "Mme de Chartres, personnage-clé de *La Princesse de Clèves*," Georges Forestier has turned the lens on Mme de Chartres as a central character.

In addition to specific actions of the princess, certain themes have attracted critical attention. For example, many critics, especially given the renewed interest brought to the novel by the field of women's studies, have been drawn to the mother-daughter relationship Lafayette creates, in particular to Mme de Chartres's lessons to her daughter. The two most frequently cited such studies are Marianne Hirsch's "A Mother's Discourse: Incorporation and Repetition in *La Princesse de Clèves*" and Peggy Kamuf's chapter in her *Fictions of Feminine Desire* "A Mother's Will: *The Princess of Clèves*."

A dominant theme in the novel is the complex notion of *repos*, or peace of mind. Stanton's "The Ideal of *Repos* in Seventeenth-Century French Literature" situates the princess's search for this personal ideal in its contemporary literary context. Critics have debated the princess's search for *repos* and her strong sense of duty. The verdict is still out on what really motivates her actions. Other themes such as the gaze and love have also generated hundreds of pages of commentary.

Since Lafayette seemingly offers an unattainable, "inimitable" model in her protagonist, many critics such as Lyons (*Exemplum: The Rhetoric of Example in Early Modern France and Italy*) and Harriet Stone ("Exemplary Teaching in *La Princesse de Clèves*") have delved into the construction and conception of aspects of exemplarity in the novel. In a similar vein, the moral quality of the novel has attracted commentary such as Helen Kaps's *Moral Perspective in* La Princesse de Clèves and Michael G. Paulsen's *A Critical Analysis of de La Fayette's* La Princesse de Clèves *as a Royal Exemplary Novel.*

Aids to Teaching

In their essays in this volume, Éva Pósfay and Julia Douthwaite identify many visual aids of use in the classroom. Students often enjoy seeing artistic renditions of the château of Coulommiers, for example. There have also been two film versions of the novel, neither of which was mentioned frequently by survey participants. Michèle Morgan has narrated excerpts from *La Princesse de Clèves* in a cassette produced by Des Femmes. Many teachers incorporate some of Valincour and Charnes's quarrel into their discussions of the novel; see appendix 1 for a selection of passages.

NOTE

Except where stated otherwise, French-language quotations from *La Princesse de Clèves* in this volume are taken from the Garnier-Flammarion edition, edited by Jean Mesnard, and English-language quotations are taken from the Terence Cave translation.

Part Two

APPROACHES

Introduction

In answering the MLA survey about teaching *La Princesse de Clèves*, respondents consistently remarked that students are most receptive to the issues and themes with which they can identify. These issues include difficulties in heterosexual relationships of love or desire, the need to keep up appearances, the restricted position of women in society, problems in mother-daughter relations, and (especially for students at small residential colleges) the insularity of the social circles. In addition, as we noted in the preface, students have difficulty understanding the historical aspects of the novel, especially in the opening pages. We try to respond to this problem in our introduction to the volume. Survey respondents also indicated that students have a hard time understanding court life, the status of marriage (and adultery) in the aristocracy of sixteenth- and seventeenth-century France, the princess's refusal to marry the man she loves at the novel's end, and key concepts tied to the seventeenth-century vocabulary such as *aveu* (confession in the form of a fidelity oath) and *repos* (tranquillity, peace of mind). Besides noting these areas of recurrent student difficulty, survey respondents voiced a desire for essays that would make the novel more accessible to English speakers, present background in cultural history, and incorporate feminist perspectives.

The essays in this section are designed to respond to these student and teacher needs. In the following synopses, we describe each essay briefly to help the reader locate which essays he or she might find most beneficial for specific situations. There is, necessarily, some overlap among essays since certain scenes (such as the princess's confession to her husband of her love for another man and her reverie in the pavilion at Coulommiers), themes (mother-daughter relations, passion versus marriage), and cultural concepts (virtue, tranquillity, plausibility) are key to understanding the novel and can be approached from numerous perspectives, leading to a wide range of interpretations.

Mirroring Society: La Princesse de Clèves *in Context*

In "Lafayette's First Readers: The Quarrel of *La Princesse de Clèves*," Elizabeth C. Goldsmith presents the critical conflicts that arose on the publication of Lafayette's controversial novel. She demonstrates how criticism in seventeenth-century France was a collective and social activity, involving and eliciting debate among many members of the literate public. This particular literary debate attests to both Lafayette's innovations in the nascent genre of the historical novel and the reading public's attempt to invent a way to read this new form.

Jansenism exerted much power over seventeenth-century French society. Louis MacKenzie explains this important religious current and how it resonates in Lafayette's novel. He argues that through a Jansenist optic the court becomes a metaphor for the world and the princess's desire, internalized from her mother's teachings, to flee Nemours and the court becomes a more fundamental rejection of the turmoil and vanity of human values. In the end her unprecedented virtue earns her the prize of moral exemplarity.

The seventeenth century in France was a period of intense social movement and volatility, both because of and despite the Sun King. Harriet Stone studies court life in *La Princesse de Clèves* as commerce, reflecting the seventeenth-century shift in France from an aristocratic to a precapitalist economy. She shows how portraits, letters, gossip, and men and women themselves in the novel are commodities of exchange. The princess, however, subverts such commodification and makes herself and her desire nonmarketable — and unrepresentable.

When one thinks of seventeenth-century France, one cannot but envision the strict social decorum at court and in society as a whole. Marie-Paule Laden analyzes virtue and civility as inscribed in the novel. Through a careful study of language, including the semantic connotations of *devoir* ("duty") and *repos*, Laden argues that the princess turns away from the courtly, collective sociability that Nemours represents toward an individual, solitary duty to self.

While many recent critics have been drawn to the feminocentric if not feminist elements in Lafayette's novel, few have focused on the construction of masculinity. Lewis C. Seifert shows how the two are necessarily intertwined. He addresses the difficulty students have understanding female heroism in *La Princesse de Clèves*. He links this difficulty to critics' tendency to overlook the question of masculinity in the novel. By analyzing how the court constructs gender identities, Seifert shows how men's social and sexual dominance depends on their knowledge about the female love object — and their controlled exchange of this knowledge. In his view the princess disrupts this crucial element of masculinity because she makes it impossible for her husband and Nemours to know her completely.

Many students throw *La Princesse de Clèves* across the room in disappointment and disgust when they reach the end. Katharine Ann Jensen offers a strategy for dealing with students' problems with the princess's refusal to marry Nemours. She suggests how key passages from the debates provoked by the novel's ending at the time of its first publication can help students both appreciate its complexity and distinguish readers' personal reactions to the ending from the ways the novel prepares for it. By showing that virtue and tranquillity form the historical and thematic frames for an understanding of the ending, Jensen argues that the heroine's renunciation of Nemours is a positive expression of her self.

Themes and Structures

In an effort to explain the princess's unconventional behavior, many recent critics have focused on her development. In "The Mother-Daughter Subtext in

La Princesse de Clèves," Michèle Longino shows how the mother-daughter relationship in the novel is crucial in this development and how it shapes the plot. In a new twist Longino argues that the mother's influence prevents the princess from articulating herself and acting on her own desire. Her rejection of Nemours signals her inability to break away from her mother's influence.

We have seen that the concept of *vraisemblance* (plausibility, verisimilitude, propriety) is the hallmark of the *nouvelle* genre. An understanding of Lafayette's use of *vraisemblance* is key to comprehending the novel and the reactions to it. In an analysis of *vraisemblance* Inge Crosman Wimmers pays special attention to the rhetorical dimensions of *La Princesse de Clèves* to illustrate how the narrator sets up a coherent logic for the princess's actions that Lafayette's contemporaries judged implausible (her confession and her refusal of Nemours).

Even though the historically grounded internal narratives can be seen to contribute to the *vraisemblance* of the novel, many critics reject them as unnecessary. Rae Beth Gordon interprets several of the internal narratives in relation to the novel's ornamental decor as episodes that can seem mere backdrop to the main plot but in fact illuminate hidden emotions crucial to the plot and help define the psychological character of the novel. She argues that a language of objects conveys what words cannot — notably, strong emotions such as erotic desire or confusion and embarrassment.

In "Mapping *La Princesse de Clèves*: A Spatial Approach," Éva Pósfay makes the novel accessible to students by concentrating on the various spaces in it. She reveals how Lafayette's descriptions of historically verifiable and culturally significant places — the court and the pavilion — chart crucial struggles for power between the sexes.

Like Pósfay, Julia V. Douthwaite asks students to focus on one aspect of the novel, the visual codes. In "Seeing and Being Seen: Visual Codes and Metaphors in *La Princesse de Clèves*," she underscores Lafayette's predilection for verbs of perception and for visual metaphors. Douthwaite shows how visual terms serve various functions in the novel, such as underlining the heroine's vulnerability in the vicious circle of court life and offering ironic commentary on characters' feelings. She argues that an alternation between public confusion and private lucidity runs throughout the novel and allows the reader to see the princess's gradual emergence as an autonomous individual.

Whereas most critics emphasize the princess's inimitability, focusing on the final line of the novel, Louise K. Horowitz takes the opposite stance in "Truly Inimitable? Repetition in *La Princesse de Clèves*." By examining the episode of the lost love letter, belonging to the vidame de Chartres but mistaken as Nemours's, and the historical space of Coulommiers, including the portrait of Nemours in the pavilion, she reveals how Lafayette's novel is structured by repetition and imitation. In Horowitz's view nothing and no one in the novel is original, and the artifice of reproduction turns love and life into death.

Specific Teaching Contexts

The increased popularity of *La Princesse de Clèves* has led to a veritable explosion of English translations. Faith E. Beasley compares and contrasts the four most frequently chosen translations of Lafayette's novel and finds often significant differences. She analyzes various terms, such as *galanterie* (politeness or love), *vraisemblance*, *repos*, and *aveu*, that pose particular interpretive problems not only for those reading a translation but also for any twentieth-century reader unfamiliar with Lafayette's cultural milieu.

In "What's Love Got to Do with It? The Issue of Vulnerability in an Anthological Approach," James F. Gaines offers an approach for teaching excerpts of *La Princesse de Clèves* found in French anthologies. As he indicates, the princess's confession is the scene most frequently excerpted from the novel. This scene takes on special meaning in the context of other classic female confession scenes from seventeenth-century texts, which are usually anthologized as well, including Corneille's *Le Cid,* Molière's *Le misanthrope* and *Le bourgeois gentilhomme,* and Racine's *Andromaque* and *Phèdre.* Notions of morality and vulnerability link these confession scenes together and distinguish them—and their heroines—from one another.

Many professors incorporate *La Princesse de Clèves* into a course on the development of the novel. Kathleen Wine demonstrates the affinities between *La Princesse de Clèves* and the romances so popular earlier in the century. Lafayette's evocation of court society provides a context for understanding the echoes of romance in her novel through an analysis of such features as marriage by means of adventure and passion as a sign of public virtue.

John D. Lyons describes teaching *La Princesse de Clèves* in an introductory course in comparative literature. He reads Lafayette's novel with Marguerite de Navarre's *Heptaméron*, a sixteenth-century novella to which *La Princesse de Clèves* explicitly refers (in the internal narrative of Anne Boleyn), thereby inscribing itself within a long tradition of storytelling. Lyons analyzes structural and thematic similarities between the two texts, raising such questions as Who is telling the story? Who is listening? What is the effect of the story on the listening character and on the reader? What are the relationships between the sexes?

Given its canonical status as the first French novel, *La Princesse de Clèves* often finds a place in a course on masterpieces of French literature in translation. Anne Callahan describes such a course whose focus is the theme of romantic love in Western literature. She analyzes the ways in which representation mediates desire and reads *La Princesse de Clèves* in the context of fatal love. Like *Tristan and Iseut*, romances by Chrétien de Troyes, and the *Heptaméron, La Princesse de Clèves* represents desire as triangular—three players change positions constantly to create new couples. Callahan shows that, unlike the earlier works from the romantic tradition, Lafayette's features a heroine whose greatest desire is to avoid the traditional fate of romantic love—death by love or a physical separation that sustains the illusion of eternal desire.

Elizabeth J. MacArthur discusses teaching Lafayette's novel in a women's studies course, specifically one on French women writers from the seventeenth century to the present. Organizing the course around the notion of interpretive communities, MacArthur seeks to create such a community in the classroom, so that students can read and discuss the novels and broaden their ideas of what life choices and gender roles are possible. MacArthur studies interpretive communities within *La Princesse de Clèves*, suggesting that the novel is largely about how the heroine uses the stories she hears to shape her own life and how her own story (her confession) gets circulated and judged publicly against her will. MacArthur also presents the interpretive communities that first read Lafayette's novel, thus returning to the subject of Goldsmith's initial essay, the quarrel.

MIRRORING SOCIETY:
LA PRINCESSE DE CLÈVES IN CONTEXT

Lafayette's First Readers:
The Quarrel of *La Princesse de Clèves*

Elizabeth C. Goldsmith

The intensity with which the artistic quarrels of the past were fought can seem strange in hindsight. How difficult to imagine, reading Victor Hugo, that his play *Hernani* could have inspired fistfights in the audience; how improbable the thought of Stravinsky's fleeing the concert hall during the first tumultuous performance of *The Rite of Spring*. And yet what insight these dramatic incidents can give us into the history of theater and music and into the public reception of art. In reading about the literary quarrel provoked by the publication of *La Princesse de Clèves*, one is first struck by the strangeness of the terms of the debate. To us the vehemence with which the author was criticized for failing to make a character sufficiently polite or for imagining a conversation between two historical figures seems both incomprehensible and exotic. But it is precisely in encountering these first responses by Lafayette's contemporaries that students can best appreciate the meaning of claims about the novel that have become almost formulaic in literary history books—that, for example, it is "the first modern novel" or a new form of historical novel.

I have taught the quarrel of *La Princesse de Clèves* in a graduate seminar on Lafayette and, in a much more limited way, in an undergraduate course called The French Classical Tradition. In both contexts I have been pleasantly surprised by how effectively the material can be made to work toward giving students a better understanding of the reading tastes and practices of the seventeenth-century literary public. Arranging access to the texts themselves, though, can be discouraging, since the only modern edition of critical essays on Lafayette that includes substantial material from the seventeenth century is Maurice Laugaa's *Lectures de Madame de Lafayette*, now out of print. John Lyons includes a few useful passages from Jean Baptiste du Trousset de Valincour's *Lettres*, as well as a paragraph from Jean-Antoine de Charnes's response, in his Norton Critical Edition. If enough time can be allotted for a discussion of the novel's critical reception, it is certainly worth preparing a packet of photocopies for students to purchase. Some key passages and their translations can be found in the appendix to the present volume. (For useful summaries of the quarrel, see Beasley, *Revising*; Harth, *Ideology*; Williams, *Valincour*.) Much more than an anthology, Laugaa's book provides illuminating readings of the texts and their significance.

During the year following the publication of *La Princesse de Clèves*, in March 1678, the literary public was treated to a critical debate over the merits of this innovative experiment in historical fiction. Within months of the novel's publication a lengthy book entitled *Lettres à Madame la Marquise de *** sur le sujet de* La Princesse de Clèves was produced by the printer Sébastien Mabre-Cramoisy, and in 1679 a response in the form of another anonymous and equally voluminous volume was printed by Lafayette's publisher, Claude Barbin, entitled *Conversations sur la critique de* La Princesse de Clèves. The first of these, it was subsequently established, was written by Valincour, a poet, critic, and historian who would later be named court historiographer by Louis XIV. He was also, for most of his career, a high-ranking official in the French naval administration. The second text has traditionally been attributed to Charnes, a clergyman who held a minor post at the court of Versailles and may also have been personally acquainted with Lafayette and her circle. Other critical discussions appeared in print or were otherwise circulated during the same period: in a series of special issues of the periodical *Le mercure galant*, edited by Donneau de Visé, readers were invited to respond to questions about their opinions on the novel's most perplexing features, and some lively epistolary exchanges between Mme de Sévigné, her cousin Bussy-Rabutin, and their friend Jean Corbinelli were circulated, read aloud, and eventually printed to form part of what we now refer to as the quarrel of *La Princesse de Clèves*.

The quarrel was launched by Valincour's profession of bafflement at Lafayette's failure to make the novel's most crucial moments believable. It must be remembered that the principal requirement for the *nouvelle historique* was *vraisemblance* (see the introduction to this volume, pp. 5–6). If the work is a history, Valincour argued, then all the descriptions of events should have been based on documentary sources, such as memoirs. In *La Princesse de Clèves* the reader is treated to conversations crucial to the development of the story that are entirely undocumented. To the extent that the work is a fiction, modeled on the epic, Valincour asserted, it should have held the characters to heroic standards of behavior. But both the princess and Nemours give in to character weaknesses that make it impossible for readers to admire them.

Responding to Valincour, Charnes stressed that *La Princesse de Clèves* was neither history nor epic but an example of a new genre, the *"galant* history," in which truth and fiction are blended together to form an image of reality analogous to life itself. He argued that this new form of historical fiction could legitimately claim to provide readers with a plausible, intelligent insight into what may have occurred behind the scenes of documented historical events. New rules had to be established to judge the new genre.

Meanwhile, readers of *Le mercure galant* provided "write-in" responses to the editor's questions much like callers to a talk show today. The topic of the most extended discussion was the key moment in the novel when the princess declares to her husband her passion for another man, a confession that Nemours, hidden in the garden, overhears. *Le mercure galant* focused the debate on issues of propriety as much as plausibility:

> Je demande si une femme de vertu, qui a toute l'estime possible pour un mari parfaitement honnête homme, et qui ne laisse pas d'être combattue par un amant d'une très forte passion qu'elle tache d'étouffer [. . .] fait mieux de faire confidence de sa passion à ce mari, que de la taire [. . .].
>
> (Laugaa 27)

> I ask if a virtuous woman, who has the highest esteem for her admirable and gentlemanly husband, but who is nonetheless ravaged by a strong passion, which she is trying to smother, for another man who loves her [. . .] would do better to confide this passion to her husband, or to remain silent about it [. . .].[1]

These debates were echoed in letters between Lafayette's acquaintances, which provide us with further evidence of the considerable renown that the novel enjoyed in public discussions and private conversations.

The textual record of this literary quarrel is substantial, and one's first task in teaching it is deciding how much of it to use and have the students read. Even the excerpted sections in Laugaa are too long to be used in an undergraduate class such as mine, where *La Princesse de Clèves* is given only two weeks on the syllabus. At this level it is most useful to focus on an aspect or two of the discussion in order to illustrate points about the original reading public for which the novel was written. The topic on which I chose to focus in my undergraduate course was the resistance of Lafayette's contemporaries to the notion of a fictional character's thoughts being conveyed directly to the reader. Bussy-Rabutin's lively remark on this issue in a letter to Mme de Sévigné is a good point of departure:

> Cela sent encore bien le roman, de faire parler les gens tout seuls; car outre que ce n'est pas l'usage de se parler à soi-même, c'est qu'on ne

pourrait savoir ce qu'une personne se serait dit, à moins qu'elle n'eût
écrit son histoire; encore dirait-elle seulement ce qu'elle aurait pensé.
(Laugaa 19)

It's like a romance [. . .] when people talk to themselves. Besides the fact
that it is not customary for people to talk to themselves, it isn't possible to
know what someone says to herself unless she writes her own story, and
even then she would say only what she thought.
(Lafayette, *Princess* [Norton ed.] 122)

Examining reader responses such as this one helps students appreciate one
of the major innovations of this "first psychological novel"—its focus on the developing inner consciousness of the heroine. This aspect of the quarrel ties in
well with earlier classroom discussions about narrative voice or omniscience,
about how characters achieve access to each other's private thoughts in the society depicted in the novel, or about the ways in which the reader is assumed or
invited to be a participant in the world the novel describes. It also allows the instructor to stress how *La Princesse de Clèves* differed from previous genres,
particularly romance.

Another feature of the quarrel that may be profitably introduced in an undergraduate course, or studied in detail in a seminar, is that all the voices engaged in it seem to be trying to invent a way of reading this new form of novel.
Two aspects of this project are particularly striking today. First, the experience
of reading the novel and the experience of passing judgment on it are both described as group activities. Reading does not seem to be an activity done in iso-
lation, and the process of forming a critical opinion is profoundly dependent on
interaction and conversation. It can be interesting to compare these aspects of
seventeenth-century literary culture with the way we read and talk about literature today. Second, the voices of Lafayette's first readers can be surprisingly
engaging—they are not, contrary to some expectations, simply the utterances
of pompous aristocrats and pedants. Encountering their individual arguments
can be a good antidote, I have found, to the stereotype of the constrained Versailles courtier, who never dares to utter a personal opinion. There is a playful-
ness to their discussions that can be both appealing and effective as an
illustration of a style of critical thinking that only people who take leisure seriously (and have plenty of it) can achieve.

The principal voices in this quarrel were not, contrary to what students usually expect, members of an academic establishment or even of the relatively
young Académie Française (though Valincour would be named to it later). The
writers state their positions on the merits or failings of the novel not with
regard to clearly established classical rules but, rather, according to much more
culturally determined notions of good taste, propriety, and verisimilitude.
Valincour, the most critical of Lafayette, does have recourse to classical

authorities, citing Vergil, Homer, and Aristotle in his critique of Lafayette's construction of plot and character. But Valincour eschews the status of *docte*, or scholar, even as he seems to lecture his readers on what makes a good novel. Like his interlocutors in the controversy, he identifies with the cultural elite of *honnêtes gens*, those cultivated members of salon and court society who were the new purveyors of literary taste (see Beasley, "Plaisir"). Charnes praises the novel while also making clear that he is a member of the social circles from which it emerged—he was in on early discussions of the story as it circulated in manuscript form; he had known what a "noise" it would make even before it hit the presses. He represents the unstoppable force of public opinion, "ce torrent de la voix publique" (Laugaa 43), that will win out against petty criticism. Charnes, in fact, denounces Valincour as an imposter, accusing him of being a *docte* and not the member of worldly society he poses as. Sévigné enthusiastically invites her exiled cousin Bussy-Rabutin to send her his opinions by mail so that she may introduce his voice into the conversations at court. The invented names of respondents to the *Mercure galant* questionnaire suggest a far-flung community of readers eager to participate in this nascent republic of letters ("l'insensible de Beauvais," "le berger des rives de Juine," "un géomètre de Guyenne"; "the insensitive person from Beauvais," "the shepherd from the shores of Juine," "a geometer from Guyenne").

It is important, I think, for students at any level to understand that the quarrel of *La Princesse de Clèves* was, like many artistic quarrels, an attempt by its participants to understand and situate a work that was universally recognized as exceptional. It is interesting to observe how Valincour's critique also could have functioned as a kind of reading manual, drawing the reader's attention to the most significant moments in the story even as he scolds the novelist for the way these scenes were written. As we read his comments on the scene in which the princess first meets her future husband, for example, we realize that we are also being given a lesson in close reading and in the value of including different voices in the project of collective interpretation:

> Les femmes habiles soutiennent qu'on n'a jamais laissé à une fille de seize ans, le soin d'assortir des pierreries; que tout ce que l'on peut faire à cet âge-là, c'est de choisir des rubans, et des garnitures; qu'on assemble toutes ses amies, et toutes ses connaissances, lors qu'il s'agit de pierreries, principalement de la conséquence de celles dont il en fallait a Mademoiselle de Chartres; et qu'enfin cela n'est pas vraisemblable. Pour moi, qui ne songeais guère à toutes ces raisons-là, je n'ai pas laissé de trouver l'aventure extraordinaire. Je n'ai pu comprendre, quelle necessité il y avait de mener Mlle de Chartres chez un Joaillier, pour la faire voir à M. de Clèves. Il m'a paru que cela était trop concerté [. . .].
>
> (*Lettres* 9–10)

Clever women are saying that no one ever gave a sixteen-year-old girl the task of matching jewels. All that a girl that age could do is choose ribbons and accessories. Where jewels are involved, especially jewels as important as those Mlle de Chartres is concerned with, one gathers all one's friends and acquaintances, and [these women] say, in short, that the situation isn't plausible. As for me, I hadn't thought of those points, but I still found the adventure extraordinary. I couldn't understand why it was necessary to bring Mlle de Chartres to a jeweler to have her see M. de Clèves. It seemed to me that it was too staged [. . .].

Not only is Valincour drawing his reader's attention to key moments in the story, but he is also showing the reader how he arrived at his interpretations through conversations and consultations with others. The reader is invited to join in and is even challenged to find something that no one else has seen, as here: "Monsieur °°° [. . .] s'est avisé de trouver à redire à un endroit que je croy qui n'a été remarqué par personne que par lui" (*Lettres* 11) ("Monsieur °°° [. . .] set about finding fault in a spot that I think has not been noticed by anyone else"). Charnes, writing as an apologist for the novel, further challenges Valincour's representation of himself as a member of salon society. He refers to him disdainfully as "The Critic." One participant in Charnes's "conversations" remarks that the epistolary and dialogical format of Valincour's book seems like a thin disguise for what amounts to a lecture or sermon: "Vraiment, dit-elle, jusques-là la Critique avait assez de l'air d'une Lettre, mais je commence à voir qu'il nous va faire un sermon dans les formes avec ses trois points" (Laugaa 56) ("Truly, she said, up until this point the criticism has seemed quite like a letter, but I am beginning to see that he is going to give us a formal sermon, complete with the three main points"). Responding to Valincour's objections to the staged quality of some of the scenes in *La Princesse de Clèves*, Charnes mocks Valincour's artificial use of social scenarios to transmit what amount to pedantic points:

> Il [va] [. . .] aux Tuileries: il y trouve un Reformateur du langage, qui y vient, non pas pour se promener, ou pour y voir le monde; mais pour y attaquer, sur le sujet de *La Princesse de Clèves*, le premier qu'il y rencontrera; et celui qu'il y rencontre le premier est justement l'Auteur des Lettres.   (Laugaa 57–58)

> He [goes] [. . .] to the Tuileries, and there he finds a reformer of language who happens to have come there not for a promenade or to see high society but to take on the first person he might meet on the subject of *La Princesse de Clèves*, and who should he meet first but the author of the *Letters*.

Charnes makes it clear that he, unlike Valincour, knows the author and knows how the novel was written. His authority derives not from academic "experts" but from simply being in the know, understanding the intentions behind this new form of novel, having his opinion shared by the vast majority of cultivated readers. Thus Valincour, "The Critic," is socially isolated—he says he was bored by the historical prelude to the story; Charnes replies that he doesn't know anyone else who felt that way (Laugaa 66). Valincour criticizes the novelist for not observing the established rules; Charnes replies, in effect, "Where have you been?": "A quelques Critiques et à quelques bizarres près, il [cet ouvrage] a eu l'avantage de plaire à tout le monde. C'est aux règles à s'accommoder au goût d'un siècle aussi poli que le nôtre . . ." (Laugaa 83) ("With the exception of a few critics and eccentrics, [this work] has had the advantage of pleasing everyone. The rules must be adapted to the tastes of an age as polite as ours . . .").

By pointing out that this kind of rhetorical packaging was substantive, and not just peripheral, in the debates over Lafayette's novel, one can link these readings with a more general discussion of the nature of the literary public in the last part of the seventeenth century. A number of secondary readings lend themselves to a more in-depth study of the quarrel (I did this only in my graduate course, but it could also be done at the advanced undergraduate level). Many of the topics introduced in the quarrel remain among those most frequently addressed by criticism, raising the question of the extent to which contemporary reactions are conditioned by these first responses. Among the many important new readings of *La Princesse de Clèves* that have appeared in the last several decades, a few treat the quarrel in some detail. Aside from Laugaa's extremely valuable edition, which also provides incisive commentary on the texts, probably the most influential is Gérard Genette's "Vraisemblance et motivation," in which Genette brilliantly and wittily undoes the notion of plausibility so dear to the heart of Valincour. Joan DeJean's "Lafayette's Ellipses" examines the question of authorial anonymity in the publication history of *La Princesse de Clèves* and analyzes the publicity strategies implicit in the *Mercure galant* questions and answers. In *Revising Memory* Faith Beasley points out that critical discussions of the function of history in the novel have generally failed to take an approach other than the one defined by Valincour, who focused on the relative measures of the historical and the fictional in the story as though they were two entirely separate forms of discourse. She argues that Lafayette carefully wove the two together to create a feminocentric *H/histoire*. In *Public et littérature en France au XVIIe siècle*, Hélène Merlin examines the arguments put forth in the literary quarrel in the context of the evolving concept of the "public" at the end of the seventeenth century. She points out the originality of this debate compared with earlier literary quarrels, such as the one that arose in response to Corneille's *Le Cid* in the 1630s. The authors of the quarrel, like the author of the novel they are discussing, all speak from behind a veil of anonymity that enables them to make of their discussion a collective representation of ideal conversation, of new ways of reading and interpreting literature that emerge from the culture of sociability.

Teaching the quarrel of *La Princesse de Clèves*, then, can provide a point of departure for the study of several larger topics in seventeenth-century French literature. The decision on how much of the material to introduce and which aspect of the debate to explore will depend, of course, on the time allotted to the novel and the level of the class. Traditionally, the quarrel has not been included as a topic for discussion in courses on French classicism, perhaps because literary histories have tended to treat it as an arcane subject of interest only to specialists. But new fields of research, including feminist criticism, the history of the book, and cultural studies on the origins of the public sphere, have suggested perspectives on the episode that are engaging to both teachers and students. For teachers who have encountered the quarrel only second-hand, listening to the voices of Lafayette's first readers will definitely be worth the trouble.

NOTE

[1]All translations are mine except where otherwise indicated.

Jansenist Resonances in *La Princesse de Clèves*

Louis MacKenzie

Among the ideological currents that nourished neoclassical French thought, Jansenism, the energetic and contentious revival of Augustinian theology, may have been preeminent. This certainly seems true when we consider Jansenism's influence on the principal literary works of the age. A quick sampling of the so-called canonical writings will underscore the extent to which Jansenism charged the creative impulses of the second half of the seventeenth century. To a more or less explicit degree, issues at the heart of Jansenist theology—free will, divine intervention, and moral prescription—can be seen in Pascal, La Bruyère, Racine, Molière, La Rochefoucauld, and, as we shall see here, Mme de Lafayette.

In the seventeenth-century survey course in which I am likely to teach *La Princesse de Clèves*, I find it most effective to deal with Jansenism in what might be called a dynamic way, that is, by using the literary text to exemplify relevant aspects rather than requiring supplemental reading or dedicating a formal lecture to it. This approach has as much to do with the relative dryness of some of the more specifically Jansenist texts as it does with the unavoidability of dealing with the subject in the first place.

It is important to point out to students that Lafayette, née Marie-Madeleine Pioche de la Vergne, came into regular and sympathetic contact with proponents of Jansenist thought at the hôtel de Nevers, a prominent salon of the period presided over by Mme du Plessis-Guénégaud, and that she held Pascal's *Pensées* in particularly high regard. It will come, then, as little surprise to students that resonances of Jansenism make themselves felt in her most successful novel. This is not to suggest that *La Princesse de Clèves* is a theological tract cloaked in literary garb. It is, rather, to visualize Jansenism as something like a conceptual aquifer, a source of sustenance hidden from view but instrumental in shaping, if only partially, the character of the novel. Put succinctly, the Jansenist aspects of Lafayette's novel may be somewhat elusive, but they are not illusory. I find it helpful to explain that Jansenism, like any theology, was not just a set of often abstract principles but also comprised a psychological and moral approach to the world. Comparing it to contemporary fundamentalist agendas, I acquaint my students with the notion that Jansenism fostered an analytical mindset that looked to pare away the trappings of personal glory or social esteem to expose an underlying tangle of self-love and a delusive sense of self-sufficiency. In class, as here, my reading of *La Princesse de Clèves* is informed, then, by two perspectives on Jansenism: the generally analytical and, to a lesser degree, the specifically theological.

The premise of Lafayette's enthusiasm for the Jansenist worldview urges the reader to revisit certain privileged moments of *La Princesse de Clèves*. The first of these moments occurs right at the beginning of the novel, where we read: "La magnificence et la galanterie n'ont jamais paru en France avec tant d'éclat que dans les dernières années du règne de Henri second" (69) ("Opulence and gallantry had never appeared so conspicuously in France as in the last years of the reign of Henri II"; since my pedagogy almost always entails semantic and etymological considerations, I provide my own translation here). At first take, the operative terms—*magnificence* ("opulence") and *galanterie* ("gallantry")— seem simply to affirm social prestige and to privilege a historical moment. Closer examination shows them losing the luster that hides their true metal. To begin with, the term *magnificence* would naturally and correctly be construed as signifying grandeur and loftiness. However, if one digs a bit more deeply into the word from which *magnificence* issues, the Latin *magnificentia*, a second, more pejorative meaning comes into play: *magnificentia* also means pomposity and boasting. In other words, while *magnificence* may indeed carry a positive connotation, it can easily slip into something of its opposite, that is, false loftiness. Similarly, the term *galanterie*, which commonly points to elegance, distinction, and civility, can be seen as cloaking coquettishness and disingenuous sweet talk. The term also refers to amorous adventure, a definition that, while not necessarily pejorative, does all the same serve to put what in the novel is called "le commerce des femmes" (70) ("the company of women" [3]) into the same kind of critical light that would question the worldly values of opulence, stylish talk, and passionate intrigue.

The third term in Lafayette's quotation that seems to hesitate between valences is *éclat* (from the French verb *éclater* 'to explode'). When Lafayette states that "magnificence" and "galanterie" had never before appeared with such "éclat," she refers first to the splendor and allure of the court. Read in this sense the word points to the plenitude of a particular moment in history. Once again, however, the term comes apart, exploding into shards (*éclats*) that may be seen as anticipating the one that will fatally injure the king and provoke a reshuffling of the power relationships at court. This privileged moment, for all its swirl and glitter, is a moment of things coming apart. This is underscored by the relentless if not always manifest critique that Lafayette deploys in the novel and that redounds to this notion of plenitude, under the sign of which the novel first orients itself.

From the outset, then, Lafayette implicitly invites her readers to analyze critically the signs of worldly accomplishment and repute; this analysis is itself part of an examination of the more general problem of the friction between appearance and reality. As is to become explicit in the novel, what appears to be real is often a distortion of reality; what appears to hold value may be holding its hollowness just out of sight. The opening signals of the novel grind the optics through which to reconsider much of what passes as exemplary. Case in point: the famous sequence of portraits that marks the opening pages of the novel. In that section, as superlatives are piled onto superlatives, they—and the courtiers they describe—become little more than clichés. The redundancy of the description serves not to distinguish but to blur distinction. The accidental prestige of being "admirablement bien faits" (70) ("wonderfully handsome" [4]), "une personne parfaite pour l'esprit et pour le corps" (70) ("a paragon of wit and grace" [4]) or "l'ornement et l'admiration de leur siècle" (70) ("the ornament and wonder of their age" [4]) loses much of its punch because it has been distributed so generously and so generally. Just as the self-destructive features of the opening words of the text establish an etiquette for reading the novel, the lack of distinction born of the redundancy of distinction asks readers to consider in an equally critical way the two central characters, Nemours and Mlle de Chartres, both promoted as models of beauty and social perfectability.

The gallery of portraits serves, then, to establish in the reader's mind an ironic backdrop in order to problematize the central love intrigue. This problematization is linked specifically to the celebration in the portraits of mere physical beauty and worldly success, once again, two inflections of the kind of vanity targeted by Jansenist thinkers. Pascal is particularly energetic in debunking vain pursuits and preoccupations. (In this regard, students will want to consider fragments 16, 23, 36, and 136 in the Lafuma French edition and the A. J. Krailsheimer English translation of the *Pensées*.) Conspicuous and significant by its absence is any hint of the most basic sense of the spiritual. What is more, as we are repeatedly told in the novel, "nature" is the source of the incomparable beauty that characterizes courtly society. There is, then, a functional link among the court, nature, and the court's perception of nature. The world of the novel—defined, at least until the very end, by the court—is wholly secular and naturalistic. Thus the questions of whether "nature" can be considered a good provider and whether natural drives and appetites are morally legitimate beg asking. Lafayette makes it clear that the court is a dangerous place. Most tellingly, when she specifies that "l'ambition et la galanterie étaient l'âme de cette cour" (80) ("[a]mbition and love affairs were the life-blood of the court" [14]), she does not simply engage in description. By conjoining *ambition* and *galanterie*, she sends a signal that would put readers as much on guard against the latter as they would logically be against the former.

Imbricated in the indictment of the court as morally suspect are nettlesome questions about personal virtue. Is it possible, for example, to be part of the court and be virtuous? Is it possible to be part of the social world without being morally compromised? It is from this perspective, where theological and sociological considerations intersect, that we will want to consider the moral pedagogy of Mme de Chartres, who sees herself both as outside the loop of the court and as attracted to it. What interests us here is the tension between antagonistic force fields—the pull of the court and the weight of experiential wisdom. If, as does indeed seem justified, we substitute *world* for *court*, the drama takes on a more clearly theological patina: refusal of the world presents itself as a viable response, perhaps the only viable response, to the pull of the world and to what is perceived to be its fatal allure. Mme de Chartres does recognize the dangers of the court but is, all the same, intent on bringing her daughter to it. The inference to be drawn here is that the primary space in the novel is exclusive. There is the court and courtly life; there is nothing else. La Bruyère, whose own affinity with Jansenism and with other inflections of conservative thought can regularly be felt in his *Caractères*, puts it this way: "Qui a vu la cour a vu du monde ce qui est le plus beau, le plus spécieux et le plus orné; qui méprise la cour, après l'avoir vue, méprise le monde" (fragment 100 in the ch. "De la cour") ("Anyone who has seen the court has seen the most beautiful, opulent, and ornate thing the world has to offer; anyone who has seen the court and is not taken by it is not taken by the world"; my trans.).

What then are the virtues that Mme de Chartres hopes to cultivate in her daughter? What are the virtues she looks to fortify in her daughter so that her daughter will be able to parry the endemic dangers of court life? Basically, the program she proposes is a social, domestic one, the fundamental tenet of which is to love and be loved by her husband. This principle, according to Mme de Chartres, guarantees happiness. That guarantee does not, however, come free of charge. The price to be paid is nothing less than whatever thrill passionate love can bring. In the simple but harsh algebra of the novel, love and marriage never do, as the old song promises, "go together like a horse and carriage." In fact, passionate love is set in almost allegorical opposition to the institution of marriage; and since marriage is specified by Mme de Chartres as the most reliable conduit to happiness, passionate love outside the structure of that institution is repeatedly posited as dangerous.

The appeal of a "loving" marriage resides in its provision of a buffer against the torment of passionate love, which, for reasons left unclarified in the novel, seems to mutate from the simply stormy to something very close to sinful. Mme de Chartres's advice is, however, wholly secular. It is given with the best intentions. It is human and commonsensical but limited in scope and efficacy; here, another resonance of Jansenism makes itself felt in the novel. Pascal, following Augustine, writes of three orders of being—the carnal, the intellectual, and the spiritual—in which regard we would want to look more closely at fragments 308 and 298. If this system were applied to *La Princesse de Clèves*, Mme de Chartres's moral advice would clearly fall under the rubric of the intellectual. Passionate love, constantly under fire in the novel, would be situated within the order of the carnal, the order of concupiscence; while the third order, the order of the spiritual (charity) would, over the course of most of the novel, be largely and significantly absent; and would, therefore, be felt all the more dramatically at the end.

The mother's words and influence take on even more weight in the scene of her death where she speaks to her daughter for the last time. In that scene, Mme de Chartres warns the princess of the inherent danger of her attraction to Nemours. Indeed, she sees the princess "sur le bord du précipice" (108) ("on the edge of a precipice" [39–40]). The term *précipice* resonates in a particularly incisive way with the Jansenist sensibility circulating in the novel. One cannot help but think of the pointed uses of this term and its synonym, *abîme* ("abyss") in the *Pensées* (fragments 44, 131, 166, 199, and 919). Mme de Chartres tells the princess that in order not to fall—or is it to throw herself?—into the abyss, "[I]l faut de grands efforts et de grandes violences pour vous retenir" (108) ("You will have to make great efforts and do yourself great violence to hold yourself back" [40]). Nancy Mitford's translation of this sentence is perhaps even more charged: "You stand on the edge of a precipice and can only hold back by making a superhuman effort" (69). The notion of "superhuman" violence to self in the service of what is held to be a higher value is altogether consonant with the Jansenist program, pointing as it does to what Pascal calls "abêtissement," a program of self-denial and -abnegation undertaken in the service of loftier principles.

Mme de Clèves is prodded by her mother to pretend not to love Nemours; she must inure herself to the siren's song of that love and proceed as if she loved her husband in something of the same way. In so doing, she will preserve the reputation that she and her mother worked to establish. Now, it could be argued that reputation is a mundane, social preoccupation and that it is simply a synonym for the very kind of *gloire* ("glory") and *honneur* ("honor") that Pascal debunks in the *Provincial Letters* (*Œuvres*). If that were the case, however, Mme de Chartres's influence over her daughter's affective and moral future would have to be read ironically, almost cynically. Precisely because the notion of reputation is, in the context we consider, linked to a refusal of the world ("Ayez de la force et du courage, ma fille, retirez-vous de la cour, obligez votre mari de vous emmener" [108]) ("Have strength and courage, my child, withdraw from the court, persuade your husband to take you away" [40]), there must be something more to it than its common acceptation, which is to say, the high regard of others. If, as is the view of Mme de Chartres, the court is duplicitous, ambitious, and mendacious (94; 26), the urge to leave the court is not only an urge to leave the imminent danger of passionate involvement with Nemours (whose very name may suggest something like the negation of love) but also a call for the renunciation of a lifestyle that defines participation in the world. As such, the notion of reputation takes on a much more personal charge. Indeed, what seems to be at stake here is less what others might think of the princess than what she might think of herself. It is as if the mother is provoking a dialogue between the princess as creature of the world and the princess as creature not of this world, between the physical and the spiritual.

We might therefore want to consider the etymology of *reputation*. In so doing, we go from *reputatio* to *putare* ("to cleanse"), arriving ultimately at the root, which is remembered only vaguely in *reputation*: that radical *pu* from which comes *purus* (clean or pure). To stay at court would be to run the very real risk of "fall[ing] like other women" (40)—and the notion of falling, itself linked both to falling in (illicit) love and, on a more psychoanalytical level, to sexual surrender cannot help but evoke resonances of the fall from grace. In other words, the image chosen by Mme de Chartres seems automatically to call on a theological and moral pre-text, one that is virtually forgotten by the magnificent and gallant heroes and heroines of Henri's court. After making her warning explicit, Mme de Chartres issues the following order to the princess: "[. . .] et souvenez-vous, si vous pouvez, de tout ce que je viens de vous dire" (108) ("[. . .] and remember, if you are able, everything I have just told you" [40]). And, let us reiterate, Mme de Chartres has just told the princess, in essence, to be watchful of her reputation and purity, to defend a state of (relative) innocence that would implicitly recall the prelapsarian state of real innocence and happiness, the memory of which goads and galls. Her beauty—her perfection, to use the precious language of the novel—cannot be defined simply in terms of the physical. It represents, rather, a condition and an ideal conspicuously at odds with the common character of the court.

After admonishing and advising the princess, Mme de Chartres literally turns away from her, eventually dying without uttering another word to her. The theological parallel is tempting, even if it works primarily on an associative level. Mme de Chartres would be analogous to the *deus absconditus*, the "hidden god" who lays down the laws and precepts and then turns away from direct or necessary intervention in the human drama. Of course, the physical eclipse of the mother does not at all mean that she disappears from the scene. To the contrary, she lingers in the princess's mind, as the pressure of the terrible charge to remember, as a primary constituent of her daughter's superego. Therefore the mother's admonition and the eventual death of M. de Clèves merge to forge a formidable moral and psychic edifice. The princess, despite the beckoning of the world—represented by the seemingly irrefutable logic of Nemours's arguments—will courageously and resolutely take up residence in this edifice.

What is more, toward the end of the novel we are told that the princess, recovering from a life-threatening illness, will remember her dead husband: "Les pensées de la mort lui avaient rapproché la mémoire de M. de Clèves" (237) ("Thoughts of death had brought home to her the memory of M. de Clèves" [154]). It is wholly implausible that the enhanced memory of her dead husband would not also invoke the words of her mother, words that bear the stamp of law. And while there can be no thought of elevating Mme de Chartres to high spiritual station—her "wisdom" is, as suggested above, predominantly terrestrial—the novel itself does seem to take an abrupt but not wholly unexpected turn toward the spiritual. The ending of the novel is intriguing not only because of the inexorability of the princess's retreat but also because it is foreshortened meaningfully. With the stroke of a pen, years pass by. During this time the princess has been up to something that, it can be inferred, is somehow different from what has already transpired in her life and from the retirement from the world that closes the novel.

Even more significant is the orchestration of the final paragraph of *La Princesse de Clèves*, in which the emphasis, at least as measured by the space allotted, is put on Nemours. It is as if, still very much within the grip of the world, he cannot help doggedly pursuing his objective. The hunt, the game, is not yet over for him; hence his ongoing attempts and accompanying misery, cured only by the passage of time. In contrast Lafayette gives the princess relatively short shrift:

> Mme de Clèves vécut d'une sorte qui ne laissa pas d'apparence qu'elle pût jamais revenir. Elle passait une partie de l'année dans cette maison religieuse et l'autre chez elle; mais dans une retraite et dans des occupations plus saintes que celles des couvents les plus austères; et sa vie, qui fut assez courte, laissa des exemples de vertu inimitables.   (239)

> Mme de Clèves adopted a way of life which dispelled any thought that she would ever return. She spent part of the year in the convent; the rest she spent at home, though in profound retreat and in occupations more saintly than those of the most austere houses of religion. Her life, which was quite short, left inimitable examples of virtue.   (156)

The cryptic cast of these "inimitable examples of virtue" and the seeming inconclusiveness of the novel have caused much ink to flow. In spite of the weighty expression "occupations more saintly," many critics have been stern in their reluctance to entertain a religious or spiritual reading of the ending of *La Princesse de Clèves*. Despite its tantalizing ellipses and apparent ambiguities, the novel does work along a rather clear teleological line. The trajectory of the princess's adventure is hardly put forth as vain, which is to say, as ironic. Nor is her adventure simply a worldly one. Indeed, it is precisely the world that she rejects in the end. The princess's refusal to cede to the common sense of Nemours's logic or to the call of worldly expectations may logically be taken as indications of something more than avoidance of discomfort and the fear of being jilted by a lover of dubious reputation. Otherwise the princess would be heroic only for her common sense and acts of self-defense, which would put her inimitability, on which Lafayette insists, into less brilliant light and would tend to render the concluding statement of the novel cloying.

    It would be shortsighted to reduce the *repos* — a term that can at once mean repose, peace of mind, and inactivity — to which she so resolutely aspires and which she so jealously protects to a simple fear of getting hurt again. To dismiss out of hand the spiritual resonances of "saintes" and "vertu" would do damage to a goodly portion of the riches embedded in the ambiguity of the novel. By the same token, one should not minimize the effect of the adjective modifying "exemples de vertu." The princess's examples are inimitable precisely because they defy and attempt to redefine prevailing moral structures, which, from a more specifically textual point of view, have to be considered in a fundamentally different light from Nemours's own inimitability, namely, his sense of fashion: "il avait [. . .] une manière de s'habiller qui était toujours suivie de tout le monde, sans pouvoir être imitée" (72) ("[h]e had [. . .] a way of dressing that always set the fashion yet could never be imitated" [5]). They fly in the face of the world as constituted and promoted by the court; to see them in this way is to agree—partially at least—with those critics, mainly feminist, who see the princess's struggle as one to achieve autonomy from male-dominated social and psychic structures. The theological currents that run just below the surface of the novel urge the reader to consider the possibility of a more fundamental(ist) refusal, one that targets not just a patriarchal order but also the entire tangle and turmoil of human values. In other words, the apparently exclusive secular cast of the novel may, in fact, be *figurative*. It may be calling for a more allegorical, more theological, and, ultimately, more "radical" reading.

The meaning of the final sentence of the novel, a sentence injected paradoxically with equal doses of understatement and exaggeration, may be situated precisely in its mystery, in Lafayette's own refusal to say just what examples of virtue the princess did in fact bequeath. For while Lafayette could easily have identified specific acts—one thinks, for instance, of what Balzac does at the end of *Eugénie Grandet*—she opts to leave the matter wide open. The reason for this may at bottom be linked to a fundamental premise of the Jansenist position on salvation (which is not, of course, meant to imply that the end of the novel in fact addresses a question of salvation). What is certain, however, is that Lafayette does direct her heroine toward some sort of reward. The princess's refusal, like her "occupations saintes," is clearly not meant to be taken as futile. Indeed, these "occupations" and their attendant acts of virtue can be read as indexes of that which is unimaginable to those given to what Pascal calls *divertissement* (diversions and the diverting of one's attention). It is for this reason also that the examples of virtue remain literally and literarily ineffable.

By the same token, however, the repeated examples of virtue could not be promoted as any guarantor of salvation; nor for that matter could Lafayette "save" her heroine without confecting an epilogue that would have ground against the historicity, fictionalized though it may be, of the novel. To have been overly explicit about the princess's virtue would have violated a theological principle. Faithful to the thought of Augustine, the Jansenists maintained that no human action, regardless of its virtuous content or intent, could necessarily indicate or guarantee salvation. Lafayette places the accent on the princess's examples of virtue, that is, on unspecifiable signs of a virtuous life. These actions, unspecifiable though they may be, indeed perhaps because they cannot be told, indicate something of a conversion, a radicalization of the refusal to compromise not only with Nemours—or with other men—but also with the world itself. And yet the princess does spend part of her time in the world ("chez elle" ["at home"]) and part of it in a place of retreat ("dans cette maison religieuse" ["in the convent"]). The princess's choice recalls the perspective taken by Lucien Goldmann in *Le dieu caché* on what he calls the tragic vision of Jansenism. The princess would be ranked among those opting for what he calls the "refus intramondain du monde" (62)—the refusal to play the game and the simultaneous refusal to quit the game altogether.

In this same perspective, one would want to rethink the notion of *repos* and, in so doing, tether it to Augustine's use of the term in his *Confessions*, where he claims that the human heart will remain in a state of disquiet until it finds repose in God. Seen in this light, *repos* undergoes a radicalization, a move away from the relative (freedom from care) to the absolute (salvation). Of course, the narrator, despite her fictive omniscience, can only take things so far. She cannot "save" the princess. She can only suggest a happier ending—one that can be inferred by another, often neglected term of the concluding expression, the verb *laisser* ("to leave," "to bequeath"). We are told that the princess left examples of inimitable virtue. That these examples are multiple and varied must be seen not only as deriving from the central plot line but also as moving beyond it. The princess is not simply the one who refused Nemours, he whose romantic attentions would have flattered any woman at court; she is also the one who, against all the apparent odds and precedents, has become virtuous. Her virtue has earned her the prize of moral exemplarity, a privilege wanting in those "perfect" creatures whose portraits graced the beginning of the novel and who, unlike the princess, have disappeared, largely unregretted, from the scene and from our memories.

Court Society and Economies of Exchange

Harriet Stone

To ensure that students weave a steady course through the labyrinthine events that Lafayette details, I have found it useful to focus on the issue of court commerce. I begin by suggesting that the novel allows us to conceive the term *commerce du monde* ("worldly commerce") as more than a metaphor for court gallantry. This concept allows us to see how the novel reflects the tension of the historic transition during the seventeenth century from an aristocratic economy to a precapitalist or more bourgeois one. One can find signs of this shift by attending to the portraits, letters, gossip, and identities that are conceived and exchanged in what I call the court's art market.

In class I refer to the critics referenced in this essay. I do not require undergraduates to read these texts. However, some of the better students, their interest piqued by class discussions, do consult these sources when preparing their papers. I expect graduate students to master the criticism along with the novel.

I start the discussion by situating the Florentine jeweler who occasions the initial meeting of the Prince de Clèves and Mlle de Chartres. I suggest that this character is exceptional because he is not a member of the court aristocracy. But I note that even this merchant is described as being so well assimilated into court society that his identity as bourgeois or foreign appears to wash away (see Tiefenbrun 35). It thus would be an exaggeration to speak definitively of the rise of the bourgeoisie in the novel's depiction of society. Nevertheless, I point out to my class that many critics have found evidence of a precapitalist economy in the novel's emphasis on commerce and exchange. Erica Harth argues that, unlike historical characters in earlier works, who served primarily to expose vice, Lafayette's characters exhibit both vice and virtue, and for this reason they seem more accessible as human beings. Consequently, the reader not only identifies these characters easily but also identifies with them (*Ideology* 216). We are moved to ask whether aristocratic ideology is not degraded by the attention to what Harth calls the "naturalization" of the historic figures. Specifically, the novel's less than virtuous portraits of court figures clearly invite a comparison with the princess's virtue. Feminist critics have stressed the princess's ultimate rejection of the traditional female role (see DeJean, "Lafayette's Ellipses"; Miller, "Emphasis"). The princess refuses to be an object handed from man to man, part of a story ordered by male desire. Referring with particular poignancy to the exchange principle inherent in this history, one critic has gone so far as to describe the subjugation of the novel's female characters as the wholesale prostitution of women at court (Greenberg 191).

I ask my students to consider seriously this characterization of court society, explaining my own mixed reaction. The emphasis on the female as an object of exchange is, I argue, certainly accurate. Moreover, it is correct to infer from this exploitation of women that the novel shows the corruption of an aristocratic ideal through a nascent capitalism. Certainly, money per se is all but absent in this novel. Moreover, with the exception of the jeweler at the beginning of the novel and, at the end, the silk merchant from whose shop Nemours watches the princess, the means of production within the economy are not specified (see Horowitz, "Tale" 27 n1). But the exchange of partners does indicate that people function much like commodities. They are consumed—used to enhance power and pleasure and discarded once they cease to perform this service. However, I suggest, the notion that only women are commodified in the novel is misguided. Women do suffer this fate. As the class reads through the novel, I am quick to point out incidents that document the subjugation and exploitation of women: Anne Boleyn is beheaded; Diane de Poitiers must share her power with the queen; Catherine de Médicis is deceived by the vidame; and, most important for our discussion, the Princesse de Clèves is victimized by her association with Nemours as this relation is further irritated by his association with the vidame. Students readily comprehend how these women are used to fulfill the ambitions of their male lovers. I encourage the class to see that the same can be said of many male characters. Sancerre mourns Mme de Tournon, only to find out that she had deceived him with his friend Estouteville. Sancerre's story can be shown to pattern from the victim's perspective the vidame's situation. I ask the students to keep track of the vidame's various lovers and deceptions. Tracing how the story unravels to show the vidame's willful violation of the queen's person and privilege, the class finds the vidame to be a victim, albeit more deserving, of the same system of exchange that victimizes the women. Ruined by the queen, the vidame can be said to have been seduced (used and discarded) by the very commerce that he so industriously employed to seduce women. Finally, I ask the class to consider whether Clèves, whom his wife respected but did not love, and certainly Nemours, whom she loves but who never enjoys the fruits of this love, are not similarly used by the court's commerce. Indeed, we see that even the king is deceived by both the queen (although it is Catherine who suffers the brunt of this infidelity) and Diane, whose liaison with Brissac causes Henri considerable pain.

I thus remind students at various intervals during our discussions that while virtue is a woman's issue—an issue imposed on women—the experience of alienation is not. Alienation is a function of the way the identities of individuals are subsumed by their role as figures represented on the court stage. I have found that representation is not a difficult concept for students to grasp once it is connected specifically to painting. The novel's initial emphasis on the brilliance (*éclat*) of court members enables the students to see that in royal society no body or person is separate from its image or persona (see Marin and Burke). Students are thus prepared to trace how Lafayette weaves the knotty threads of official court portraiture, which shows that the court preserves its power through the reproduction of its own image, with the broader-based, and, appropriately, baser, commerce of exchange that patterns the heroine's history at court. By "official portraiture" I refer to commissioned paintings, which reflect the hierarchy of relations because they extend from the king, the unifying sign behind all the portraits that circulate in the novel. I explain to my students that in this aristocratic economy the more images there are produced—the more paintings made in tribute to the king—the more extensive is the power realized by the court. In contrast, under the bourgeois economy the value of the thing or person exchanged is diminished in direct proportion to the number of reproductions made. Thus the more often a story is told, the more the individuals involved in it are degraded. The princess must negotiate the labyrinth of these economies as they intersect.

In our discussions we acknowledge how both economies can be said to dissimulate, if by *dissimulation* we understand the power of the image in correcting or enhancing the real. Each economy cultivates a seeming (*paraître*) that contrasts sharply with being (*être*). Yet the more commercial economy, in which no single image but rather a full cast of images comes into play, denies the value of the individuals whose identities it exchanges. I suggest to the class that the princess in the end rejects the bourgeois commerce outright. Interestingly, however, she uses the aristocratic currency—official portraiture—to perform a consummate act of exchange that allows her to escape the court's grip. The class considers how the princess eventually transforms rather than extends the court's power by subverting its unique reliance on self-reproduction, the circulation of many copies of its own image. We discover, however, that she does so without subjecting herself to the new economy.

The historical portrait takes two forms. The first relates to the glorification of court history, to the novel's idealistic, rather than realistic, portrayal of people and events (see Beasley, *Revising*). The second form relates to what Harth ascribes not to the novel but to seventeenth-century print culture in general. Harth specifies that, unlike the ancients, who could not reproduce images through printing and engraving, the French monarchy used these techniques as a means of "multiplying infinitely a given discourse and of displaying the image of one thing in various places" (*Ideology* 259). She observes that printed reproductions made the king's glory visible to those who were unable to see the various objects produced to honor him. I invite my class to consider how, just as engravings later advanced the mission of Louis XIV, so in Lafayette's work official portraits make ubiquitous Henri II's presence.

Specific examples help illustrate this point. The reine dauphine commissions miniatures of various members of society for her mother, who is absent from court (135; 63). Students quickly understand that the portraits "make the court visible" and make its power felt by those removed from it. Turning then to the paintings commissioned by the duchesse de Valentinois, the class examines how these representations function to commemorate and to celebrate the king's authority. I use the following passage to illustrate the court's extension of its power through art:

> [La princesse] s'en alla à Coulommiers; et, en y allant, elle eut soin d'y faire porter de grands tableaux que M. de Clèves [*sic*; "elle" in all other French editions] avait fait copier sur des originaux qu'avait fait faire Mme de Valentinois pour sa belle maison d'Anet. Toutes les actions remarquables qui s'étaient passées du règne du roi étaient dans ces tableaux. Il y avait entre autres le siège de Metz, et tous ceux qui s'y étaient distingués étaient peints fort ressemblants. M. de Nemours était de ce nombre et c'était peut-être ce qui avait donné envie à Mme de Clèves d'avoir ces tableaux.   (205)

> [The princess] went away to Coulommiers, taking care to give instructions that a set of large paintings should go with her: these were copies she had had made from originals that Mme de Valentinois had commissioned for her fine house at Anet. All of the noteworthy events that had taken place during the reign of the late King were represented in these paintings. One of them depicted the siege of Metz, with lifelike renderings of all those who had distinguished themselves there, including M. de Nemours: this was perhaps what had made Mme de Clèves want to have the paintings.   (125)

The history of the commissioned paintings appears mainly to set up the personal story of the princess. Still, this episode allows us to see how the art market at court has none of the bourgeois overtones that the art market would later have, for example, in the novels of Balzac, where copies are devalued with respect to the original. If, as Walter Benjamin has shown, in industrial society identical reproductions are devalued, the reverse is true in the court economy. Or, more precisely, if the original held by the court still retains the primary value, the copies are valued all the more because the court has authorized them and their dissemination into the homes of the courtiers. Lafayette's depiction of the aristocratic economy thus reveals the king's hold on his subjects through the privilege accorded to the copies.

I ask my students to consider the size of the paintings commissioned by the king's mistress. They note that the paintings seem larger than life because the king functions in them more as an idealized figure than as a real soldier on the battlefield. Hung in her chateau outside Paris, the paintings further illustrate the physical distance that the court bridges through its art. The class discusses how Diane venerates Henri by decorating the chateau that he has built for her with signs of his glory. The duchess is in many instances the real power behind the throne, and, even in her lesser moments, she offsets through her influence on the king the queen's officially sanctioned power. Diane's privilege is reflected in the images with which she surrounds herself. The class analyzes how the connection between power and privilege is affirmed yet again when the Princesse de Clèves has replicas of these paintings made for herself. Such replication flatters the crown. The obverse relation—namely, that the princess would risk offending Diane or the king—is inconceivable. Thus the class comes to understand why the assumption grounding the royal economy is that nothing causes the supply curve to shift under the weight of a fickle or inconsistent demand from the king's loyal subjects. There is a market for every image that the court produces of itself. In this economy more is, quite simply, better, for more is always more of the same idealized image of the king.

The new, bourgeois economy as it relates to the history of Nemours and the princess is another matter entirely. Substituting one lover or intrigue for another, the members of court society in effect trade one image for a more empowering one, and it for another, and so on (see Greenberg). The cast of characters expands as new figures, such as the princess, assume their roles on the court stage. In presenting this new commerce, I point out that the king's subjects are alike in how they differ from the king. For Henri participates in the "commerce du monde" not only as Diane's lover—that is, as one who, like the other court figures, is engaged in gallantry—but also as the sole primary image maker and principal subject of representation in the aristocratic economy.

The princess's story involves her becoming an object of exchange. To understand this intricate story, the class needs to unravel the events of the princess's famous confession to her husband (see DeJean, "Lafayette's Ellipses"). The princess is unknowingly observed by Nemours declaring to Clèves that she loves a man whom she nonetheless refuses to name. The class discusses each of the subsequent events in detail: the duke recounts the remarkable confession in veiled terms to the vidame, who tells it to his mistress, who repeats it to the reine dauphine, who eventually tells it to the princess. I suggest to the students that, beyond what it says about the princess's desire for Nemours and about his own pleasure in confirming that desire from his voyeuristic vantage point as secret observer, the princess's extraordinary confession takes its significance from being framed by two other portrait scenes: the scene in which Nemours steals the miniature of the princess belonging to her husband and the scene at Coulommiers in which the princess contemplates the painting, described above, that includes a representation of Nemours.

Both episodes reveal the decline of the court's ability to control its art market. In the earlier scene, which takes place as the reine dauphine unveils her commissioned paintings, Nemours's theft of the miniature of Mme de Clèves literally steals away from the royals the right of unique privilege—the exclusive authority to dispense the royal image. While the princess's portrait is the private property of M. de Clèves, it is connected in this scene to the unveiling of the portraits by the reine dauphine and thus to the idea of royal privilege. Nemours opens up the self-contained world of official art, in which all court figures bask in the light of the king's image, by thrusting the princess's portrait into the more scurrilous domain of spying, theft, and voyeurism. Moreover, the rivalry between Nemours and Clèves evident both in this episode and in the confession scene devalues the object of their love, the princess herself. Her importance to both men notwithstanding, the princess appears less consequential in this acting out of the love triangle than does the male rivals' struggle for dominance (see Girard, *Mensonge*). Indeed, the male identification is so complete that in the confession scene we find Nemours rooting for Clèves as Clèves implores the princess to reveal her lover: "[Nemours] était si transporté qu'il ne savait quasi ce qu'il voyait, et il ne pouvait pardonner à M. de Clèves de ne pas assez presser sa femme de lui dire ce nom qu'elle lui cachait" (173) ("He was so carried away that he could scarcely grasp what he was witnessing, and he could not forgive M. de Clèves for not pressing his wife hard enough to divulge the name she was hiding" [97]). Not only is the Clèves' privacy violated by the undetected presence of Nemours here; the normally serene and judicious husband loses his sangfroid. I ask the students to compare Clèves's response, his oppressive insistence that his wife complete her confession by naming her lover, with Nemours's voyeuristic presence. Both attitudes reveal the violence of the men's actions, their violation of her privacy.

This scene is, of course, a prelude to the nocturnal visit of Nemours to Coulommiers, where he has the distinct pleasure of watching the princess fawn over his portrait. The latter event provides a unique perspective into the crossing of economies. I point out to the class that the similarity between the male rivals is again evident here. For just as Nemours is surreptitiously watching the princess, so is he surreptitiously being observed by the gentleman hired by Clèves to spy on him. The reader is likewise caught in the web of spying: we watch Nemours watch Mme de Clèves look adoringly upon his portrait, unaware that he is watching her watching him. The court history captured in the portrait is subordinate to the highly erotic history enacted, as critics have duly noted, through the multiple gazes that make this scene the most sexually fulfilling encounter of the princess and Nemours's relation (see Butor; DeJean, "Female Voyeurism"; Greenberg; Miller, "Emphasis"; Schor; Weinstein). Significantly, however, the fulfillment represented here is that of lovers who remain separated.

I encourage the class to consider how each of the portrait scenes can be blocked into a triangle. In the first diagram I situate the princess (doubled by her painted image), Nemours, and Clèves. The princess mediates the scene by refusing to expose Nemours's theft of her portrait. Her complicity in the theft complicates the issue of her virtue: she begins to be identified through her image, which enters the court economy as a stolen and hence degraded object. In the second triangle I place the princess, Nemours, and the image of him on which her attention is fixed. By superimposing the two triangles, I suggest that Nemours's image has come to assume the regulatory role, first assigned to Clèves, of limiting the princess's desire. For if the princess can indulge her passion by contemplating Nemours's image here, it is because such an expression of passion substitutes for the actual consummation of her love for him. The image thus represents the princess's decision to remain virtuous, to limit her desire at least insofar as her public actions are concerned. But I go on to suggest that the triangle, by isolating the important function of Nemours's image, ultimately allows us to construe a relationship between the princess and this image that is potentially even more significant than her relationship with Nemours himself.

At Coulommiers the princess becomes empowered by bringing the image of Nemours into the pavilion. This act subordinates Nemours himself to her fantasy; it makes him a mere accessory to the princess's desire (see DeJean, "Female Voyeurism"; Schor). In a recent class, one student argued that the princess does not love Nemours so much as the idea of being in love. That is, the princess loves not Nemours but rather what Nemours represents to her. I further suggest that the scene, by separating the real lover from the image of the lover that the princess extracts from the painting of the siege of Metz, echoes the Cartesian formula "Je pense [. . .]": I think, and this representation constitutes the sole proof of my being. Significantly, consistent with Descartes's famous utterance, nothing in this moment proves a resemblance between the princess's consciousness and the world around her. Nothing signifies outside her representation (her mind's eye) and in the world of objects (in nature). Thus her experience in this scene is not modeled in the gaze as it originates in the male spy and lover, in this economy of images that devalues the subject. Nor is it the product of official history, which makes the princess a consumer of the king's glorious image and a consumer of Nemours only as an accessory to this royal image making. Instead the scene captures the princess's own desire. Indeed, she does not know initially that Nemours is even there (see Stone, *Classical Model* 162–66).

Does the princess's fascination with Nemours's image not mean that she is still dependent on the court? In our final discussion of this scene, students argue that to a certain extent she is. Such dependency reflects the intersection of aristocratic and bourgeois markets. But, the students insist, the princess has to separate her image of Nemours from the painting that pays tribute to the king. And this image is separate from the flesh-and-blood man who observes her from outside her window. That is, if this flesh-and-blood man is the model for the painting, the painted image in its regal splendor bears little resemblance to the real man as he performs in this scene. Moreover, the painting models not only Nemours's court-enhanced image but also the princess's own imagination, the conception of an idealized lover that she projects onto the canvas. To the extent that the real is severed from the image here, the princess ultimately controls the economy. She represents to herself not the official story of the court any more than she does the actual history of the lover who spies on her and violates her solitary pleasure. Rather, she revels in the quiet contemplation that permits her, at last, to enjoy a purely private and nonmarketable self whose knowledge of itself cannot be exchanged.

Virtue and Civility in *La Princesse de Clèves*

Marie-Paule Laden

Teaching *La Princesse de Clèves* to undergraduates is like administering cod-liver oil to a child; it requires a lot of coaxing. The students' initial reaction to the novel echoes Antoine Adam's opening statement in his introduction to his edition: they feel cheated. They expect a beautiful love story, and instead they find themselves plowing through several pages of court intrigues among a host of characters whose names are not only unpronounceable but also usually unfamiliar. Although the key to the historical figures that I provide increases the students' self-confidence, the world portrayed by Mme de Lafayette remains foreign to them until I draw their attention to lexical issues. Emphasis on the obsessive usage of superlatives in the opening pages of the novel and the recurrence of words such as *magnificence, galanterie, grandeur, valeur, mérite extraordinaire, estime, éclat* ("brilliance"), and *bienséance* ("propriety") allows the students to understand that they are entering a coded world in need of deciphering.

To begin our analysis, we look at definitions of *galanterie, bienséance, mérite,* and *honnêteté* taken from Furetière's and Richelet's dictionaries to help the students understand that these words are all inextricably interconnected; the definition of each word draws on the others. To create a dialogue between Lafayette's novel and the literary scene of the time, we read the first section conjointly with contemporary responses to *La Princesse de Clèves*. They include comments from l'abbé de Charnes and Bussy-Rabutin, as well as extracts from Valincour's *Lettres à Madame la marquise de °°° sur le sujet de* La Princesse de Clèves. I draw this background information from an edition of *La Princesse de Clèves* and from Maurice Laugaa's *Lectures de Mme de Lafayette*. Once they have understood the vocabulary and are properly impressed by the atmosphere of *grandeur* that pervades the apparently homogeneous and immutable world of the court, I introduce the notion of "civility" — the word recurs in the definitions we look at — as linked to a literature of sociability that flourished in the seventeenth century. I mention the influence of Baldassare Castiglione's *The Book of the Courtier* (1528), which I present briefly as a how-to book aimed at teaching would-be courtiers how to build a social figure based on the primacy of appearing over being. Hence the necessity of dissimulation, without which one does not survive in the public world of the court, where one is condemned to live under the perpetual gaze of the other. The ideology that took shape at the beginning of the seventeenth century in France owes a lot to the doctrine of *The Courtier*, a debt amply illustrated through our reading of the opening section of the novel. At the same time, however, a countermodel was elaborated: it opposed the public world of the court, the manners of which were judged unrefined by the select aristocratic circles of private salons such as Mme de Rambouillet's famous "chambre bleue." In the private space of the salons women played a decisive role in promoting a new kind of civility—*honnêteté, galanterie,* or *urbanité*—which distinguished itself from the regulated sociability that had become the rule at court. (See Brooks; Lougee.)

The students can now be alerted that the representation of courtly society introduced in the opening section of the novel is more problematic than they first thought or than the author would have us think when she describes the novel as "une parfaite imitation du monde de la cour et de la façon dont on y vit" ("a perfect imitation of the world of the court and of the way people live there") in her famous letter to the chevalier de Lescheraine (*Correspondance* 2: 62–64). This description may refer as much to the court of Louis XIV as to that of Henri II, in the same way that the terms used to convey the splendor of Henri II's court are ambiguous, since they reverberate with vying conceptions of civility and *galanterie. Galanterie* is linked to outer splendor, the primacy of appearing over being, and to a world in which beauty, high birth, and favor are the main components of *éclat* (brilliance) and *mérite.* Civility transcends social, aesthetic, and moral categories; it evokes a world imbued with a private sense of duty.

> Il parut alors une beauté à la cour, qui attira les yeux de tout le monde. [. . .] Son père était mort jeune, et l'avait laissée sous la conduite de Mme de Chartres, sa femme, dont le bien, la *vertu,* et le *mérite* étaient extraordinaires. [. . .] [E]lle ne travailla pas seulement à cultiver son esprit et sa beauté, elle songea aussi à lui donner de la *vertu* et à la lui rendre aimable. [. . .] [E]t elle lui faisait voir [. . .] combien la *vertu* donnait *d'éclat* et *d'élévation* à une personne qui avait de la *beauté* et de la *naissance.* Mais elle lui faisait voir aussi combien il était difficile de conserver cette *vertu,* que par une extrême défiance de soi-même et par un grand soin de s'attacher à ce qui seul peut faire le bonheur d'une femme, qui est d'aimer son mari et d'en être aimée. (76; my emphasis)

> There appeared at court in those days a young woman so beautiful that all eyes turned to gaze upon her. [. . .] Her father had died young and left her in the safe keeping of his wife Mme de Chartres, a lady of extraordinary wealth, *virtue,* and *merit.* [. . .] She sought not only to cultivate her wit and beauty but also to make her love *virtue* and be virtuous. [. . .] She told her how much *brilliance* and *distinction virtue* bestows on a woman who is *beautiful* and *well-born*; but she also taught her how difficult it is to preserve *virtue* except by an extreme mistrust of one's own powers and by holding fast to the only thing that can ensure a woman's happiness: to love one's husband and to be loved by him. (9–10; my emphasis)

At this point, even the most unperceptive students notice that the word *virtue* appears for the first time when Mme and Mlle de Chartres make their entry into the novel and that its repetition—four times in the same paragraph—establishes a sharp contrast with words already used to describe other courtiers: *mérite, beauté, éclat, élévation, naissance.* In the homogeneous world of the court, where everyone shines through a mixture of merit, beauty, and high birth, Mme de Chartres emphasizes virtue in her daughter's education as a way to set her apart, thus creating "un exemple différentiel" ("a counterexample") as Sylvère Lotringer puts it (507).

The idea of a counterexample is further emphasized throughout the paragraph in the contrasting parallelism of a series of adverbial phrases—"elle ne travailla pas seulement à cultiver son esprit et sa beauté, elle songea aussi"; "elle lui faisait voir [. . .] mais elle lui faisait voir aussi [. . .]" ("She sought not only to cultivate her wit and beauty, but also"; "she taught her [. . .] she told her [. . .]")—as well as direct oppositions: "La plupart des mères s'imaginent [. . .] Mme de Chartres avait une opinion opposée. Elle lui contait le peu de sincérité des hommes [. . .]; et elle lui faisait voir d'un autre côté [. . .]" (76) ("Most mothers imagine [. . .] Mme de Chartres believed the opposite. She spoke to her of men's insincerity [. . .]; she painted for her, on the other hand [. . .]" [9–10]). The idea of exemplarity is also conveyed through the repetition of "faisait voir" ("she told/taught her"). (See John Lyons's discussion of exemplarity in *Exemplum.*)

The unusual (differential) aspect of the education received by Mlle de Chartres is thus doubly emphasized; by its nature, first, since, unlike other girls of her rank, she was raised by her own mother, away from the court. (This absence from the court marks the beginning of another series of oppositions, this one spatial, movements to and from the court, which will punctuate the novel after the princess meets Nemours.) Second, it stands out by its content: unlike other mothers, Mme de Chartres does not hesitate to talk about love to her daughter: "elle faisait souvent à sa fille des peintures de l'amour" (76) ("She often gave her daughter descriptions of love" [10]).

By stressing that virtue will give her daughter "éclat" and "élévation," Mme de Chartres reintroduces moral values to a world of sociability in which merit is no longer linked to virtue (even though the *Dictionnaire de l'Académie,* in 1694, will still define *mérite* as a synonym of *vertu*). Virtue, according to Mme de Chartres's precepts, will bring the same perfection to her daughter's private life as civility will bring to her public life. Moreover, by emphasizing how difficult it is to "conserver cette vertu que par une extrême défiance de soi-même" (76) ("to preserve virtue except by an extreme mistrust of one's own powers" [10]), the mother points to virtue not only as a sort of interiorized civility but also as the only way to happiness and tranquillity in a world in which "l'amour était toujours mêlé aux affaires et les affaires à l'amour" ("love was always entangled with politics and politics with love"), where "personne n'était tranquille" (81) ("no one was tranquil" [14]), and where "ce qui paraît n'est presque jamais la vérité" (94) ("what you see is almost never the truth" [26]).

Strategically placed after the passage just discussed, such sentences make obvious the uniqueness of Mlle de Chartres's position at court; furthermore, they showcase Mme de Chartres's insistence on virtue as a different code of conduct, pointing to a revision of the courtly code. The students are now ready to understand why the novel caused such a controversy when it appeared in 1678. The rebuke Bussy-Rabutin gave to a novel that he said had "plus songé à ne pas ressembler aux autres romans qu'à suivre le bons sens" (qtd. in Genette, "Vraisemblance" 77) ("tried harder not to resemble other novels than to follow common sense"; my trans.) echoes his contemporaries' puzzlement on reading Mme de Clèves's confession to her husband. It is, however, particularly illuminating to read the remark in the context of a discussion of Mlle de Chartres's education, since it stresses the notion of a deliberate deviation from a norm he calls "bon sens" ("common sense"). If what Bussy-Rabutin means by common sense refers to the conformity of the reader's expectations with what he reads, his remark bears a striking resemblance to P. Rapin's definition of *vraisemblable* ("plausible") as "tout ce qui est conforme à l'opinion du public" (qtd. in Genette, "Vraisemblance" 73) ("that which conforms to public opinion"; my trans.). Mme de Clèves's confession violates both social and novelistic conventions, since it is not proper for a woman to disrupt her husband's peace of mind and since there is no example of such a fiction.

The students find particularly useful Genette's discussion of the confusion between *vraisemblance* ("plausibility") and *bienséance* ("propriety") in the seventeenth century: Genette traces their fusion ("amalgame" [72]) to the ambiguity of *devoir* ("duty"), which expresses both obligation and probability. It gives students a deeper understanding of the public's reaction to *La Princesse de Clèves* while highlighting Mme de Lafayette's conscious manipulation of, and deviation from, the codes of fiction and conduct. With that background, when they are confronted with Bussy-Rabutin's exclamation — that "l'aveu de Mme de Clèves à son mari est extravagant et ne se peut dire que dans une histoire véritable, il est ridicule de donner à son héroïne des sentiments si extraordinaires" (qtd. in Genette, "Vraisemblance" 71–72) ("Mme de Clèves's confession to her husband is extravagant and could occur only in a true story, so it is ridiculous to give such extraordinary emotions to one's heroine"; my trans.) —they rebut it themselves by pointing out that the princess's unusual behavior has been carefully prepared and foreshadowed at various levels in the text: through the narrator's reiterations of her singularity, through the counterexamples given by the inserted stories, and, most directly, through the princess's and other characters' comments on her conduct. For instance, the reine dauphine's exclamation, "Il n'y a que vous de femme au monde qui fasse confidence à son mari de toutes les choses qu'elle sait" (164) ("You are the only woman in the world who confides to her husband all the things she knows" [88]), comes before the famous scene of the confession. Above all, Mme de Clèves's comments on her own conduct point to the internal logic of the text: "je vais vous faire un aveu que l'on n'a jamais fait à son mari" (171; see also 172, 174, 175) ("I will make you a confession which no woman has ever made to her husband" [95;

see also 96, 98, 99]); "il n'y a pas dans le monde une autre aventure pareille à la mienne; il n'y a point une autre femme capable de la même chose" (187) ("there could be no other story like mine in the world, no other woman capable of doing such a thing" [110]); and especially her outcry, "Cette histoire ne me paraît guère vraisemblable" (183) ("That story hardly sounds plausible to me" [106]), when she hears her own story told at Mme la dauphine's.

The students need little guidance to remark that in the world of the court, where one is condemned to make a show of appearances, the princess's desire to retire to her own quarters or to escape to Coulommiers represents a serious violation of decorum, and her husband, who is a perfect courtier, tells her as much on several occasions (122, 130, 178; 51, 57, 100). They therefore perceive her confession as inscribed in the text because she remembers M. de Clèves's words to Sancerre (117 [46]) and because after her mother's death M. de Clèves is her last resort in her attempt to salvage her virtue. By confessing, however, she casts him in an extremely ambiguous role, not just because he cannot "quitt[er] le personnage [. . .] de mari, pour la conseiller et pour la plaindre" (117) ("abandon the role of [. . .] husband in order to offer her [his] advice and [his] compassion" [46]) but also because he cannot abandon the role of the courtier who needs to know everything yet has to conceal his inner thoughts. Hence the increased pressure he puts on his wife to keep up appearances at court. M. de Clèves's death underscores the impossibility of straddling the world of virtue and the world of sociability.

This realization helps the students understand the ending of the novel. Guilt, contrary to what they thought initially, has very little to do with Mme de Clèves's decision to refuse Nemours and to retire from the world. Neither does she follow her mother's precepts in doing so, as some of them thought. First, by showing her daughter "combien la vertu donnait d'éclat et d'élévation" (76) ("how much brilliance and distinction virtue bestows on a woman" [10]) and by insisting on the outer representation of virtue—"pensez que vous allez perdre cette réputation" (108) ("reflect that you are on the point of losing the reputation you have earned for yourself" [40])—Mme de Chartres places virtue in a context of social appearances that Mme de Clèves will reject. Second, by linking virtue to tranquillity and happiness, she locks her daughter in a double bind, since she mandates a course of conduct that proves impossible to follow in a world in which social and political considerations take precedence over the personal. For a fleeting moment Mme de Clèves contemplates such a utopic scenario: "Plus de devoir, plus de vertu qui s'opposassent à ses sentiments" (223) ("No duty, no virtue could now stand in the way of her feelings" [142]). But such dreams are short-lived, and they dissolve during her final confrontation with M. de Nemours.

It comes as no surprise that the novel ends with a verbal joust revolving around Mme de Clèves's and M. de Nemours's interpretations of *devoir* ("duty"). This linguistic struggle echoes the slippery nature of the vocabulary used to describe the court of Henri II, in the concatenation of alternative codes of behavior, one linked to the public space of the court and the other to a more personal conception of civility. When Mme de Clèves invokes "les règles austères que mon devoir m'impose" (228) ("the austere principles my duty imposes on me" [146]), it is clear that she refers to an internalized sense of duty that clashes with the social context in which M. de Nemours repeatedly casts it: "il n'y a plus de devoir qui vous lie, vous êtes en liberté" (228) ("no duty ties your hands now, you are free" [146]).

It is worth noting that it is in the name not of virtue but of duty that Mme de Clèves refuses M. de Nemours. While she appeals to her *devoir* and her *repos* ("peace of mind"), it is Nemours who brings in the notion of virtue: "cette vertu ne s'oppose plus à vos sentiments. [. . .] Vous seule vous imposez une loi que la vertu et la raison ne vous sauraient imposer" (232–33) ("your virtue is no longer opposed to your feelings [. . .] you alone have made for yourself a law that virtue and reason could never impose" [150–51]). By rejecting or at least ignoring virtue and by finally emphasizing *repos* over *devoir*—"Les raisons qu'elle avait de ne point épouser M. de Nemours lui paraissaient fortes du côté de son devoir et insurmontables du côté de son repos" (236) ("Duty seemed to her a powerful reason for not marrying M. de Nemours, her peace of mind an insurmountable one" [153])—Mme de Clèves turns away from Nemours and his world of courtly sociability, a world he more than ever represents through his framing of virtue and duty in a social context. Her decision to retire from the world in the name of her *repos* may also be interpreted as a direct answer to her late husband's claim that "le repos [. . .] n'est guère propre pour une personne de votre âge" (170) ("rest and tranquillity [. . .] are hardly what a woman of your age needs most" [94]). She also sets herself apart from her mother, who not only emphasized virtue as a way of being in a world of appearances but also linked it to happiness, thus setting a trap from which her daughter can escape only by dividing her time between a "maison religieuse" and "chez elle" (239) ("convent" and "at home" [156]): that is, away from two different kinds of collectivity, the court and the convent, thus again affirming her difference through "des exemples de vertu inimitables" (239) ("inimitable examples of virtue" [156]).

Since *La Princesse de Clèves* is the first text I teach in an introductory course on the novel from Mme de Lafayette to Benjamin Constant, we spend some time discussing this curious association of virtue and happiness, which the eighteenth-century novel will challenge by presenting dramas of virtue that portray the individual's relation to the moral and social codes as one of tension rather than harmony. In the context of the course, Mme de Clèves's decision to retire from the world points to the increasing divorce between individual and collective happiness. It illustrates the shift from a virtue allied with and dependent on freedom to a virtue of constraint and imprisonment.

Masculinity in *La Princesse de Clèves*

Lewis C. Seifert

My students are almost always deeply divided on how to interpret the princess. One faction, usually small, contends that she is a protofeminist heroine who succeeds in escaping the constraints of marriage and patriarchal society. The other group (usually the majority) holds that she is victimized by an aristocratic "traffic in women" that condemns her to emotional anguish and physical solitude. Of course, these two points of view are not necessarily incompatible—or at least not completely incompatible. The question, then, is how can we help students (and ourselves) grasp the extent *and* limits of the princess's "heroinism"? What textual grids might we propose to help students view the novel as a whole and take into account the complexities of the princess's actions? To be sure, the illuminating readings of prominent feminist critics provide many such grids (see DeJean, "Lafayette's Ellipses"; Hirsch; Kamuf, *Fictions*; Miller, "Emphasis"; Stanton, "Ideal"). But although these insights are fundamental—indeed they are integral to my teaching—they approach *La Princesse de Clèves* primarily from the point of view of the heroine and the question of femininity. In fact, to date, few critics have confronted head on the question of masculinity in the novel. To do so is not only to discover a new and important interpretive grid by which to measure the princess's narrative persona but also to heed the novel's extensive commentary on masculinity. Moreover, to consider the place of masculinity in *La Princesse de Clèves* is to uncover some of the most basic conflicts underlying any definition of sexual difference.

A reading that seeks to understand the construction of gender identities in *La Princesse de Clèves* must deal with the court setting in which all the novel's characters exist. In my experience, however, students are readily inclined to discount this "background" in favor of concentrating on the "real" plot (as I've sometimes heard the princess's story called). It is no easy task to show that Mme de Clèves's (or any other character's) narrative existence can only be understood in relation to the social dynamics of the court. For all characters in *La Princesse de Clèves* social identity—including masculinity and femininity—is acquired, maintained, and often endangered within the closed world of the court and its intensely competitive rivalries. Moreover, these rivalries are fueled by and contribute to tightly controlled circuits of exchange channeling the knowledge and thus the power that govern life at court. Divided into neatly drawn factions, the members of Henri II's court are obsessed with reputations—their own and, of course, others'. Everyone gives and receives such knowledge; consequently, all the characters are constantly obliged to dissimulate truth potentially damaging to themselves and to divine fact from the misleading fictions of others. Characters exist insofar as they are able to maintain an acceptable discursive image, which involves keeping abreast of the courtly exchange of knowledge, so as to attempt to control their public personae.

The novel makes clear that the knowledge continually ferreted out and circulated in this court society is a sexual knowledge that is indistinguishable from political interest. "L'amour était toujours mêlé aux affaires et les affaires à l'amour" (81) ("[L]ove was always entangled with politics and politics with love" [14]), declares the narrator while describing the political influence of women at court. The oft-mentioned internal narratives are doubtless the most prominent examples of such knowledge and its circulation; but hardly a moment passes without a character's worrying about news of a faux pas or avidly seeking to discover who is loved by whom among fellow courtiers.

Precisely how such knowledge is circulated in the novel can be illuminated through the notion of the erotic triangle proposed by René Girard (*Deceit*) and refined by Eve Kosofsky Sedgwick. In its most basic formulation, this notion contends that desire be understood as a relation not between subject and object but rather between two rival subjects caught in a spiral of mimetic one-upmanship. How and what knowledge is exchanged or withheld is of crucial significance in the struggle between desiring subjects. When the two friends, the Prince de Clèves and the chevalier de Guise, discover that they both love Mlle de Chartres, they not only grow distant from each other but also make their passion public so as to stake a claim to her hand (82–83; 15–16). The model of triangular desire on the interpersonal level (the rivalry between Guise and Clèves for Mlle de Chartres) never functions in a vacuum but always occurs as part of larger court intrigues and rivalries. Guise's older brother, the cardinal de Lorraine, opposes a match between Guise and the princess out of hatred for Mlle de Chartres's uncle, the vidame de Chartres; and Mme de Chartres considers it an affront to her family that the Prince de Clèves's father publicly denounces his desire to marry her daughter. When made into news, amorous intrigues or even possible intrigues become political affairs that can alter these same liaisons, these erotic triangles, as well as the power relations at court.

In the midst of these rivalries masculinity and femininity emerge as hierarchical and discrete entities with respect to each other. Women first appear to wield an unusual amount of power in the novel. At the outset, the gendered positions of male and female characters are somewhat blurred, as is apparent in the narrator's assertion that "[l]'ambition et la galanterie étaient l'âme de cette cour, et occupaient également les hommes et les femmes" (80–81) ("[a]mbition and love affairs were the life-blood of the court, absorbing the attention of men and women alike" [14]). And yet what appears to be symmetry between masculine and feminine positions at court is in fact asymmetry. While women are divided into power *cabales* led by the queen, the reine dauphine, the queen of Navarre, Madame, and Diane de Poitiers and while male courtiers necessarily ally themselves with one or more of these groups to advance their own positions, ultimate authority rests with the king. Thus if Diane de Poitiers is at the center of the rivalry between the Guises and the connétable at the beginning of the novel, it is because of her privileged link to Henri II (see, e.g., 72–74; 6–8). Although undeniably powerful, then, women at this court are intermediaries through whom men establish and maintain the homosocial bonds necessary for their hegemony. It is hardly an accident that the novel's opening descriptions devote far more space to the male than to the female courtiers (see, e.g., 70–72; 3–5). Even more telling is the narrative's own insistence on this disproportion: after introducing "les plus grandes princesses" ("the greatest princesses"; my trans.), the narrator turns to "les plus grands princes" ("the greatest princes"; my trans.) by making the men about to be described the superlative superiors of superlative women: "Mais ce qui rendait cette cour belle et majestueuse était le nombre infini de princes et de grands seigneurs d'un mérite extraordinaire" (70) ("Yet what gave the court its splendor and majesty was above all the infinite number of princes and great nobles whose qualities surpassed the common measure" [4]). Given this imbalance, the circulation of knowledge at court is always already in the service of male homosocial bonding. What is at stake here is the preservation of a particular patriarchal order that enlists all participants — regardless of gender — through the exchange of sexual and political knowledge.

If students consider the function and organization of the court as I have suggested, then they are in a position to define what, in a normative sense, characterizes masculinity and femininity in *La Princesse de Clèves*. Indeed, the difference between these gendered identities can be explained at least in part by their roles in the court's economy of exchange. In the end, masculinity affords far more latitude than femininity does. To understand this difference, we might consider two ways in which men's relation to the circulation of knowledge diverges from women's.

First, compared with women, men would seem to have greater freedom to narrate their own sexual intrigues and thus fabricate their public identities. Even if the novel displays the failure more than the success of this freedom, characters such as the vidame de Chartres and even the duc de Nemours do not shy away from discussing their exploits. For instance, the vidame de Chartres indirectly flaunts his sexual conquests by boasting of the well-written love letter that, after falling into the wrong hands, will eventually mar his reputation at court. Contrary to what the vidame's misfortune might lead us to think, sexual intrigue is an accepted part of masculinity at this court: Nemours's exploits are widely known (if not admired), and, even more significant, Mme de Chartres's "lesson" to her daughter has as its most basic premise "le peu de sincérité des hommes, leurs tromperies et leur infidélité" (76) ("men's insincerity, [. . .] their deceptions and infidelity" [10]). By contrast, women can only stand to suffer from public love affairs. The heroine's own experience, confirming her mother's explicit warnings, is ample proof of such danger; but other allusions clearly make this point as well. The story of Anne Boleyn, told by the reine dauphine, and in fact the reine dauphine's own involvement in the imbroglio over the vidame's love letter reveal how dangerous (and in Anne Boleyn's case fatal) the discursive exchange of a woman's desire can be for her. That these two women suffer because of false love affairs contrived by their enemies only further accentuates the difference between masculine and feminine roles in the circulation of sexual knowledge.

This difference can be understood in another sense as well. I have already noted that all the members of Henri II's court are constantly searching for and proffering new knowledge. Yet, compared with women, men have a particular advantage and a peculiar stake in finding out who loves whom. It goes without saying that, as men, both M. de Clèves and the duc de Nemours have many more means at their disposal to meet with and even spy on the princess than she does in relation to them. And while the queen seems to have her own sources of information about the vidame de Chartres's comings and goings (149–59; 75–83), her example is not only exceptional, because of her elevated status, but also fundamentally different from that of the novel's two male protagonists. If Clèves is obsessed with discovering the identity of the man who has captured his wife's affections and if Nemours takes pleasure at witnessing, repeatedly and voyeuristically, the princess's expressions of her love for him, it is because men are fundamentally dependent on women for psychic and social dominance. Masculinity in *La Princesse de Clèves*—as in psychoanalytic theory—bespeaks mastery and the foreclosure of lack. For these two men, ignorance of the princess's innermost thoughts is tantamount to lack, to failed masculinity. To (attempt to) penetrate and recuperate Mme de Clèves's desires is to (attempt to) keep the upper hand in the struggle for the mastery of knowledge that is masculinity. It is also to defend one's ground in the rivalry that pits man against man in the erotic triangle. Knowledge about the female love object and the controlled exchange of that knowledge are crucial to the preservation of masculine dominance in love as well as in the homosocial bonds of the court.

No matter how inexorable the regime of masculine privilege might appear, there is a gulf between its theoretical underpinnings in the novel and its actual representatives, Clèves and Nemours. In fact, these two leading characters are in many respects eccentric exceptions to the norms of masculinity at court. Through them, the novel stages disruptions in the networks of knowledge that construct masculinity.

To consider this question, we need to place the triangular relationship of Nemours, Clèves, and the princess over and against the workings of the court. Specifically, for all the three main characters, the quest for knowledge about others ultimately leads back to the self, thereby shattering the certainty of self-knowledge and self-mastery. If the court as a whole is, as Mitchell Greenberg has put it, "a locus of paranoia" (180), then Nemours, Clèves, and the princess are surely the most extreme examples of this malady. With the *coup de foudre* (love at first sight) that strikes Nemours and the princess, all three are thrown into a struggle for knowledge that threatens to undo them. Nemours is so taken by the princess that he strays from his earlier womanizing and sets out to satisfy his desires fully. Clèves, as I have already mentioned, becomes obsessed with knowing whom the princess loves and in the end falls victim to the false certainty that she has been unfaithful to him.

No less anguished by her love, the princess now facilitates, now hinders the mimetic rivalry between her husband and her suitor. She gives various signs of her love for Nemours, both wittingly, by refusing to go to a ball and by acquiescing to the theft of her portrait, and unwittingly, when she is spied confessing to Clèves her love for Nemours and, later, gazing on his portrait with his cane at Coulommiers. So doing, she encourages Nemours's love and his rivalry with Clèves. She supplies Nemours with the knowledge he needs and desires in order to compete with Clèves. In fact, she herself becomes the objectified knowledge that Nemours possesses and, through the famous confession scene, puts into circulation at court. Her shock at hearing her story told and her bewilderment at how it could have become general knowledge (other than through Clèves) are vivid examples of how women are victimized through male homosocial bonding. And yet she is not the sole victim. Both Nemours and Clèves suffer from the exchange of the confession scene—Nemours because he realizes that it mortifies the princess and Clèves because he cannot understand how it happened or abide that this most secret moment of his marriage is widely known.

What this suggests, and what students often have a difficult time comprehending, is that the princess is not only a victim in the court's economy of exchange but also its opponent in both a theoretical and a practical way. In other words, we need to help students understand that she is both a participant and a detractor in the homosocial construction of masculinity at court. Her penchant to be wary of Nemours and the love he evokes must be traced to the apprenticeship in the ways of the court she receives from her mother. Although critics have noted, justifiably, the profoundly negative consequences of this "lesson" (see Hirsch; Kamuf, *Fictions*), it should be noted that Mme de Chartres proposes for her daughter, on the one hand, a counterknowledge that exposes the dangers of love affairs for women and, on the other hand, a counterexchange— a relationship of friend to friend and not mother to daughter—that is designed to prevent the princess from becoming an object of public scandal. If the princess's apprenticeship with her mother is unable to ward off the desire that the very sight of Nemours instills in her, it is also the basis from which she performs a profound critique of masculinity. By first giving her husband the role of maternal adviser and then, on his death, assimilating it as what Nemours calls a "fantôme de devoir" (229) ("phantom of duty" [147]), the princess adopts her mother's skeptical vision of the homosocial bonding in courtly intrigue. Even before Clèves's death, she has internalized enough of her mother's warnings to attempt to put a stop to the narration of her confession when she hears it at court, asserting that the story is implausible (183; 106). We might say that she is intent on short-circuiting the masculinist exchange of knowledge—at least as far as her own story is concerned. It is in her final face-to-face rejection of Nemours, however, that she accomplishes the most definitive deconstruction of masculinity. In her only verbal declaration of love for him, the princess returns to her mother's counterknowledge to refuse his love:

> Je sais que vous êtes libre, que je le suis, et que les choses sont d'une sorte que le public n'aurait peut-être pas sujet de vous blâmer, ni moi non plus, quand nous nous engagerions ensemble pour jamais. Mais les hommes conservent-ils de la passion dans ces engagements éternels? Dois-je espérer un miracle en ma faveur; et puis-je me mettre en état de voir certainement finir cette passion dont je ferais toute ma félicité?
>
> (230–31)

> I know that you are free, that I am free also, and that, in all the circumstances, the world would perhaps have no reason to blame either of us if we were to bind ourselves together for life. But how long does men's passion last when the bond is eternal? Can I expect a miracle in my favour? If not, can I resign myself to the prospect that a passion on which my happiness depended must infallibly come to an end?   (148)

By invoking public opinion, this passage suggests that the princess fears not only male infidelity but also public knowledge of that infidelity and, one might conclude, humiliation. It is not entirely unexpected, then, that this demystification of masculine desire is followed by a complete and absolute end to all communication with Nemours. To attain the *repos* ("tranquillity") she so ardently strives for, she must withdraw herself and knowledge of herself from the exchanges of court life. Unless she takes herself out of circulation, so to speak, she has no hope of regaining her self-knowledge.

If the princess is at least partially successful in regaining her sense of self-control, the same cannot necessarily be said for Nemours and certainly not for Clèves. The princess is able to fashion a femininity that resists homosocial exchange and the victimization of women it entails, while the rival male protagonists actually fall prey to the structures of mimetic desire on which masculinity depends in this novel. Love for the princess causes both Nemours and Clèves to violate the prescribed codes of masculinity. We can identify at least two transgressions.

First, both men confuse the roles of lover and husband, which are intended to be distinct. Christian Biet has shown that moral prescriptions for marriage in sixteenth- and seventeenth-century France forbade the presence of "amour-passion" between spouses and that much of the plot turns on this question (see esp. Biet 44, 46). The roles of husband and counselor were to be kept distinct from those of lover and friend. M. de Clèves himself admits to blurring these distinctions when, after his wife's confession, he declares, "J'ai tout ensemble la jalousie d'un mari et celle d'un amant. Mais il est impossible d'avoir celle

d'un mari après un procédé comme le vôtre. [. . .] [I]l me console même
comme votre amant" (172) ("I am jealous both as a husband and as a lover; yet
it is impossible to feel a husband's jealousy after a gesture such as yours. [. . .]
[I]t consoles me even in my role as lover" [96]). In his final conversation with
the princess, the duc de Nemours in effect asks her to join marriage and passion. And it is precisely this prospect that she cannot accept because, as she explains, Nemours will in the end be unable to remain both husband and lover,
faithful to her alone.

> [V]ous êtes né avec toutes les dispositions pour la galanterie et toutes les
> qualités qui sont propres à y donner des succès heureux. Vous avez déjà
> eu plusieurs passions, vous en auriez encore; je ne ferais plus votre bon-
> heur; je vous verrais pour une autre comme vous auriez été pour moi.
> (231)

> [Y]ou were born with a great susceptibility to love and all the qualities re-
> quired for success in love. You have already had a number of passionate
> attachments; you would have others. I should no longer be able to make
> you happy; I should see you behaving towards another woman as you had
> behaved towards me.   (149)

Beyond the consequences to her personally, the princess's reply suggests the
social disorder that could be caused by the confusion of the roles of husband
and lover. In a sexual and political economy such as the court's, which treats
family ties as strategy (if not property) and which puts love in the service of ambition, men must be free to manage their kinship arrangements as social—and
not affective—affairs and, further, to move from intrigue to intrigue as circumstances warrant. Only by preserving this freedom are men able to maneuver
within the risky exchanges of knowledge and power.

Second, to varying degrees, neither Nemours nor Clèves is able to maintain
the lucidity and thus the freedom necessary to function properly at court. This
transgression of the novel's codes of masculinity concerns the psychological
disarray that both men experience because of their love for the princess. The
husband and the lover are taken to the threshold of madness; they are afflicted
by an utter loss of self-control. Unable to force the princess to confess her
lover's identity, Clèves is overcome by violently contradictory passions.

> [J]e n'ai que des sentiments violents et incertains dont je ne suis pas le
> maître. Je ne me trouve plus digne de vous; vous ne me paraissez plus
> digne de moi. Je vous adore, je vous hais; je vous offense, je vous de-
> mande pardon; je vous admire, j'ai honte de vous admirer. Enfin il n'y a
> plus en moi ni de calme, ni de raison.   (204)

> I have fallen prey to violent, shifting emotions which I cannot master. I
> no longer consider myself worthy of you; you no longer seem worthy of

me. I adore you, I hate you, I offend you, I beg your forgiveness; I admire you, I am ashamed of my admiration. There is, in short, no last shred of tranquillity or reason in me.   (124)

As Nemours resolves to meet with the princess for what will be the last time, he too is plagued by self-doubt: "Est-il possible que l'amour m'ait si absolument ôté la raison et la hardiesse et qu'il m'ait rendu si différent de ce que j'ai été dans les autres passions de ma vie?" (225) ("Can love have deprived me so absolutely of reason and courage? Can it have made my behaviour so different from what it used to be in my other attachments?" [143]). The turmoil that both Clèves and Nemours find themselves in is exacerbated (if not caused) by the princess's refusal to play her part, especially at the end of the novel, in the mimetic rivalry between them. Withdrawing her knowledge and her very presence, the princess renders both Clèves and Nemours ineffective within the circuits of exchange that make up the world of the court. Rather than mediate between the two men, the princess disrupts the homosocial bond of patriarchal dominance. Rather than facilitate the struggle for control between the two leading male characters, she contributes to the loss of their self-control—the loss of mastery over self and other through knowledge that is the illusion of masculinity.

In the final pages of *La Princesse de Clèves*, the narrator seems to take over the princess's role in exposing the dysfunction of homosocial exchange. After the final meeting with Nemours, the princess dims from our view, retiring from the court and the world. The narrative pace quickens and third-person narration dominates; it is as if Mme de Clèves's exceptional, inimitable example is incomprehensible, unknowable not only to Nemours and Clèves but also to patriarchal regimes of reading and knowledge generally. By withholding the detailed knowledge about the princess that is provided up to this point, the novel seems to invite readers to reflect on their own stake in the exchange of knowledge represented in the text and (re)enacted in criticism and the classroom. How and what do we know about Mme de Chartres, the princess, Nemours, and Clèves? How and what do we know about femininity and masculinity in the novel? Consideration of questions such as these will not lead to simple answers. It may, however, be a first step in helping students become aware of the role of literature and knowledge in the construction of gender identities, a first step in encouraging them to rethink the relation of masculinity and femininity to the exchanges of knowledge that structure our world.

Making Sense of the Ending:
Passion, Virtue, and Female Subjectivity
Katharine Ann Jensen

I have taught *La Princesse de Clèves* in a variety of graduate and undergraduate courses at a large state university in the South over the last eight years. All too often, the end of the novel signals the end of my students' patience. Invested in the Hollywood happy ending of consummated passion in marriage, the students have such a hard time reading any other kind of story or imagining any other kind of happiness that they often think the princess or Lafayette is "weird" or "masochistic." This difficulty stems, I believe, from the unfamiliar historical terms that define women's identities in the novel. In this essay I suggest one strategy for dealing with students' resistance to the ending and offer a reading of the heroine's story that sees her renunciation of Nemours as a positive expression of her subjectivity rather than as an impenetrable or self-punishing action.

From the beginning of our study of *La Princesse de Clèves*, I try to gauge how open students are to historical and cultural differences. I ask questions such as How would you describe life in the court? What are the differences between men's and women's lives in the court? How do aristocratic people marry in the ancien régime? Why does Mlle de Chartres come to court? Their answers (and their questions) help me emphasize, elaborate, and reiterate points from earlier discussions as we proceed with the novel. I have found, however, that no matter how well students seem to grasp the complexity of the novel, no matter how well they seem to appreciate the princess's dilemmas, the ending is almost always a stumbling block to their earlier understandings. So once students have finished reading the novel, I begin the class period by asking, Why did the princess refuse to marry Nemours? I write down the usually diverse responses on the board or underscore them verbally. I stress the diversity of students' interpretations to suggest that it is itself a clear indication of the richness of Lafayette's novel. Indeed, I emphasize that to debate the heroine's choice shows how literature lives beyond the time it was written and extends beyond the pages of a book. I then explain that as responsive and responsible readers, however, we must distinguish between how the novel explains the heroine's choice and our reactions to it. We might not like the princess's decision or not want to adopt it for our own lives, but we can still try to understand it in the terms of the text and its cultural context and thereby learn about our own contexts.

Next, I present key passages from debates that the novel's ending provoked at the time of its first publication. When students learn that the princess's decision not to marry Nemours has posed problems since the seventeenth century, they tend to feel more confident about their responses, interested in considering the reasons for other responses, and less resistant to examining the assumptions they hold. These debates, which sometimes uncannily echo students' criticisms, demonstrate that readers' difficulties with the princess are not exclusively due to her historical remoteness, since even some of Lafayette's contemporaries could not fathom her heroine's motivations.

After *La Princesse de Clèves* appeared in 1678, two prominent men of letters, Roger de Bussy-Rabutin and Jean-Baptiste de Valincour, pronounced the heroine's actions unbelievable or implausible for different reasons. Bussy-Rabutin found it hard to believe that a woman would remain faithful to her husband during his lifetime when she was passionately in love with another man, for in his view her passion would naturally overpower her virtue. Bussy maintained that once M. de Clèves died, since the princess was still in love with Nemours, "she would be delighted ['ravie'] to be able to bring [love and virtue] together by marrying a man of [Nemours's] quality [. . .]" (Laugaa 18; my trans.). Valincour, although not actually in dialogue with Bussy, answers Bussy's objection, quoting the princess's reason for her refusal: "Ce que je crois devoir à la mémoire de M. de Clèves serait faible s'il n'était soutenu par l'intérêt de mon repos" (224) ("What I believe I owe to the memory of M. de Clèves would be a feeble resource were it not sustained by self-interest, namely my desire for tranquillity of mind"; my trans.). He goes on to explain, following Lafayette's text, that the princess fears that after marrying Nemours, she would lose peace of mind because he would cease to love her in preference for another woman. Valincour derides this fear, for he considers the princess a "coquettish prude" (*Lettres* 223; my trans.). In other words, he moves from criticizing the plausibility of the ending to condemning her character: either she should act on her passion for Nemours and marry him or she should repress her feelings and remain silent (223). She should not speak of her passion to Nemours if it is only to refuse him on the grounds of his probable infidelity: "This *seems to her such a horrible misfortune* that she takes seven or eight pages to depict it in terms of the most refined coquetry. Isn't that a lovely reason not to marry a man?" (224; my trans.; emphasis added). According to Valincour, then, the princess's fear of Nemours's infidelity and her attempt to explain that fear are just so much teasing and prevarication.

I ask the students, On what do Bussy and Valincour base their allegations of implausibility? With whom or what do they identify when they criticize the heroine's actions? The students are generally able to see that the critics identify with a male perspective, perhaps Nemours's in particular. I remind them of Bussy's objection that a woman's virtue could never have withstood her adulterous passion and point out that virtue and, more specifically, the tranquillity it brings are the keys to understanding the princess's actions. Virtue and tranquillity thus form the historical and thematic frames for the following reading of the novel's ending.

I begin by explaining that for women in *La Princesse de Clèves* virtue means chastity before marriage and fidelity after it—at least ideally. In ancien régime

France, aristocratic families arranged their children's marriages in the interest of class insularity. Once married, the wife was obligated to provide male heirs to ensure the continuation of her husband's lineage and to keep money and property in the family. Because marriages were not made for love and passion, both men and women often sought to satisfy such desires outside marriage. The emphasis on male bloodlines, on paternal property and its transmission, resulted in powerful strictures against female adultery because of its potential for producing illegitimate children, notably bastard sons who would threaten the "proper" succession of wealth. Though infidelity was common, women risked paying a much higher price for it than men did. In fact a husband had the right, although it was not always exercised, to kill his wife were he to find her with another man. At the very least, the unfaithful woman would lose her good name, having dishonored her husband, herself, and their families. The ideal of female virtue in marriage thus worked to ensure the stability of a patriarchal structure.

When we first meet Mlle de Chartres, what role has virtue played in her education? Her widowed mother, who has been uniquely responsible for raising her, developed an exceptional strategy to instill virtue in her daughter. Departing from the norm of maternal silence on sexual matters, Mme de Chartres portrays the pleasures of illicit entanglements, all the better to highlight the dangers and unhappiness of such involvements. In contrast to the pain and disruption of adultery, Mme de Chartres shows "quelle tranquillité suivait la vie d'une honnête femme, et *combien la vertu donnait d'éclat et d'élévation à une personne qui avait de la beauté et de la naissance*" (76; emphasis added) ("the tranquillity that a woman of good reputation enjoys. She told her *how much brilliance and distinction virtue bestows on a woman who is beautiful and well-born*" [10; emphasis added]). On the one hand, virtue reaps peace of mind and tranquillity of soul; on the other, it distinctly enhances a woman's identity, or more specifically her *reputation*, since identity in the world of the court where Mlle de Chartres will circulate is a relentlessly public issue. Whereas beauty and nobility are qualities a woman like Mlle de Chartres is given at birth, virtue is something she can achieve. Achieving virtue is far from the only means through which an aristocratic woman can exercise an ambitious wish, but it certainly is the only safe one. Examples in the novel show that both men and women hold political ambitions, desire power, and use marriage, love affairs, and affiliations with powerful figures to pursue their own ends (81; 14). Yet when duplicity of this kind is exposed, it has dire, even fatal, consequences. Moreover, precisely because adultery and duplicity are the order of the day, virtue constitutes exceptional behavior; and the desire to be exceptional through virtue is another form female ambition might appropriately take.

Certainly, Mme de Chartres, who is described as "extrêmement glorieuse" (77) ("exceptionally proud and ambitious" [10]), wants her daughter to distinguish herself through virtue. For Mme de Chartres, virtue means erotic inviolability. Portraying marital love, which in arranged marriages consists in respect and appreciation, as a woman's only chance at happiness—"ce qui seul peut faire le bonheur d'une femme [. . .] est d'aimer son mari et d'en être aimée" (76) ("the only thing that can ensure a woman's happiness: to love one's husband and to be loved by him" [10])—Mme de Chartres posits an ideal that, were it realized, would safeguard her daughter from the emotional havoc that desire wreaks, even desire for one's husband. According to Mme de Chartres's account of "le peu de sincérité des hommes, leurs tromperies et leur infidélité" (76) ("men's insincerity, [. . .] their deceptions and infidelity" [10]), husbands no less than lovers can betray and wound those who desire them. In the Prince de Clèves, for whom her daughter feels "reconnaissance" (86) ("gratitude" [19]) but no "inclination" (87) ("attraction" [20]), Mme de Chartres thus makes a strategic choice. Meanwhile, the prince's unusual passion for his wife—which will in time destroy him physically and emotionally—provides further grounds for the daughter's dutiful appreciation of her husband (89; 22). The mother wagers that her daughter, married to the prince and wholly devoted to conjugal virtue, will remain free from erotic and emotional investment and the pain that such investment invariably brings.

Before tracing the fate of Mme de Chartres's wager, let us look more closely at her ideal of female happiness. What, other than virtuous behavior and, therefore, a brilliant reputation, does conjugal fidelity—freedom from desire—mean? In presenting her ideal for happiness, Mme de Chartres evokes the tranquillity that results from virtue, that is, from the absence of desire's agitating pains and pleasures. Students, who often equate tranquillity with boredom, need help here to see that tranquillity, or *repos*, constituted a prominent ethical value in seventeenth-century France, where passions came to be seen as antithetical both to happiness and to knowledge of self, God, and human existence. By freeing oneself from the agitations and conflicts of desire, one might attain *repos* and through it insight and knowledge into oneself and others (see Stanton, "Ideal").

Although a general human ideal, *repos*, I would argue, held out particular interest and advantages to women. As we have seen, marital and sexual relations in the ancien régime were governed by a rule of male privilege. Thus the woman who yielded to desire and its momentary fulfillment in physical union—whether conjugal or adulterous—subjected herself not only to the self-undermining vagaries of desire but also to the self-defeating structure of the double standard: a woman's husband or lover would inevitably betray her. In other words, the nature of desire and the structure of heterosexual relations left women with very little *self* at all. By contrast, the tranquillity that could result from lack of desire, from the absence of emotional dependence and of the agony of abandonment, would afford women the chance to be subjects for themselves rather than objects of men's seduction and betrayal.

Indeed, as I contend to my students the Princesse de Clèves's story is one of becoming a subject for herself. She can only begin to assert herself, however, after her mother's death, for Mme de Chartres, in life, arrests her daughter's development through her own narcissism. Her ambition to create a daughter known for exceptional virtue is, after all, also, or even primarily, a wish to distinguish herself through that daughter. After marriage, for example, when the princess continues to be the object of many men's desire, her mother, agent of the daughter's actions, achieves her ideal: public recognition that her daughter, who appears unassailable, is absolutely virtuous (89; 22).

The princess not only appears to be unattainable but is also desireless. Free of erotic, emotional attachment to a man, she remains exclusively attached to her mother. Mme de Chartres's emotional and ambitious desires, we see, are inextricably bound together, and they depend completely on the daughter for satisfaction. This dependence makes the mother most vulnerable; for she can achieve her desires only as long as her daughter complies with her narcissism. The princess incarnates her mother's desireless ideal not by choice but by default. Until she meets Nemours, she has no basis for choosing for or against desire, since her sense of self is utterly reflective, uniquely defined by her mother's wishes for desirelessness. Nemours gives the princess access to a desire distinct from her mother's; thus she begins to gain a sense of self that is separate from her mother's construction of her. While this separation heralds the beginning of the Princesse de Clèves's story, it signals Mme de Chartres's undoing.

Before falling in love with Nemours, the princess followed her mother's instructions to confide in her mother about all matters of "galanterie" (82) ("love" [15]); these confidences facilitated Mme de Chartres's protective and possessive desire to guide and control her daughter. With the burgeoning of desire, the situation changes.

> Elle ne se trouva pas la même disposition à dire à sa mère ce qu'elle pensait des sentiments de ce prince qu'elle avait eue à lui parler de ses autres amants; sans avoir un dessein formé de lui cacher, elle ne lui en parla point; mais Mme de Chartres ne le voyait que trop, aussi bien que le penchant que sa fille avait pour lui.   (100)

> She found herself to be less disposed to tell her mother what she thought about the Duc de Nemours's feelings than to speak to her of the other men who were in love with her; without deliberately intending to hide anything, she said nothing about it. But it was all too evident to Mme de Chartres, as was her daughter's liking for him.   (32)

Mme de Chartres recognizes immediately that her daughter is no longer the transparent reflection of maternal wishes, no longer the passive vessel of maternal authority. She also recognizes Nemours—a ladies' man with a reputation for being irresistible (100; 32)—as the object of the princess's desire. On both counts, the daughter has dealt her mother what turns out to be a fatal narcissistic blow. With the advent of the princess's passion, Mme de Chartres is no longer the sole emotional focus or the unique authority. She has also failed in her ambition to create a woman who is erotically inviolable, that is, absolutely virtuous and thereby exceptional. The princess's virtue is not just tainted; she is subject to the worst kind of desire: adulterous desire. In the mother's world of absolutes, her daughter can only be either erotically inaccessible or forever fallen; either the mother has an exclusive emotional authority over her daughter or she has nothing. Unable to attenuate these absolute terms, the mother sickens and dies as a result of her daughter's illicit desire and newfound subjectivity.

After her mother's death, the princess is left to contend with her desire and to define herself. Sometime after she returns to court following the initial mourning period for Mme de Chartres, she experiences desire in such a way that it will inform her subsequent choices to privilege *repos* over turmoil, self over Nemours. One evening, the princess is given a letter by the dauphine who tells her it is a letter written to Nemours by "cette maîtresse pour qui il a quitté toutes les autres" (142) ("the mistress for whose sake he has abandoned all his other mistresses" [70]). The dauphine instructs her to read it to see if she recognizes the handwriting and can identify the mysterious woman. The princess is stunned by "une [. . .] douleur insupportable" (143) ("an intolerable pain" [70]), for Nemours himself had given her to understand that *she* was this woman; yet another had written the letter. The princess recognizes that the excruciating pain she feels is "la jalousie avec toutes les horreurs dont elle peut être accompagnée. Elle voyait par cette lettre que M. de Nemours avait une galanterie depuis longtemps" (145) ("jealousy with all its attendant horrors. The letter showed her that M. de Nemours had long been engaged in a love affair" [72]). Where earlier that day the princess had experienced her disordering desire for Nemours as pain mixed with "quelque sorte de douceur" (142) ("a kind of sweetness" [69]), now it has become the pure pain of betrayal and the ravaging agony of jealousy. Her loss of self to this emotional torture is exacerbated by the humiliation of loving a man unworthy of her. Worse than this, she had let him see she loved him, thereby making herself vulnerable to his egotism and perfidy. Recalling her mother's deathbed advice to take whatever drastic actions necessary to avoid the miseries of adultery (108; 40), she berates herself for not confessing her illicit desire to her husband, with whom her secret would have been safe (146; 72).

By reading herself into the misplaced letter, the princess sees herself reduced to an object in the service of male self-aggrandizement, subjected to a man "qui ne pensait à être aimé d'elle que par un sentiment d'orgueil et de vanité" (146) ("who only wanted her love in order to nourish his pride and vanity" [72]).

Although the princess recovers her composure somewhat when she learns that her uncle, the vidame de Chartres, not Nemours, is the addressee of the letter, the trauma of the episode provides motivation for two singular actions, which mark crucial steps in her development of self-consciousness. First—to the amazement of many of the novel's first readers—she does confess her desire for another man to her husband. Designating this act as one that sets her apart from all other wives (171; 95), the princess reveals that she wants to distinguish herself through virtue just as her mother had wished. Yet whereas her mother was primarily invested in the public, external benefits of such distinction, the daughter is motivated by more-private, internal concerns, for underlying this ambitious wish to be singular among women is her wish to be free of the controlling force of desire. She confesses in order to minimize this force, to preserve her marriage and, thereby, to some degree, her tranquillity and sense of self.

In her mother's economy of absolutes, desire of any kind mitigated the princess's virtue; the Princesse de Clèves avows her illegitimate desire, however, as proof of her marital devotion. By distinguishing between adulterous feelings and virtuous actions—the interpretation of the confession that I present to my students (171; 95)—the princess attempts to resolve an ethical contradiction: extramarital passion can coexist with wifely fidelity. Similarly, passion, when properly subordinated to virtue, need not overwhelm the self.

In her effort to gain some control over desire and herself, the princess, paradoxically, must subordinate that self to her husband's will as an act of wifely virtue. During her confession she asks him to allow her to withdraw from court life and all its private and public dangers, but the prince demands that she go back into circulation, all the better for him to discover the object of her desire—whom she consistently refuses to name.

Finally, when the prince dies of jealousy, the princess is free to exercise more control than ever before over herself and her life. She is free, that is, from her mother's narcissistic investment in her virtuous actions and from her husband's rule over her behavior. Rather than resubmit herself to another man's control, she chooses to remain alone, autonomous. In her only private face-to-face meeting with Nemours, she justifies her refusal to marry him on the basis of his amorous history and her excruciating experience of jealousy during the letter episode: "Vous avez déjà eu plusieurs passions; vous en auriez encore. [. . .] J'en aurais une douleur mortelle [. . .]" (231) ("You have already had a number of passionate attachments; you would have others. [. . .] I should be mortally wounded" [149]). By refusing the pain that she believes marriage to the ladies' man Nemours will inevitably bring her, the princess privileges her subjectivity over male social and sexual prerogatives.

Her refusal to marry the man she desires is an exceptional act—one that Bussy and Valincour charged with implausibility—because it defies patriarchal norms according to which women act in men's interest, not on behalf of their own desires. Though the princess, in fact, concedes to these norms by enlisting her duty to her husband to shore up her argument against Nemours and to achieve self-preservation and peace of mind (232; 150), her refusal of Nemours is, finally, a profoundly self-conscious, self-affirming act based on experience and on insight into the destructive consequences of male sexual privilege, the disempowering force of desire, and the confining structure of marriage. While signifying to a singular degree her wifely virtue, her devotion to a dead man—rather than reengagement with a live one—is a clear means of winning female autonomy (which Bussy and Valincour may have sensed since they were not satisfied by the princess's preference for one *man* over another; as noted, they may have had the virile Nemours's interests closer to heart than those of the fragile Prince de Clèves). What the princess wants more than the momentary pleasure of sexual fulfillment is the lasting benefit of a self and a life she can control.

To give students an alternative—positive—reading of the ending, I emphasize that the heroine's stunning act of self-affirmation through refusal is not the end of her story. In a world where female subjectivity is an anomaly, the princess must work to insure herself against the prevailing forces of corruption and desire. To avoid Nemours, she withdraws from court and takes refuge in the space that, historically, provided aristocratic women with the most complete autonomy: the convent. After Nemours's passion dies and he no longer threatens her independence, the princess modifies her living situation, spending half the year in the convent and the other half at home. In either dwelling, assured of tranquillity and autonomy, the princess is able not only to be but also to act productively—albeit briefly. As the novel's final lines record, she spends her time "dans des occupations plus saintes que celle des couvents les plus austeres; et sa vie, qui fut assez courte, laissa des exemples de vertu inimitables" (239) ("in occupations more saintly than those of the most austere houses of religion. Her life, which was quite short, left inimitable examples of virtue" [156]). The brevity of the heroine's life could be seen as a measure of the traditional limits of fiction: what makes a novel is adultery and desire, not a woman's independent life and productivity once her struggle with passion is over. At the same time, the terms of her productivity—virtuous deeds—reflect how history, culture, and class limit women's work. Nonetheless, that the princess does lead some sort of productive life after she secures her autonomy suggests, perhaps, that the ultimate benefit of subjectivity is agency, that is, the chance to act in and on the world. Finally, then, the inimitable nature of the princess's virtuous acts might measure her own and her author's ambitious wish to leave, on this world, an indelible trace.

The Mother-Daughter Subtext in *La Princesse de Clèves*

Michèle Longino

It is one of the great ironies of the profession that in the literature class students can be taught only what in some sense they already know. For this reason, there can be a considerable difference between teaching *La Princesse de Clèves* to generally more naïve undergraduate students and to more experienced graduate students. The distance between these two groups mirrors that between the princess's innocence at the beginning of the novel and her mother's worldliness, except that the graduate student will, like the undergraduate, identify with the heroine, as guided by the narrator, and will not necessarily subscribe to the mother's opinions. This does not, however, mean that introduction to the novel should be delayed. The sooner students begin to read *La Princesse de Clèves*, the better. For it is a classic and bears repeated reading, yielding new insights at each contact. Students need to grow into it and out of it. Timing, then, is crucial to the kind of reading the text will bear. And most often students will learn best to appreciate the novel not from the teacher but from one another and from their own experience outside the classroom.

The mother delivers her cautionary words both too soon and too late. They miss their moment, that moment when the daughter experiences precisely that against which the mother has cautioned her. Mlle de Chartres has everything yet to learn about love and courtship, while Mme de Chartres speaks to her from vicarious and unacknowledged (it is speculated) experience, sharing positions and proffering lessons couched in generalities and stories about particular individuals. In the same way the teacher's words inevitably miss their moment.

But while the classroom does not afford coincidence of experience, it is the place where insight can be had on prior experience and where ground can be laid for future insight.

The ideal, then, is to teach the novel to mature students who have read it before and who can bring to it their own experiences, to encourage a praxis of recognition. Then one can concentrate on the complex structure and subtleties of the plot and from there move on to the theoretical issues of narrative and psychology at play. Undergraduate students must often be helped through the historical apparatus, the abstract language, and the elliptical grammar, so that it is a struggle to move beyond the level of comprehension to analysis and interpretation. This can be done, but it means privileging one reading over others so as not to overwhelm the students. And I believe that if one reading is to be privileged, it is that which highlights the crucial role of the mother-daughter relationship in the formation of the princess and the shaping of the plot.

In both the undergraduate and the graduate class, my approach is to begin with a close reading of the novel, to analyze this seventeenth-century artifact exhaustively as constructed text, to highlight the passages most pertinent to my reading, and only afterward to look at how twentieth-century feminist theory illuminates representations of the mother-daughter relationship then and now; finally, we consider the greater familial, economic, and political scheme that frames the relationship.

The two most illuminating essays—founding and by now classic readings—on the mother-daughter subtext in *La Princesse de Clèves* are those by Marianne Hirsch ("A Mother's Discourse") and by Peggy Kamuf ("A Mother's Will"). Again and again I am struck with the richness of these essays, and I combine teaching them as fine examples of literary criticism with my presentation of the novel. Their insights inform this essay if only obliquely. I recommend assigning these readings for discussion toward the end of the study of the novel, so that the students are allowed first to formulate their own interpretations.

As for presentation of the textual evidence, I first point out that direct allusions to the mother end at page 146 (72), shortly before the end of volume 2, approximately halfway through the novel. From there it is a question of investigating the nature of her presence and role in the first half and eventually analyzing the remainder of the novel, specifically the princess's key relationships with the men in her life—M. de Clèves and the duc de Nemours—in that light. Thus what is above named the subtext, the underpinning of the plot, can also be understood as the pretext: what happens first and determines what follows. Below I focus on the pressure points of the text that yield insight on the mother-daughter subtext, the passages my students and I discuss at length.

The unfurling of historical pageantry that characterizes the first pages of the novel is interrupted by the introduction of the fictional heroine into the world of the court (76; 9). Her story, as it unfolds in turn, respects a precise political, economic, and familial order and offers salient supporting facts. First is presented the anonymous beauty, Mlle de Chartres—the object of exchange brought to market. Her appurtenance to the family of the vidame de Chartres sets out the court loyalties that must be hers, and her wealth marks her desirability as a match at court, suggesting that there will be competition for her hand. Next, significantly, her father is named for the sole time in the novel; he will thus function as at once absent and present throughout. Although he is dead, at his death he had confided his daughter to his wife, her mother, and transferred to his wife his paternal authority over their daughter, thereby ensuring the continuance of his influence in the daughter's life and augmenting the mother's. The empowerment of the mother's voice and the shaping of the daughter's life takes place, then, under the aegis of the father. Deathbed pronouncements, first the father's, then the mother's, and finally the husband's, will set psychological limits on the options available to the princess as she eventually structures her life. Mme de Chartres thus has a double function: she represents not only the maternal element but also the continuing paternal one—her role in her daughter's life is doubly charged. Since she has lived alone with Mlle de Chartres in the country, far from court, the daughter has been subjected to her exclusive influence in her formative years and now at sixteen is distinctly a product of her upbringing.

Mlle de Chartres's education is described at length (76; 9–10) and is key to appreciating what follows. Mme de Chartres is most concerned with immunizing her daughter against gallantry and passion. She does not hold a high opinion of women: she seeks to exempt herself and her daughter from her harsh judgment on their kind by cultivating difference; one can only suspect that her attitude covers some doubts concerning her own worth and perhaps even some guilt for past transgressions of her own. The mother does not want herself or her daughter to be like other women. The distinction between other mothers ("la plupart des mères" ["Most mothers"]) and Mme de Chartres ("Mme de Chartres avait une opinion opposée" [76] ["Mme de Chartres believed the opposite" (9–10)]) indicates the mother's concern for her daughter's exceptionality, which will surface spectacularly at her deathbed: "si quelque chose était capable de troubler le bonheur que j'espère en sortant de ce monde, ce serait de vous voir tomber *comme les autres femmes* [. . .] (108; my emphasis) ("Were anything capable of troubling the happiness I hope for in leaving this world, it would be to see you fall *like other women*" [40; my emphasis]).

To nurture such a sense of exceptionality and to make her daughter impervious to amorous advances that could bring about her downfall, Mme de Chartres takes the unusual course of describing love in great detail; as a result, she thinks, the daughter will be prepared when it strikes, able to combat it and maintain not only an appearance but also an essence of virtue. But it is telling that the preponderance of the mother's discourse is given to describing the foibles of men, the dangers and disappointments of love—indeed, she produces a precise inventory—and very little to describing the pleasant aspects, which remain vague, abstract, unspoken. The mother's insistence on the negative and guilt-producing aspects of passion, the danger of involvement with all men save one's husband, is explicitly stated, the easier to seize. Her words register in her daughter's conscience.

Such an education was certainly in keeping with the Catholic position on marriage, a position held even more strongly under the reign of Henri II, the setting of the novel, than in Mme de Lafayette's time. What is more, between that time and the penning of the novel the wars of religion had further defined and embittered dogmatic differences between Catholics and Protestants. Add to this that the novel was written during a period of particular severity, under the influence of the strict Jansenists, who believed in predestination and the corrupting nature of the senses (they considered all sensual experience debasing and sinful), and it becomes even clearer that Mme de Chartres's lessons to her daughter, even if they were not intended as particularly religious, were in accordance with the prevailing views on marriage (virginity until marriage, no tolerance of adultery, no possibility of divorce). These considerations, of course, affected attitudes more markedly than they affected actual practices.

Given Mme de Chartres's views on the dangers of love, it follows that her main concern should be to marry her daughter to someone *she* loves, so that passion might be contained within the sanctioned relationship. But two concepts of love are at play here, the one of attraction (*inclination*) and the other of appreciation (*reconnaissance*). And also two beings: for the ambiguity of the "she" emphasized above emblematizes the problem of identity between mother and daughter: separation issues and ego boundaries, such as Hirsch discusses and Nancy Chodorow elaborates, are at stake even at the level of grammar. They explain the mother's undue influence and the daughter's susceptibility reciprocally and reveal that Mme de Chartres, as the mother, has the dominant, authoritative role in the couple. The daughter is young, only sixteen (77; 10), and she has led a sheltered existence under her mother's exclusive tutelage. She is not equipped to know whether or in which way she loves someone until or unless it happens. The mother, who must exercise the paternal prerogative as well in identifying a suitable husband is, we learn, "extrêment glorieuse" (77) ("exceptionally proud and ambitious" [10]). Her main concern is not simply to find a love match for the daughter but to engineer a marriage worthy of the family. This effort turns out to be complicated in the extreme, given the factions that divide the court and the familial obligations that render certain suitors ineligible.

During this period of husband seeking, Mme de Chartres requests her daughter's complete confidence, so that she might advise her in any situations that arise and might help sort them out. In this way, she hopes to maintain control over her daughter and to continue to shape her as she sees fit (82; 15). One sees to what extent the daughter is truly the mother's creation. Just as Mme de Chartres had been forced by circumstances to take on the role of father in addition to that of mother, here she attempts to take on the role of friend in place of that of mother: "elle la pria *non pas comme sa mère, mais comme son amie, de lui faire confidence*" (82; my emphasis) ("she begged her, *not as a mother but as a friend*, to tell her if anyone ever talked to her of love" [15; my emphasis]).

These role signals indicate that there exist at the time clearly prescribed comportments for each of the relations (mother, father, friend), and the consequences for the princess of stepping in and out of them suggest the dangers of collapsing the roles. The signals foreshadow her eventual husband's claim that if he saw his wife distressed because she was taken with someone else, he would step out of his role of husband: *"Je quitterais le personnage d'amant ou de mari,* pour la conseiller et pour la plaindre" (117; my emphasis) (*"I should abandon the role of lover or husband* in order to offer her my advice and my compassion" [46; my emphasis]). We know that his ultimately impossible avowal prepares the way for the princess's—a moment of sincerity that produces disastrous results for all. Apparently society is organized according to roles, and individuals function smoothly in society only as long as they respect those roles. The assumption, discarding, doubling, confusion, and collapsing of the roles put persons at risk and confound the social fabric. But adherence to given roles stifles, stunts, and equally jeopardizes the well-being of men and women. This effect is illustrated throughout the novel by Mlle de Chartres, the Princesse de Clèves, who remains quintessentially the mother's daughter.

When the proud mother sees her ambitions for a distinguished match with the Prince de Montpensier disintegrate (84; 17) and the enamoured M. de Clèves suddenly becomes available thanks to his father's death (86; 19), the marriage question appears to be resolved. However, it is M. de Clèves who voices the concerns that should be the mother's when he approaches Mlle de Chartres—it is he who fears to constrain her in a relationship that appears to inspire only polite appreciation. Mlle de Chartres's conversation with her mother concerning M. de Clèves's interest is like an exchange with a deaf—or selectively deaf—person (87; 19–20). The mother claims that if her daughter "sentait son inclination portée" ("felt an inclination") to M. de Clèves, this would be an excellent match. Mlle de Chartres's negative response is clear: "elle n'avait aucune inclination particulière pour sa personne" (87) ("she felt no particular attraction for his person" [19–20]). Her words are entirely unacknowledged. Mme de Chartres proceeds to negotiate with the prince the very next day as if the daughter's words, the very opinion she had been soliciting, had never been stated. This failure to hear sets the stage for a tragic mismatch.

Further, Mme de Chartres acts in the place of the father, but because she too is a woman she acts also in the place of her daughter and of herself. As Kamuf points out, the marriage is contracted between the two adult parties, M. de Clèves and Mme de Chartres, who excludes her daughter from consideration almost entirely (75). She is merely the object of exchange. It should also be noted that as the mother arranges her daughter's marriage, her perception of M. de Clèves suggests that he too does not fit the proposed role: "il faisait paraître tant de sagesse pour son âge" (87) ("[he shows] a wisdom beyond his years" [19]). M. de Clèves is not young at heart but staid and mature beyond his years. He fits the bill of father or uncle more appropriately than that of husband or lover; he is a more suitable match for the mother than for her daughter.

All the clues set in place in this exchange between the mother and her daughter, as well as in the preceding one between the young girl and M. de Clèves, indicate that this is clearly not a good match for Mlle de Chartres. But the mother insists that the princess should be grateful to this man for having courted her, since he did so at a time when no one else could (89; 21). The politics of matchmaking and of negotiating the maze of court life has made this marriage so attractive to the mother that she chooses to ignore the very factor of love—"inclination" (87; 20)—on which she herself had so firmly insisted in her earlier lessons to her daughter and about which she claimed to be concerned when her daughter first mentioned M. de Clèves's interest.

The mother further binds the daughter to her standards after the marriage (89; 22). It is evident that the princess is not in love with her husband. He and the mother are both aware of this, but the princess, who has had no experience of attraction, is not, and is alone ignorant of her deficiency as wife. And so it is even more important that the marriage be cemented by feelings of duty, gratitude, and devotion, that the daughter's behavior be irreproachable and that it advertise her as unattainable (89; 21). This façade the mother encourages her daughter to cultivate.

When the princess dances with M. de Nemours, those who care—specifically, the mother and the chevalier de Guise—immediately see that she is smitten (92; 24–25). Curiously, M. de Clèves is missing in these pages; apparently he has failed to register the scene of mutual attraction to which he has nevertheless also been a witness. And this failure suggests a defective attachment on his part. What is missing in his feelings for the princess so that he is not on the alert too? Since, according to the novel, it is love that attunes one's sensitivities to those of others, where are his? Is it his *sagesse* ("wisdom") that acts in the place of *sentiment* ("feeling") and that blinds him to the evidence before his eyes? A deaf mother and a blind husband do not augur well for the marriage.

The maternal instruction of the daughter continues after her marriage, in the form of cautionary stories about some of the personages of the court, in particular Mme de Valentinois, and in warnings about the deceptiveness of appearances in this society. A curious anecdote imbricated in the tale of Mme de Valentinois (93–99; 26–31) operates as a permanent tease in the text: Mme de Chartres recounts the story of a lady who was amorously involved with the duc d'Orléans. Both he and the woman's husband died at the same time, so that her legitimate mourning for the one covered her mourning for the other. She retired to the country in her grief and henceforth lived a life of exemplary virtue, and, according to the mother's ethical code, because she had succeeded so well in maintaining appropriate appearances, she deserved to go unnamed and to preserve her good reputation. As Hirsch points out, this anonymous lady might well be Mme de Chartres herself—nothing in the text contradicts or confirms this speculation (85–86). But it does make sense of the ending the princess invents or perhaps borrows for her own story, one of distancing, concealment, and silence, and it is offered by the guiding mother here as a model she approves, even if she does not admit it as her own.

Mme de Chartres combats the passion she recognizes in her daughter for M. de Nemours surreptitiously, without indicating her knowledge, and when the princess is about to betray her inclination by showing marks of affection for the duke, Mme de Chartres diverts the exchange. She reroutes those signs so that feigned illness is understood as real (104; 35–36) and not as a response to the duke's cues. She speaks of the duke at length and, without showing animosity toward him, paints a picture of a charming, unreliable seducer—a portrait that is supported by the rest of the story with the notable exception of his constant and long-lived if not eternal attraction to the princess (well, it lasts until the last page of the book—that's pretty good!). "Louanges empoisonnées" (104) ("poisoned compliments" [36]) characterize her discourse as she attempts to deflate her daughter's opinion of the duke without giving away her motives.

Perhaps most crucially, in the same conversation, Mme de Chartres jeopardizes the friendship that the princess is developing with the reine dauphine, a relationship with another woman that would counteract the exclusive hold of the mother and help the daughter develop a greater sense of autonomy. She does this by suggesting that the duke is actually in love with the reine dauphine. Although the princess makes her peace with her friend through direct conversation and learns that the duke and the reine dauphine do not have an understanding, she cannot entirely dismiss the mother's damning words about the duke or her own experience of jealousy. They will haunt her throughout her life, helping make it impossible for her to risk ever contemplating an attachment to him.

The mother drives her lesson home with all possible force in the deathbed scene (108–09; 39–40). There her authority is absolute, and her final words are etched in the princess's soul forever. She reveals that she is aware of Mme de Clèves's attraction to Nemours—she mentions it for the first and last time and enjoins her daughter to do all in her power to resist it. Marital duty and reputation are at stake. The princess must muster all her strength and not allow this to happen, must leave the court, and must turn to her husband. As a final blow, the mother adds that this is her only deathbed concern, that she would rather be dead in any case than see her daughter engage in an illicit affair such as this one, that is, fall like other women. Ironically, she terms her monologue, one of the longer ones in the novel, a "conversation" (108; 40) as she announces its conclusion. Tears are the only contribution the daughter is allowed in the supposed exchange, and the mother abruptly refuses further contact: "Elle se tourna de l'autre côté en achevant ces paroles et commanda à sa fille d'appeler ses femmes, sans vouloir l'écouter ni parler davantage" (109)

("She turned away when she had said these words and ordered her daughter to call her women, refusing to listen to her or to say anything more" [40]). As at the crucial moment of the marriage decision, here at the deathbed the daughter is not heard. The mother has the final word, and the daughter has none (109; 40).

M. de Clèves, who has been notably absent from the text, resurfaces at the mother's death, as if to take her place (Kamuf 84–85). He will serve as his wife's guarantor as her mother had served as her guardian. When he protests her tendency to flee the crowds at court, she will claim that without her mother she can no longer permit herself to circulate as freely (171; 95). She does not recognize that her married status and the presence of her husband should police her virtue just as effectively as her mother's company had. This discrepancy reveals how inadequate M. de Clèves's conjugal hold on her is. He replaces the mother as storyteller, recounting the tale of Mme de Tournon; he claims that he would welcome sincerity in his wife even if it meant learning that she loved another and that he would step out of the role of husband in order to console her (117; 46). He is thus unwittingly inviting Mme de Clèves to confide in him as she had in her mother before, although there her one glaring silence had always been that concerning her attraction for Nemours. Indeed, her friendship with the reine dauphine and her attraction for Nemours are the sole indications of autonomous feeling in her. Since her dying mother had advised her to take whatever measures necessary to combat her passion, it occurs to the princess that the most effective means of containing her passion is to confess it to her husband, to pass the burden and responsibility for her behavior on to him (171; 95). That is, the husband is envisaged as a stand-in for the mother, and this role substitution has the same disastrous consequences as the others.

The mother's words are firmly etched in the daughter's soul, and it is memory rather than conscience that guides the princess's decisions and actions henceforth: "Enfin elle pensait tout ce qui pouvait augmenter son affliction et son désespoir. Quels retours ne fit-elle point sur elle-même! Quelles réflexions sur les conseils que sa mère lui avait donnés!" (146) ("Her mind fastened on everything, in fact, that could possibly increase her distress and despair. How severely she judged herself, how painfully she recalled her mother's advice!" [72]). Her initiation into the pains of jealousy when the misplaced letter falls into her hands and is attributed to a mistress of the duc de Nemours confirms for her the truth of her mother's admonitions and affirms her belief in maternal wisdom. Even after having obtained clarification and spent an intimate afternoon in the company of the duke, having experienced the pleasureful aspect of her attachment, the princess heeds her mother's warnings and seeks in every way to avoid further involvement (168; 92).

Here is the last direct allusion to the mother and her influence in the novel, but the psychological apparatus is completely in place; there will be no further evolution in the character or behavior of the princess. She is unable to break out of or away from her mother's lessons, and so they will guide the plot to its predictable and inexorable conclusion. M. de Clèves's deathbed words reiterate and reinforce the dying mother's admonitions, just as he had taken up the place of the mother in the princess's affective life. And against these two ghosts, which echo each other and which have behind them the will of the father and the weight of official family and court positions, the princess cannot forge for herself her own voice.

Therefore, even though she is free in her widowed state, has observed an appropriate period of mourning, and has the blessing of her remaining relative—the vidame de Chartres—the princess persists in refusing Nemours and sets about deliberately distancing herself from him, from the court, and from her own passion. The daughter has taken to heart the mother's lessons. The lively debate about whether the princess's retreat and the ending of the novel represent a victory or a defeat seems emptied of meaning when the importance of the mother's role in shaping the plot of the daughter's life is underscored, for it is no longer the princess's decision that punctuates the novel but the extent of the mother's influence over the princess that brings the princess's life to closure.

I do not believe a ready-made blueprint of how to teach these points can be applied in all classrooms. The teacher can assign the passages noted above for the students' particular attention and can set forth certain concepts regarding the maternal, but it is in discussion, in the participation and the contributions of the students, that meaning will be made collectively of the mother-daughter story. And the meaning will inevitably be at the least slightly different each time it engages a new group of students bringing their own experience and insight to the classroom, since they will do their share of the teaching.

Conflicting Emotions:
Personal and Cultural *Vraisemblance*
in *La Princesse de Clèves*

Inge Crosman Wimmers

When *La Princesse de Clèves* was first published, in March 1678, it gave rise to lively discussions. Of major interest in these first responses was the behavior of the central character, the princess. The novel's progressive focus on the personal needs of its heroine set up a new kind of verisimilitude for the seventeenth-century public, raised on conformity and respect for the norm. The text reinforces its own authority by exposing these conventions as untenable. The novel's shift in emphasis from public opinion to personal discovery constitutes a claim for a new order of belief. That the depiction of such a new order met at first with considerable resistance is obvious from the initial responses. Such evidence is proof that readers bring culturally conditioned frames of reference to their reading of novels. Mme de Lafayette's seventeenth-century readers found Mme de Clèves's exceptional conduct hard to accept, since it challenged their society's foremost social code. *Bienséance* ("propriety"), defined by one authority as "non pas ce qui est honnête, mais ce qui convient aux personnes" ("not what is decent, but what is appropriate to a person") (Jean Chapelain, qtd. in Bray 227), is here defined as "non pas ce qui convient aux personnes, mais ce qui me semble honnête" ("not what is appropriate to a person, but what seems decent"). Diametrically opposed to social convention, such a radical departure from the norm was not likely to be taken as *vraisemblable* ("plausible"). If, as Wolfgang Iser claims in *The Act of Reading*, the central function of literary texts is to make us aware of norms and conventions by questioning and negating these norms in order to encourage us to imagine something new (208), then *La Princesse de Clèves*, by rewriting *vraisemblance* and *bienséance*, is an excellent example of a fictional work that takes the reader of its time beyond habitual frames of reference and by doing so makes for active reader response. The involvement of today's readers is equally intense, but its focus is elsewhere: on the close depiction of the character's inner life rendered vivid and persuasive through rhetorical and narrative strategies. Given this framework for reading the text, I focus class discussions on both the historical, cultural setting of the characters and the novel's rhetorical strategies to show how, through emphasis and other techniques, the narrator sets up a coherent logic for the princess's actions and reactions. Since I teach *La Princesse de Clèves* in an undergraduate course on the French novel that emphasizes reader response, we pay particular attention to the interaction between reader and text, first in a sequential reading, centered on the pages assigned for each class session, then retrospectively during the final discussion, as we examine reader response to the novel's overall rhetorical strategies and narrative logic.

From the beginning I focus the students' attention on how, in various ways, Lafayette prepares for Mme de Clèves's unusual confession to her husband. We pay particular attention to the narrator's description of the confession, a passage that makes us aware that the princess herself is the first to call attention to her unusual behavior by prefacing her confession with remarks that prepare both her husband and the reader for what is to come: "je vais vous faire un aveu que l'on n'a jamais fait à son mari; mais l'innocence de ma conduite et de mes intentions m'en donne la force" (171) ("I will make you a confession which no woman has ever made to her husband. Only the innocence of my conduct and my intentions gives me the strength to do it" [95]). What could be more explicit than this built-in glossing, which overtly tells us that Mme de Clèves is well aware of what is done and what is not — a fictional fact worth noting for the evaluation of her character and conduct? I ask the students to pay attention to such interpretive remarks in assessing the princess's feelings and actions. In considering these we constantly refer back to the cultural codes of *bienséance* and *vraisemblance*, since they provide the logical background for the elaborate rhetorical framework set up by the narrator and give us insight into seventeenth-century reader response to the novel. Although the narrator explicitly presents the princess's behavior as extraordinary — hence implausible under ordinary circumstances — and uses rhetorical mediation to take the reader gently from conventional to unconventional conduct, the *aveu* ("confession") was simply not accepted. The modern reader, in contrast, may well wonder why such a fuss was made over it. What surprises us today is not Mme de Clèves's behavior but rather the many justifications for it. What we learn from them, however, is the importance of contemporary cultural codes so crucial to an understanding of the central character's frame of mind and the narrator's rhetorical ploys.

While the extensive use of historical and cultural references gives the impression of verisimilitude so important to the novelist's central purpose, to offer a convincing account of an unusual person in an unusual situation, equally important is the intensifying focus on the inner life of Mme de Clèves, which initiates the reader into her way of thinking and feeling. Though we know that other people's thoughts and feelings are inaccessible to us and that novelists who depict them are fabricating, we nonetheless find, as Dorrit Cohn has shown, that the "special life-likeness of narrative fiction [. . .] depends on what writers and readers know least in life: how another mind thinks, another body feels" (5–6). To afford the students a better grasp of the techniques novelists use to give readers insight into characters' minds, I have them read the introduction of Cohn's *Transparent Minds* (3–17), paying special attention to her distinctions among "psycho-narration," the narrator's omniscient description of a character's consciousness; "quoted monologue," "reference to the thinking self in the first person, and to the narrated moment (which is also the moment of locution) in the present tense" (13); and "narrated monologue" (also known, I point out, as *style indirect libre* or "free indirect speech"). In addition, I distribute a handout I prepared on the different narrative functions, which is based on the five functions discussed by Gérard Genette in *Figures III:* "la fonction narrative," "la fonction de régie," "la fonction de communication," "la fonction émotive," and "la fonction idéologique" (261–65) ("narrative function," "the function of register," "the function of communication," "the emotive function," and "the ideological function").

To understand how the reader is gradually initiated into Mme de Clèves's dilemma and how it is made believable, we must take a closer look at the principal joints of the novel's rhetorical framework. When we do so, we realize that through foregrounding, repetition, and built-in interpretive models, the author sets up the framework for reading the novel. The central character stands out not only in the title but also in the gallery of portraits that opens the novel. It is significant that the only other person singled out as truly outstanding is the duc de Nemours, so that the reader may jump to the conclusion from the start that these two exceptional people are made for each other. In fact, the narrator draws this conclusion for us while describing their first impressions of each other when they meet at the ball: "De sorte que, se voyant souvent, et se voyant l'un et l'autre ce qu'il y avait de plus parfait à la cour, il était difficile qu'ils ne se plussent infiniment" (93) ("In consequence, since they frequently met and recognized in each other a perfection unequalled at court, it was difficult for them not to be infinitely attracted to one another" [25]).

That the private life of the princess is at the center of the book becomes more and more obvious as we progress in our reading. The focus is on Mlle de Chartres once the historical cadre has been set up, and we soon realize that the entire narrative is built around her: all episodes and events are linked to her, while the narrative focuses increasingly on her inner life through summary narration of her consciousness, through narrated and quoted monologues, and through conversations in which she reveals her thoughts directly. We are also given inside information into anything that plays a role in her moral and sentimental education. For example, we witness firsthand the moral guidance given her by her mother and husband, we hear each of the four stories told her about problematic aspects of love, we read verbatim the entire text of the lost letter through which she learns about betrayal and jealousy, and we follow each step of her relationship with the duc de Nemours. In assessing twentieth-century reader response to the novel, we discuss the attention feminist critics have paid to the importance of maternal discourse (Hirsch; Miller, "Emphasis"). At crucial moments, we receive insight into her reactions and inner debate, so that we are in a position to understand her unusual confession to her husband and her final, unshakable decision to withdraw from the life of passions—a decision she arrives at through close reasoning, witnessed by the reader, who is familiar with all the evidence for the irrevocable decision. Thus verisimilitude, a new kind of *vraisemblance*—based on personal needs and not on cultural norms—is built up in *La Princesse de Clèves*.

To take a closer look at this convincing rhetorical strategy, I focus class discussions on how strikingly similar the husband's role is to the mother's, a similarity underscored through narrative pattern: like Mme de Chartres, he tells a story about an unhappy love affair, he encourages Mme de Clèves to turn to him for help and advice, and he gives her his views on love and marriage just before he dies. After pointing out these parallel developments, I focus the discussion on the various internal narratives and their effects on the princess and the reader. Taking this comprehensive view, we see that each one is calculated to give a negative image of love and as such is an important part of her sentimental education. The reader is bound to be sensitive to such narrative overdetermination through repetition of a message.

I devote at least thirty minutes of class discussion to these internal narratives once we have read all of them. In a retrospective reading we first focus on what they have in common: they are secondary stories told by one character to another. Then we take a close look at the narrative situation, specifying who narrates and who listens to each, which makes it obvious that each tale of insincerity and infidelity is told to Mme de Clèves: Mme de Chartres tells her daughter about the king's stormy relationship with Mme de Valentinois, who constantly gives him cause to be jealous; M. de Clèves tells his wife about the suffering caused by Mme de Tournon's insincerity; tales of inconstancy, jealousy, and murderous revenge are told by the reine dauphine to the ladies at court, including Mme de Clèves, to familiarize them with the private affairs of the English court; and finally the story of the vidame's amorous intrigues is retold by M. de Nemours to Mme de Clèves, a story showing how someone she likes and respects has repeatedly betrayed a woman's trust.

Most of the discussion is focused on the second internal narrative, since it is of central importance for the princess's subsequent decisions and actions. M. de Clèves's story is set in the same period and place (the court of Henri II) as those of the main narrative. Though the story is about the private life of one of his friends, the love affair between Sancerre and Mme de Tournon, it has an exemplary function: it gives Mme de Clèves and the reader further insight into how people in love behave. Mme de Tournon's misleading conduct—pretending to mourn her husband while having an affair with Sancerre, then pretending to love Sancerre while secretly planning to marry another—confirms Mme de Chartres's advice about the masked appearances at court that make it difficult to distinguish between être (reality) and paraître (appearance).

How deeply this story affects Mme de Clèves is obvious from the detailed description of her reaction to it, especially when M. de Clèves gives a verbatim account of his advice to Sancerre, namely, that Sancerre should be open to any confession from Mme de Tournon, even if she were to confess her love for another; M. de Clèves adds that he himself follows this advice in his own life, since he values sincerity above all else (116–17; 45–46). The importance of this passage is already apparent in a first, linear reading of the novel, since M. de Clèves's "ode to sincerity" stands out in the text as a separate paragraph. Similarly, our attention is drawn to Mme de Clèves's reaction to this plea for sincer-

ity, which is also set in relief as a separate paragraph. Such emphasis underscores the significance of this scene for the characters in the story world and in
the reader's interpretive constructs. It helps prepare the way for the princess's
confession to her husband, which, though unusual, seems convincing and
verisimilar against the background of all that she has seen and heard and that
we, as readers, have witnessed as well.

The repeated focus on the same character makes it obvious that incidents,
like the one involving the lost letter, and internal narratives all acquire meaning
in relation to her. Even the narrative technique is closely geared to the progressive stages of her self-awareness. While in the beginning of the book the pre-
dominant mode is omniscient narration of her inner life, there is a marked
difference after the lost love letter's mistaken attribution to the duke, which
subjects the princess to intense feelings of jealousy, an emotion she had never
experienced before. We are suddenly given insight into her mind through a
more direct method, either through quoted interior monologue, which is the
most direct way of rendering consciousness, or through narrated monologue,
the *style indirect libre*, which allows the character's mental speech to infiltrate
the narrator's discourse. The most revealing passage is the one describing Mme
de Clèves's state of consciousness just after she has realized that the change in
her attitude toward M. de Nemours—a change brought about by the inner turmoil caused by the lost letter—is a sign of her passion for him. Because of her
newly experienced jealousy she also realizes, of course, how vulnerable a position she is in, since someone like the duke is unlikely to be capable of a stead-
fast love. It is remarkable how, within one paragraph, the narrator's omniscient
narration of her consciousness suddenly switches to interior monologue just as
the princess, at a moment of rare insight, fully comprehends her situation and
is able to put it in a broader perspective and settle on a plan of action that foreshadows her future attitude and conduct: to avoid M. de Nemours at all cost by
retreating to her country estate and to tell M. de Clèves everything if he opposes such action. It is quite clear, from her repeated inner questioning, that
the emphasis is on what she herself wills and wants, since no fewer than seven
times she asks herself "veux-je" ("do I want to"):

> Elle trouva qu'il était presque impossible qu'elle pût être contente de sa
> passion. Mais quand je le pourrais être, disait-elle, qu'en *veux-je* faire?
> *Veux-je* la souffrir? *Veux-je* y répondre? *Veux-je* m'engager dans une
> galanterie? *Veux-je* manquer à M. de Clèves? *Veux-je* me manquer à
> moi-même? Et *veux-je* enfin m'exposer aux cruels repentirs et aux
> mortelles douleurs que donne l'amour?   (167; my emphasis)

> She felt that it was almost impossible for her to find happiness in his love.
> But even if I could, she said to herself, what can I want with it? Do I re-
> ally want to tolerate it? respond to it? Am I ready to embark on a love af-
> fair? to be unfaithful to M. de Clèves? to be unfaithful to myself? Do I

wish to expose myself to the cruel remorse and mortal sufferings that love
gives rise to?   (91–92)

From this detailed account of her inner life it is obvious that the moment of self-
awareness is of capital importance. It also provides the key to all further developments in the novel by initiating the pattern of flight and entrapment, which
dominates the episodic structure of the rest of the book. One of the first consequences of her flight from love is the confession to her husband, which, in turn,
sets up a vicious causal chain leading to his death. This unexpected turn of
events prompts M. de Nemours to ask for her hand, a final temptation that she
escapes by withdrawing to a far-off country estate and by entering a convent.

To focus the students' attention on how narrative technique and logic make
the princess's final decision more plausible, I select certain passages for close
analysis in class. For instance, I point out that, significantly, the narrator most
frequently chooses the word *trouble* to describe Mme de Clèves's frame of
mind after her first step toward self-awareness, since this emphasis on her
inner turmoil lays the groundwork for one of her major arguments for retreat
from love, inner calm (*repos*). Ironically, by pursuing her, the duc de Nemours
continually revives this troubled state, which plays so important a role in her
final choice. We pay attention to how, by giving us insight into Mme de
Clèves's emotional state and by familiarizing us with her reasoning, the narrator deeply implicates us in her situation: we not only learn to trust her judgment but also build up a fair amount of sympathy for her inner struggle. When
she opts out by renouncing love, we are likely to understand and empathize,
not condemn her. Suffering through jealousy is obviously her main reason for
retreat and is rhetorically (vis-à-vis Nemours, vis-à-vis the reader) her strongest
point, since she backs up her reasoning with concrete detail. In basing her argument on the inconstancy of love and the turmoil it causes, she draws on her
experience, which as readers we have shared.

Yet throughout her "debate" with the duke, she repeatedly brings in a second reason, duty to her husband. She closely links the two reasons to reinforce
her argument. That she does this not only to convince her interlocutor but also
to strengthen her own decision is quite apparent. We take a close look in class
at one of the most crucial passages in this amorous debate. Here she frankly admits, in reply to M. de Nemours's objection that he cannot see how her "vertu
austère" (232) ("virtue so austere" [150]) could oppose her feelings any longer,
that she finds herself in a paradoxical situation where she is constantly torn between scruples and the desire to love. The direct quotation of her speech allows the reader to follow each step of her reasoning and thus to share fully the
emotional impact. Her choice of words and the chiastic development of her argument is a persuasive verbal translation of the no-exit situation in which she
finds herself:

—Je sais bien qu'il n'y a rien de plus difficile que ce que j'entreprends, répliqua Mme de Clèves; je me défie de mes forces au milieu de mes raisons. Ce que je crois devoir à la mémoire de M. de Clèves serait faible s'il n'était soutenu par l'intérêt de mon repos; et les raisons de mon repos ont besoin d'être soutenues de celles de mon devoir. Mais, quoique je me défie de moi-même, je crois que je ne vaincrai jamais mes scrupules et je n'espère pas aussi de surmonter l'inclination que j'ai pour vous.   (232)

"I am well aware that there is nothing more difficult than what I propose to do," replied Mme de Clèves. "I put little faith in my own powers, despite all the reasons I can muster. What I believe I owe to the memory of M. de Clèves would be a feeble resource were it not sustained by self-interest, namely my desire for tranquillity of mind; likewise, the reasons that speak in favour of tranquillity need to be supported by those that duty prescribes. Little as I trust myself, however, I believe that I shall never be able to vanquish my scruples, nor can I hope to overcome my attraction to you."   (150)

Though she admits her love and the difficulty of overcoming it, she uses this admission as an additional argument to avoid seeing the man she loves at all cost. It is quite clear—from her emphatic speech and her circular argument—that there is no way out. The duke, having learned from what she has said, finally understands her line of reasoning. What moments earlier he called a "fantôme de devoir" (229) ("phantom of duty" [147]), in reference to her alleged duty to her husband, he now understands to be a personal duty. He realizes that this emphasis on the personal threatens their love, since there are no ready-made arguments for defeating opinions based on personal needs. By now it is evident to him and the reader that Mme de Clèves is not influenced by contemporary cultural notions of *bienséance* and *vraisemblance*, that she has, instead, replaced such social codes of behavior with a private ethics of personal honor and inner peace. The novel is thus brought to its logical conclusion. We can accept this conclusion, even if our own view of love is different, since we have been led to it through narrative logic and emphasis.

Getting Inside:
Digression, Entanglement, and the Internal Narratives

Rae Beth Gordon

How do students read the passages of *La Princesse de Clèves* that do not seem directly connected to the principal narration, the love story? What is the purpose of the internal narratives, intercalated within the central narrative? As many others have pointed out, the tales within the tale, in which various members of the court are shown engaged in marital infidelities, political intrigue, and treachery on a grand or less grand scale, offer moral lessons for the *éducation sentimentale* of the princess. She herself notes, "[J]'ignore si entièrement [les divers intérêts et les diverses liaisons de la cour]" ("I am so ignorant of [the various interests and liaisons of the court]"), at which point her mother recounts one of the "choses de la cour du feu roi qui ont même beaucoup de rapport avec celles qui se passent encore présentement" (94) ("matters concerning the late king's court which are in fact quite closely connected with things that are happening at present" [26]). It is not difficult to demonstrate to students the importance of the tales within the tale, portraits of various members of the court who are shown from the point of view of moral lessons recounted for the benefit of the princess.

Therefore I do not dwell on this function of the portraits here. It is their appearance of being digressions that interests me. Paradoxically, only by conceiving of them as digressions can one show how important they are to the central problem of the novel: passion, what to do with it, and how to express it. Long seen as a defect in the novel's structure, they complicate the architecture of the otherwise sober, spare, restrained recounting of the story of the princess and the duc de Nemours.

After all, the workings of the psyche are not so simple, and putting its complexity into words is far from easy. In this first of psychological novels, the task of finding an adequate means of expression for the princess's feelings must have been daunting. In fact, Lafayette is often forced to confess that words can't describe feelings: "Aussi ne peut-on représenter ce qu'elle sentit" (124) ("it is impossible to describe what she felt" [53]), or "Le trouble et l'embarras de Madame de Clèves était au-delà de tout ce que l'on peut s'imaginer" (184) ("[her] confusion and embarrassment were greater than it is possible to imagine" [107]), and so forth. Words seem inadequate to express strong emotions and the author often resorts to hyperbole or understatement. Despite the impotence of words, the reader feels the force of the heroine's desire, like that of the duc de Nemours. Another language here conveys what words cannot. It is the language of objects and of the decor, forms that are repeated by the interwoven structure of the novel.

I have taught *La Princesse de Clèves* three times, twice in a French literature in translation course. In each class students were surprised when the apparently peripheral aspects of the text opened up insights into the central problems of the novel, and some were even excited by the discovery that paying attention to the decor and to the architecture of the text revealed notions that were absent or underplayed elsewhere.

I use slides to make the setting of the novel vivid and familiar to my students: Chenonceaux and its two gardens, one for the mistress and the other for the queen; Chambord; ornamental details on façades; and Renaissance dress. I also show portraits of François I and other Renaissance figures.

"La magnificence et la galanterie n'ont jamais paru en France avec tant d'éclat que dans les dernières années du règne de Henri second" (69) ("Never has France seen such a display of courtly magnificence and manners as in the last years of the reign of Henri II" [3]). I begin teaching the novel by asking the students, "What are the first things mentioned in the text?" We clarify their definitions of *magnificence* and *gallantry*, and I remark that the first words in the text link the love affairs at court to rich ornamental finery and decor. Both seduction and finery are "display[ed]" and Henri's "violent" "passion" for Diane de Poitiers is "advertised" as "openly" as the jewels and the gorgeous lace and satin brocades worn by lovers (3). Pomp, opulence, and pleasure are inseparable. And among the pleasures available at this court are the arts, erotic entanglements, and the pleasure of telling secrets.

"Jamais cour n'a eu tant de belles personnes et d'hommes admirablement bien faits. [. . .] Ceux que je vais nommer étaient, en des manières différentes, *l'ornement* et l'admiration de leur siècle" (70; emphasis mine) ("No court has ever brought together so many beautiful women and wonderfully handsome men. [. . .] Those I shall name here were, in their different ways, the *ornament* and wonder of their age" [4; emphasis mine]). It is clear that these players are not mere extras. Yet this impressive cast of characters is certain to cause confusion for the student embarking on the novel; students often feel as though they are lost in a forest of names. I supply them with a genealogy of French royalty as well as a schema of the relationships among the characters (see p. 196 of this volume for a genealogy of *La Princesse de Clèves*). But the confusion effect is there, and it plays into my reading of the text. The prized qualities of the noblemen, as dazzling as they may be, prepare the way for the description of the duc de Nemours, which I ask the students to present. "[C]e prince était un chef d'oeuvre de la nature. [. . .] [C]'était l'homme du monde le mieux fait et le plus beau" (71–72) ("M. de Nemours was nature's masterpiece. He was the most handsome and the most nobly built man in the world" [5]). He possesses a certain style "qui faisait qu'on ne pouvait regarder que lui" (72) ("that made it impossible to look at anyone else when he was present" [5]. In giving their impressions of the duke, the students realize that there is no physical description of him; instead, we are given hyperbole: "masterpiece," "inimitable," "incomparable value" (5). This is very nearly true of the heroine: the text describes only her fair complexion, honey-blonde hair, and classical features, and hyperbole takes on the task of presenting Mlle de Chartres to the reader: "c'était une beauté parfaite, puisqu'elle donna de l'admiration" ("peerless indeed her beauty must have been, since it aroused wonder and admiration"); "un éclat que l'on n'a jamais vu qu'à elle" (76–77) ("a lustre no other girl could equal" [9–10]). Her beauty arouses "wonder." "[Elle] attira les yeux de tout le monde" (76) ("all eyes turned to gaze upon her" [9]). Even the discreet Prince de Clèves on seeing her for the first time can't help staring at her. If the students haven't yet noticed how important the gaze and the pleasure it brings are, it is time to point it out to them.

The education that Mme de Chartres has given her daughter regarding the dangers of passionate love as opposed to the other path a woman can choose (virtue, honesty, a peaceful and upright comportment, and reciprocal love in marriage) prepares the way for her marriage to the Prince de Clèves. Yet what drives and stimulates everyone else is the energy of creating or unraveling the complications (intrigues) involved in erotic and political liaisons. "[U]ne sorte d'agitation sans désordre" (81) ("a kind of orderly unrest" [14]) reigns at court. I ask the students why this would be pleasurable.

"Si vous jugez sur les apparences en ce lieu-ci, [. . .] vous serez souvent trompée: ce qui paraît n'est presque jamais la vérité" (94) ("If you judge by appearances in this place, [. . .] you will frequently be deceived: what you see is almost never the truth" [26]), advises Mme de Chartres. But what appears on the surface is constantly valorized, and the princess herself is no exception, since she and the man to whom she is attracted are the most perfect ornaments of the court. Brilliant outward appearance attracts and dazzles the eye. At the ball where the princess and the duke dance together before even being introduced, they are infinitely pleasing to each other. Until now, the princess has been completely honest and transparent, but as she *watches* the duke for signs of his love for her, she *hides* her feelings from her mother. The theme of the hidden is consistently tied to the themes of looking and of passion. The desire to unveil or unravel what is hidden is everywhere in the novel. I ask the students to watch for passages where Lafayette unveils and reveals what the princess is feeling and for passages where she stops short of doing so.

What is the point of the internal narrative (of Diane de Poitiers), told to the heroine by her mother? One answer is that one hides sentiments to keep one's reputation. (This is not the reason that the princess conceals her desire for the duke.) Another answer is that Diane's extraordinary story (she gives her virginity to save her father's life; she is first François I's mistress, then his son's; she is treated with deference equal to the queen's, yet she is unfaithful to Henri), despite all its immorality, does not prevent the king's enduring passion (over twenty years) for her. Contrary to what Mme de Chartres has underlined in past "lessons," a man can be sincere and faithful outside marriage. This internal narrative cannot therefore serve later to dissuade the princess from accepting the duke's offers of love.

The second long internal narrative concerns the exploits of the newly deceased Mme de Tournon, whom the princess had thought to be wise and good; the story, told to the heroine by her husband, proves once again that appearances are meant to deceive. Mme de Tournon was exceptionally clever in deceiving everyone by giving false appearances: she was able to pretend to the world to be in mourning *and* pretend passion for one of her admirers. It is in this "digression" that M. de Clèves proclaims to Sancerre that he values sincerity above everything else: "la sincérité me touche d'une telle sorte que je crois que si ma maîtresse, et même ma femme, m'avouait que quelqu'un lui plût. [. . .] Je [. . .] la conseiller[ais] et [. . .] la plaindr[ais]" (116–17) ("sincerity moves me so profoundly that, if my mistress, or even my wife, confessed to me that she was attracted to another man. [. . .] I should [. . .] offer her my advice and my compassion" [46]). This narrative motivates the confession, and it goes much further in enriching our understanding of the text. Passion is not only dangerous for one's reputation or position at court; it can lead to madness and death. We had learned this in an earlier scene, in which Marie Stuart, the reine dauphine, gives a one-page history of her mother to the heroine, but it is brought home with more force here. There is more. Sancerre had hidden his affair with Mme de Tournon from his friend the Prince de Clèves. The prince discovers the secret and is angry he wasn't trusted with it. But let's pay attention to the way he finds out. The king had given Mme de Valentinois (Diane de Poitiers) a ring, a pretty little ornament that is a token of his love. She gives the ring to her lover, the maréchal de Brissac, and when the king realizes this, he is enraged. M. d'Anville tells this secret to M. de Clèves. M. de Clèves tells the secret to his good friend Sancerre but begs him to keep it to himself (114; 43). The students will remark that M. de Clèves has already betrayed d'Anville's confidence, and one can cite the queen's words: in one of the internal narratives (told by the vidame de Chartres to his best friend, the duc de Nemours), she is distressed that no one in France "eût du secret" (149) ("[is] capable of keeping a secret" [76]), and this robbed one of the pleasures of telling secrets. I try to show the students why secrets are so important in this text. Like the little jeweled object that encircles the loved one's finger and is a token of desire, secrets are a substitute for desire. One can possess a secret, and that is highly exciting and pleasurable. And all these secrets have to do with erotic desire. One cannot possess desire: it is elusive and mobile, always bound to move on. This is perhaps signified by the way the ring circulates from one love object to another. Mme de Clèves, in possession of herself as no other characters in the novel are, knows that desire is bound to move on. Hence, her determination to seek *repos*, the opposite of movement, of desire (and, ultimately, of life itself).

In the last session on the novel, I ask the class to choose sides for a debate. One side will argue the duke's case, the other side the princess's. I encourage students to draw on the examples of other courtiers in the internal narratives. The debate always arouses much enthusiasm and passionate pronouncements.

Later in the novel, the letter that falls from the vidame's pocket and is thought to have fallen from the duc de Nemours's circulates from hand to hand even more often than the ring and d'Anville's secret. As it does so, it takes on incredible complications (143–53, 162–167; 70–81, 86–90). As the path of the letter, which contains the internal narrative of the vidame de Chartres and the queen and which refers back to details of Diane de Poitiers and Brissac's love affair in the first internal narrative (93–99; 26–31), becomes more and more complicated, it is embroidered on by several characters whose destiny is caught up in the implications and interpretations it is given along the way. Everyone wants to possess this letter. It contains a lover's secret, of course, but one the vidame was preparing to reveal to his friends despite the negative portrait it contains of him: the sheer weight of his mistress's strength of character shows that if such a woman loves him, he must be desirable. The twists and turns in the plot resemble the imbroglios recounted in the narratives. The letter revealing the entanglements of the vidame (the heroine's uncle) unexpectedly brings the duke and the princess together; in other words, it is intrigue and the pleasure of intriguing together that bring them into a playful intimacy for the first time.

The internal narratives in the text are not autonomous little interludes but are interwoven (thanks to the repetition of characters) and tied thematically to the principal narrative, not only through the moral questions they pose but also because they present the reader with verbal portraits of the courtiers. Two painted portraits, one of the heroine and one of the hero, will be of extreme importance in revealing the feelings that were hidden until the moment that the portraits appeared in the novel. And they will cause the plot to change course (like passionate love, which makes one "entièrement opposé à ce que l'on était" [127]) ("[into] the very opposite of what one was before" [56]). *These* portraits are clearly crucial to the narrative (yet they can't help but remind us of the "portrait digressions"). The scene of the stolen portrait is in fact prepared by the appearance at court of the painted portrait of Queen Elizabeth and then by the verbal portrait of her mother, Anne Boleyn. These works of art also remind us that the duc de Nemours is "nature's masterpiece" and that the princess is the most beautiful ornament of the court.

How does the stolen portrait of the princess tie in with two of the principal themes of the novel, the gaze and concealment (the theme of the hidden)? In this scene, the emphasis on the pleasure of the gaze is enormous, as in the scene in which M. de Nemours is present while Mme de Clèves is having her portrait painted: he "n'osait pourtant avoir les yeux attachés sur elle [. . .] craign[ant] de laisser trop voir le plaisir qu'il avait" (136) ("dared not keep his eyes on her [. . .] afraid that his pleasure [. . .] might be too apparent" [63]). The pleasure of the gaze is erotic, so much so that it sometimes must be hidden: "Lorsqu'il vit [le portrait] qui était à M. de Clèves, il ne put résister à l'envie de le dérober" (136) ("When he saw [the miniature portrait] belonging to M. de Clèves, he could not resist the temptation to steal it" [63]). The princess sees him do this, and he realizes that she has probably seen him. At the same time as the joy of possessing the portrait enhances every nuance of

en France" (194) ("the most magnificent spectacle ever seen in France" [116]), that the ties between them will be knotted. The colors that M. de Nemours wears as he enters the lists are a private language between them: "M. de Nemours avait du jaune et du noir. On en cherchera inutilement la raison. Mme de Clèves n'eut pas de peine à la deviner: elle se souvint d'avoir dit devant lui qu'elle aimait le jaune, et qu'elle était fâchée d'être blonde, parce qu'elle n'en pouvait mettre" (194) ("M. de Nemours wore yellow and black, no one could discover why. Mme de Clèves had no difficulty in guessing: she remembered having said in his presence that yellow was a colour she loved and that it vexed her to have fair hair because she could not wear it" [116]). No one other than the hero and heroine would be able to guess whom the colors designate; it is their secret. The princess feels "une *émotion extraordinaire* et, à toutes les courses de ce prince, elle avait de la peine à cacher sa joie" (195) ("an *extraordinary emotion*, and each time he jousted, she found it hard to conceal her joy" [117; emphasis mine]). These colors reappear a few pages later in the narrative, introduced — and, as it were, framed — by a short descriptive passage. Mme de Clèves tries to distance herself from the court by returning to Coulommiers, where she feels protected from these passions. Yet despite the "very high" fences, M. de Nemours finds a way through and sees the lights burning in her favorite alcove. "[T]outes les fenêtres étaient ouvertes et, en se glissant le long des palissades, il s'en approcha avec un trouble et une émotion qu'il est aisé de se représenter" (208) ("all the windows were open and, slipping silently along the garden fence, he approached the pavilion in a state of trepidation and emotion which one may readily imagine" [128]).

Perhaps easy to imagine, but not easy to depict — and this is precisely my point: Lafayette *does not* depict these emotions explicitly. They are transferred to the decor and to an ornamental object. Nemours spies on the princess through the window.

> Il faisait chaud, et elle n'avait rien, sur sa tête et sur sa gorge, que ses cheveux confusément rattachés. Elle était sur un lit de repos, avec une table devant elle, où il y avait plusieurs corbeilles pleines de rubans; elle en choisit quelques-uns, et M. de Nemours remarqua que c'étaient des mêmes couleurs qu'il avait portées au tournoi. Il vit qu'elle en faisait des noeuds à une canne des Indes, fort extraordinaire, qu'il avait portée quelque temps et qu'il avait donnée à sa soeur, à qui Mme de Clèves l'avait prise [. . .] pour avoir été à M. de Nemours. Après qu'elle eut achevé son ouvrage avec une grâce et une douceur que répandaient sur son visage les sentiments qu'elle avait dans le coeur, elle prit un flambeau et s'en alla proche d'une grande table, vis-à-vis du tableau du siège de Metz, où était le portrait de M. de Nemours; elle s'assit et se mit à regarder ce portrait avec une attention et une rêverie que la passion seule peut donner.
> (208–09)

It was hot, and on her head and breast she wore nothing but her loosely gathered hair. She was reclining on a day-bed with a table in front of her on which there were several baskets full of ribbons. She picked out some of these, and M. de Nemours noticed that they were of the very colours he had worn at the tournament. He saw that she was tying them in bows on a very unusual malacca cane which for a while he had carried [. . .] and which he had then given to his sister; it was from her that Mme de Clèves had taken it without showing that she recognized it. [. . .] She completed this task with such grace and gentleness that all the feelings in her heart seemed reflected in her face. Then she took a candlestick and went over to a large table in front of the painting of the siege of Metz that contained the likeness of M. de Nemours. She sat down and began to gaze at it with a musing fascination that could only have been inspired by true passion.   (128)

We have to note, for the last time, the author's avowal of inadequacy to describe these feelings:

On ne peut exprimer ce que sentit M. de Nemours dans ce moment. Voir, au milieu de la nuit, dans le plus beau lieu du monde, une personne qu'il adorait, la voir sans qu'elle sût qu'il la voyait, et la voir tout occupée de choses qui avaient du rapport à lui et à la passion qu'elle lui cachait, c'est ce qui n'a jamais été goûté ni imaginé par nul autre amant.   (209)

It is impossible to express what M. de Nemours felt at this moment. To see a woman he adored in the middle of the night, in the most beautiful place in the world, to see her, without her knowing he was there, entirely absorbed in things connected with him and with the passion she was hiding from him — what lover has ever enjoyed or even imagined such delight?   (128)

The emotions may be "impossible to express," but they are present—we feel them and the students feel them. The instructor can ask students to point to elements in these passages that convey the duke's and princess's passion and then can note the act of entangling, intertwining, here. What does it have to do with passion? What does it have to do with intrigue? And what does it have to do with the plot and with the structure (the interwoven internal narratives and the central narrative) of the novel?

The duc de Nemours impulsively moves forward a few steps with the intention of speaking to the princess, but he advances so nervously that his scarf gets entangled in the window, and the princess hears the noise. Woven objects, like the portraits that seem to frame the love story, get tangled up in the central tableau, here the scene framed by the window. These objects aren't here simply to frame or set off the central figures or events; they are inextricably woven into these events and the psychology of the characters. The lover's scarf *does* frame and repeat the image of the ribbons knotted around the cane: woven objects that carry the same desire, the first as it is felt by the princess and the second as it is felt by the duke.

Certainly, the ribbons entwined around the cane carry a sexual symbolism that students will grasp. Ribbons, other ornaments, colors, and portraits can serve as a language. The love entanglements and the interlacing of characters and episodes in *La Princesse de Clèves*—including the inserted portraits—underline the importance of intertwining. The internal narratives' tales of passion and intrigue are perhaps examples of text within the text, texts of unbridled passion in a "sober" narrative, but that they are too inextricably intertwined signifies that the "sober" narrative can't possibly "protect" itself and keep out emotion, confusion, and digression, just as the fences can't keep out the lover. Passion involves entangling and connecting. It is complication and confusion; it doesn't follow the straight line of logic. It is the contrary of *repos*.

What about the style and structure of the novel? Restrained in its language and in its expression of emotion, the novel appears clear and limpid, always in control of its means. But "if you judge by appearances [. . .] you will frequently be deceived." By entangling the central narrative and the "digressions" Lafayette makes the latter necessary. She, it seems, like her heroine, takes pleasure in the acts of interlacing, entangling, and knotting. She, like her hero, strays from the main path. If the notion of decorum tries to rule the novel, limiting and reining in passion, the decor, including the "historical decor" in the internal narratives, spills over into the surrounding territory, showing what cannot be told.

Mapping *La Princesse de Clèves*:
A Spatial Approach

Éva Pósfay

A spatial approach can be engaging, enlightening, and gratifying for students studying *La Princesse de Clèves*, a novel often considered among the most challenging works of French classicism. Teaching an upper-level seventeenth-century French literature survey at a liberal arts college regularly allows me to explore the novel with small groups of students, usually ten to twelve people a class, most of them majors. The course is structured chronologically, so that by the time we reach Lafayette toward the end of the term, after authors such as Pascal, Molière, and Racine, students feel more at ease with seventeenth-century French. This increased sense of confidence, however, does not usually last beyond the first pages of *La Princesse de Clèves*. Because students are unaccustomed to Lafayette's sometimes treacherous syntax (the initial lengthy description of the court is not exactly encouraging either), I like to turn for assistance to an attribute of theirs that they often choose to rely on: their visual skills. Nurtured by television and computer technology, this generation of students seems quite receptive to visualization. I believe that this affinity for the visual is what makes the spatial approach to *La Princesse de Clèves* fruitful and particularly popular among students.

Given the remarkable multiplicity of and insistence on spaces in *La Princesse de Clèves*, the spatial approach is most appropriate. Its main presupposition is that spaces (a study, a garden, a convent, for example) reveal crucial textual meanings. The approach analyzes how spaces operate, how they govern group interactions and define individuals. It is also flexible; the teacher, or the class, can relate the concept of space to a variety of topics, including language, history, politics, gender studies, sociology, architecture, and ethics. Students report that identifying, evaluating, linking, and comparing different spaces in the novel make *La Princesse de Clèves* more accessible, more tangible to them. A spatial perspective helps them grasp a text removed from their own frame of reference. They delight in creating what they call a "spatial argument" based on their close literary analyses of spaces. After such analysis, they usually feel comfortable venturing into more sophisticated readings of the novel.

Before our spatial exercises with Lafayette, I find it useful to devote some time (at least one whole class) to two spaces unique to seventeenth-century France: the Parisian literary salons and Louis XIV's Versailles. Each, in its own way, sets the stage for *La Princesse de Clèves*. At the heart of my first presentation lie the salons, in particular their *précieuses*' defiant determination to direct their own lives. An excellent illustration of the *précieux* mindset is Madeleine de Scudéry's "Carte de Tendre" (1: 398). This map of the land of Tenderness presents a female point of view on gallantry, one that instructs men about how women wish to be wooed (see DeJean, *Tender Geographies* 56–57, 87–90). Later on, we regularly refer back to Scudéry's map when we discuss Mme de Clèves's desire to control her own (female) space.

Leaving the realm of female-run salons, we discuss how political power can be expressed through space and architecture, using examples from the students' own experience, such as the White House. Then I go on to introduce students to Versailles, often seen as the symbol of patriarchal and absolutist rule. With the help of engravings, paintings, and photographs of the château and its gardens taken from Robert W. Berger's *A Royal Passion* (53–72) and Kenneth Woodbridge's *Princely Gardens* (197–223) (views of the opulent *fêtes* of the 1660s and 1670s work well), I lecture on how Versailles helped consolidate royal power and weaken most other social scenes, including the Parisian literary salons. The focus on Versailles as a political space prepares us for the pivotal role played by Henri II's court at the beginning of Lafayette's text.

Our reading of *La Princesse de Clèves* itself takes about two weeks; one sixty- to seventy-minute class is devoted to each of the novel's four parts. From the start of our investigation, I suggest that students pay special attention to any reference to space as they read. I even advise them to make a list of the different spatial elements they encounter. Though this task may sound daunting, it proves wonderfully effective. It provides students with a solid thread to follow —even through those early interminable descriptions of the court's factions— and the carefully collected data can lead to telling insights about the meaning of *La Princesse de Clèves*.

We concentrate next on applying the spatial approach to two specific locations: the court and the pavilion at Coulommiers. Among all the spaces in Lafayette's novel—the jeweler's store (77; 10), the silk merchant's shop (222; 140), the garden outside the city limits (223; 141), and so on—these two offer the most revealing contrast between public and private spaces.

The Court

Armed with their spatial findings and a distributed chart outlining the personal dynamics in Henri II's royal household (Catherine de Médicis vs. Diane de Poitiers, the Guise family vs. the Montmorency family, etc.), students are ready at last to evaluate the first space presented in the novel: the court. Its importance undoubtedly cannot be ignored, as it stages crucial events ranging from royal intrigues to Mme de Clèves's fateful meeting with the duc de Nemours. That this "space" is presented without much information about *physical* spaces seems naturally disconcerting to the students, who, more often than not, expect to find descriptions of buildings. Lafayette, however, never describes the court as a building. While the court can be perceived as a unique entity with its own peculiar atmosphere, throughout the novel it remains spatially unstable, for it is a mobile court traveling to and fro between the Louvre, Chambord, and

Fontainebleau. The only spatial indications to be found are discreet allusions, such as those to the salon-like "chez la reine" (70) (the queen's "apartments" [4]), which is one of the most popular social centers in the court.

These rare glimpses into the physical space of the court eventually spur discussions about Lafayette's apparent disinterest in spatial descriptions. At this point I ask students to contrast the baroque style with Lafayette's classical *écriture* (writing style). Georges de Scudéry's *Almahide* contains, for instance, unbelievably extensive baroque spatial descriptions:

> En effet, sans redire tout ce que ie vous ay desia dit de ce beau Bastiment, & sans m'arrester mesme aux Phrises qui sont sur la Porte, que l'on voit couvertes de Crocodiles, d'Hypopothames, de Tritons, de Syrenes & d'autres Figures aquatiques, propres aux ornemens des Phrises & des Arrabesques: ie vous diray seulement, que l'on voit d'abord en entrant, sur le haut de l'Escalier, à droit [sic] & à gauche, deux grandes Statuës de Marbre blanc, qui representent des Fleuves [. . .].   (2: 309–10)

> In effect, without reiterating all that I have already told you about this beautiful building, and without even dwelling on the friezes on the door, which are covered with crocodiles, hippopotamuses, tritons, sirens and other aquatic figures, as befits the adornment of friezes and arabesques, I will only tell you that upon entering one first sees at the top of the staircase, to the right and to the left, two large statues of white marble representing rivers [. . .].   (my trans.)

Invariably, somebody points out that while Lafayette does not expand on the court in spatial terms, she does seem to relish describing—in the greatest detail—the characters who constitute the court. This observation prompts us to explore the court as a human structure rather than an architectural entity. We interpret the court as a *social* space whose human actors provide our only access to its inner workings.

Keeping in mind Lafayette's famous characterization of the court ("il y avait une sorte d'agitation sans désordre" [81]; "there reigned at court a kind of orderly unrest" [14]), along with her assertion that both men and women are responsible for the destabilizing intrigues in Henri II's domain, we bravely set out to examine the characters' spatial use of power. To be sure, spatial details disclose great struggles between people of the same sex; Catherine de Médicis, for example, forces herself to "approcher cette duchesse de sa personne, afin d'en approcher aussi le roi" (70) ("keep Mme de Valentinois close to her person in order to draw the King himself closer" [3]). But far more frequently are power and space coupled and problematized at the court (as well as in the rest of the novel) when the two sexes come into contact with each other.

To tackle the issue of spatial power between the sexes at the court, we use Michael Danahy's helpful study on *La Princesse de Clèves* in which he compares the movements of men and women in various settings of the novel. The critic presents data on "their entrances and exits, comings and goings, encounters and interventions" (*Feminization* 103–04) before discussing important issues such as spatial initiative and spatial precedence in Lafayette's work. Following his lead, we reflect on the characters' spatial access and behavior in order to analyze the dynamics of their meetings. Soon our debate focuses on Mme de Chartres's claim that a woman—Diane de Poitiers—rules both the king and his empire (98; 30) and Danahy's contradictory view that the court is a genderized space covertly dominated by men, though only the king "exercises absolute topographical priority as part of his birthright" (105). Our consensus tends to be that women's spatial might is real but terribly precarious. Diane de Poitiers can be powerful—as long as the king allows it. Once Henri II dies she is banished from the space she had just dominated.

But what is Mme de Clèves's perspective on spatial power at the court? For the novel's most scrutinized character, the court—the public space par excellence—is an overwhelming context in which she feels dire discomfort. In the course of *La Princesse de Clèves*, she will gradually distance herself from this most public zone replete with dangerous temptations, tumultuous hostilities, and tragic misunderstandings.

The Pavilion

Following Mme de Clèves in her removal from court, we turn next to Coulommiers, the Clèves' private country estate just outside Paris. Though the pavilion may have been Lafayette's invention, the estate itself was historical, and we draw on Micheline Cuénin's work in examining its rich history. Cuénin suggests (in her section of an article cowritten with Chantal Morlet-Chantalat [118–21]) that Lafayette's choice of the setting may not have been coincidental, given its association with certain women, including Catherine de Gonzague (a founder of convents) and Marie d'Orléans-Longueville (an active participant in the Fronde war), both of whom retreated to Coulommiers. Cuénin also points out that the château was decorated with the busts of historical and mythological female figures. (For an interpretation of the château's history, see Beasley, *Revising Memory* 224–26.) Interestingly enough, while the château (the "public" part of Coulommiers) remains unportrayed, the pavilion (the "private" area) receives a great deal of descriptive attention.

This formal realization leads us to conclude that Lafayette's text continues to deemphasize the public (as it did in depicting Henri II's court) to privilege and celebrate the private. Before we examine Mme de Clèves's increasing desire to leave courtly public life for privacy in Coulommiers, I ask students to meditate on what their private spaces mean in their own lives (What do these spaces provide? How important are they and why?). The purpose of the exercise is to contrast the students' and the heroine's experiences with privacy.

Students tend to consider privacy commonplace and to take it for granted. In the princess's world, however, public life takes precedence over private, so to yearn for privacy is to rebel. Just as it is politically audacious of the princess to withdraw to Coulommiers rather than to attend the coronation of François II in Rheims (200–01; 121), so it is unusual that Lafayette valorizes privacy at all. I like to remind students of the taste for the public and the ceremonial under the Sun King. We generally use Norbert Elias's *La société de cour* for anecdotes about court life, and we discuss why *home* has no French equivalent.

At this juncture, we study the singularity of the pavilion. Unlike the château of Coulommiers, this garden structure is Mme de Clèves's private territory, her personal project, and her source of pleasure. We naturally emphasize that the pavilion area stages two unique events: the princess's confession to her husband "sous le pavillon" (169) ("in the pavilion" [93]) and her enunciation of passion before M. de Nemours's portrait "dans le cabinet" (208) (in one of the side rooms of the pavilion [128]). Given the extraordinary emotional connection between the pavilion and the princess, we conclude that it is hardly surprising that the duke would attempt to take control of this space that symbolizes, in some ways, Mme de Clèves herself.

It is immensely productive and amusing to visualize M. de Nemours's four trips to the pavilion by drawing them collectively on the blackboard. We make simple sketches of the character's routes (see my diagram). These drawings inform the spatial—and social—dynamics at work between the duke and the princess. Here is my text accompanying the diagram:

1. The duke enters the pavilion and witnesses in secret Mme de Clèves's confession, which is held inside the small structure. At the end of the confession, he returns elated to the forest (169–75; 93–98).
2. M. de Nemours observes the princess from outside one of the French windows of the pavilion. He then tries to penetrate the pavilion, but he is foiled when his scarf gets caught in the window. He withdraws (208–10; 128–30).
3. The duke is welcomed by closed doors, possible signs of Mme de Clèves's refusal to see him. To find solace, he spends the night wandering around the garden of Coulommiers (210–12; 130–32).
4. Instead of approaching the pavilion from the forest as he did the other three times, M. de Nemours enters now through the official door of the château in the company of his sister to dissipate the princess's suspicions about his intentions. Mme de Clèves thwarts his wish to visit the pavilion. The duke is forced to leave Coulommiers without being able to see the princess in private (213–14; 132–34).

From our spatial vantage point, it emerges that the pavilion of Coulommiers occupies a crucial place in *La Princesse de Clèves*: it is truly the first space in Lafayette's text to call into question M. de Nemours's infallibility. Initially, the

A Tantalizing Destination: Coulommiers

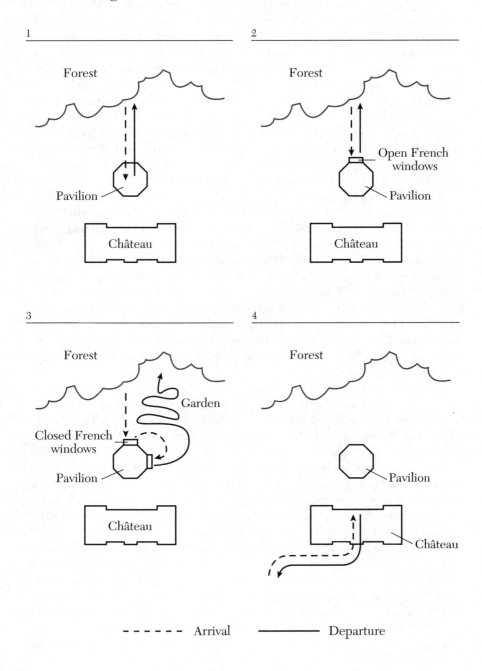

duke is a self-assured and resolute explorer on the Clèves' property who has always enjoyed freedom of movement; earlier, he even convinced M. de Clèves to let him enter the princess's Parisian bedroom while she was lying in bed! Nevertheless, after his first trip to the pavilion, the duke suffers a progressive loss of spatial power in Coulommiers, for he has less and less access to the pavilion and to Mme de Clèves. The princess, on the contrary, seems to grow stronger; she devises increasingly effective defensive strategies against the duke's incursions. By the end of his fourth visit to Coulommiers, M. de Nemours has become a different person. He looks ill and desperate: "Mme de Mercœur lui demanda s'il se trouvait mal; mais il regarda Mme de Clèves, sans que personne s'en aperçût, et il lui fit juger par ses regards qu'il n'avait d'autre mal que son désespoir" (214) ("Mme de Mercœur asked him if he felt ill, but he looked at Mme de Clèves without anyone noticing and his eyes told her that his illness was nothing other than despair" [134]).

It is perhaps the spatial humiliation endured by M. de Nemours that is responsible for the efforts of Jean-Baptiste Trousset de Valincour, the most vocal seventeenth-century critic of Lafayette's novel, to belittle the pavilion. In his *Lettres* Valincour judges much about the pavilion meaningless (as he does for all the novel's other spaces except the convent), from its architecture (allegedly incomprehensible [42]) to its confession scene (accused of being held in an arbitrarily chosen place [46]). This antagonistic perspective acquaints students with the well-known brouhaha that surrounded *La Princesse de Clèves* at its publication. Thus they learn about the uneasiness and even anger that can develop in readers who are unsympathetic to the heroine's spatial yearnings and triumphs.

If the pavilion valorizes the princess's successful management of a serious spatial crisis, its possible penetrability incites Mme de Clèves to search for a safer space of her own, a territory whose limits she can control. This idea of spatial domination takes us to recent feminist critics such as Nancy K. Miller, who suggests that the princess chooses to reject the duke in order to preserve passion "on her own terms" and govern her own plot ("Emphasis" 30). The parallel between Miller's interpretation and the spatial approach is clear: in both arguments the heroine dreams of control. It is this desire that makes her the defiant, subversive, and controversial character who greatly distressed Lafayette's contemporaries and still troubles many readers today.

Despite his decreasing self-confidence M. de Nemours persists (admirably) with his agenda, giving up only after repeated rejections. Mme de Clèves, in contrast, perseveres in her spatial quest until she achieves her objective: the power to draw her own boundaries. By the time she finds her peace of mind (and her space?) and settles down in her final dual residence, my students and I are also ready to end our pursuit, not without gleefully reminding each other that while no one conquers the princess, we have just conquered together *La Princesse de Clèves*.

Seeing and Being Seen:
Visual Codes and Metaphors
in *La Princesse de Clèves*

Julia V. Douthwaite

The concern with sight (seeing and being seen) and insight or interpretation plays a crucial role in the plot and the social context of *La Princesse de Clèves* (1678). While ostensibly set in the last years of Henri II's reign (the late 1550s), the novel presents a world very reminiscent of Lafayette's own milieu, the court of Louis XIV in the 1670s. Louis XIV demanded that his noble subjects live at court, under his seemingly omniscient gaze, to remain in his good graces and thus maintain their place in *le monde* ("the world" of aristocratic society). Obliged to be on permanent display and to undertake no meaningful occupation, the courtiers in their idleness developed a complex repertoire of social gestures. Mastering this coded language of word, glance, and gesture constitutes the biggest hurdle facing the young heroine of *La Princesse de Clèves* and serves as a metaphor for her internal struggle as well; her story follows a movement from blindness (an inability to "read" social codes and a lack of self-knowledge) to sight (public astuteness) and insight (private lucidity). Before turning to our reading of Lafayette's novel, let us first consider the implications of this etiquette of sight in the everyday living conditions of seventeenth-century France.

Concepts of public and private, like standards of cleanliness and elegance, are historical constructions, relative to particular times and places. While extremely sensitive to issues of public civility and linguistic refinement, Lafayette's contemporaries seem oblivious to some elements of modesty and hygiene that we take for granted. Our concepts of privacy and notions of specialized room usage, for example, would seem quite odd to the seventeenth-century French. In those days the bedroom was the focus of household activities—the place where visitors assembled and business was transacted. Both men and women received visitors while in bed, sometimes fully dressed, sometimes in *négligé*. More intimate friends joined the master or mistress of the house in the space between the bedside and the wall called the *ruelle*—whence comes the expression *courir les ruelles*, to frequent ladies' chambers. To illustrate further in the classroom this peculiar aspect of seventeenth-century domestic space, I show slides of period interiors and daily life in which the bed features prominently. Particularly useful are two plates from Peter Thornton's *Seventeenth-Century Interior Decoration in England, France, and Holland*: "Parisian interior of the 1630s" (pl. 2) and "A Parisian woman receiving female friends in her bedchamber in the 1630s" (pl. 4).

La Princesse de Clèves bears witness to this custom in two scenes of social gatherings in the apartment of the princess, who receives callers while lying or sitting on her sumptuous bed. The first occurs after the death of her mother; M. de Nemours waits to pay his respects until all the other visitors have left and finds the princess appealingly arranged "sur son lit" (126) ("lying on her bed" [55]). Although somewhat flustered by his arrival in her bedchamber, the princess does not propose a change of place; her tête-à-tête with the duke ends only with the arrival of her husband, who appears undisturbed to find a male caller sitting alongside his wife's bed. The bed is also integral to the scene in which M. de Nemours steals the princess's portrait (136–37; 63–64). Here the reine dauphine — usually the shrewdest of observers — is sitting on the princess's bed and has her vision blocked by its heavy drapes. The dauphine's obstructed vision makes possible M. de Nemours's theft and his covert exchange of glances with the princess. The artful arrangement of the characters on and around the bed can be read as a metaphor for the conflicting emotions of the princess, caught between the demands of courtly etiquette (the reine dauphine) and private desires (M. de Nemours). I use slides to clear up any confusion over the intricate logistics; there are excellent illustrations of the scene in the 1891 English translation (see fig.) and the 1820 edition of *Œuvres complètes de Mesdames de La Fayette, de Tencin et de Fontaines* (2: front.).

Perhaps even more than issues of personal space, seventeenth-century practices of personal hygiene hold many surprises for the twentieth-century reader. Students are often shocked to learn that Louis XIV continued the time-honored custom of receiving important visitors while seated on his *chaise percée*, or closestool. This chair was no doubt beautifully upholstered, covered with morocco leather, velvet, or even tapestry. I like to show slides of similarly decorated *chaises* to illustrate this point; Thornton includes representative examples (pls. 312–14). Although the very idea of conversing while sitting on a toilet strikes us as patently unsuitable, the king's conduct is merely one manifestation of the period's rather nonchalant attitude toward sexual modesty and bodily functions. "In those times," writes Annik Pardailé-Galabrun, "nobody was offended by having to use a commode seat in common view, or urinating in the ashes of the hearth, or by chamber pots emptied out of windows" (144). Elegant Versailles was not exempt, as a German visitor commented in 1702: "There is one dirty thing at Court that I shall never get used to: the people stationed in the galleries in front of our rooms piss into all the corners. It is impossible to leave one's apartments without seeing somebody pissing" (Princess Palatine 110).

What seems paradoxical is that the same people who invited outsiders into the most intimate corners of their homes and did not flinch at relieving themselves in social settings should attach immense importance to such seemingly insignificant practices as polite conversation and eye contact. But we, in our anonymous industrialized society, need to remember that the aristocratic milieu represented in *La Princesse de Clèves* was extremely competitive and that sociability was crucial to maintaining one's place at court (and one's royal pension or livelihood). A courtier might piss with impunity in the hall at Versailles

Illustration of Nemours's theft of the princess's portrait, drawn by Jules Garnier and engraved by A. Lamotte (Lafayette, *Princess* [Perry trans.] 1: 177).

and remain largely unnoticed, but if he were to pass without greeting the wife of a peer or to exchange glances repeatedly with a superior at court, his gestures would invariably elicit much curiosity and speculation. Subtle changes in speech or even in body language—in gestures, glances, and physical proximity or distance between persons—were highly significant, for they suggested new alliances and shifting configurations of power. In *The Court Society* the sociologist-historian Norbert Elias tells us, "A shift in the hierarchy that was not reflected in a change of etiquette could not occur. [. . .] For this reason each individual was hypersensitive to the slightest change in the mechanism, stood watch over the existing order, attentive to its finest nuances" (88). Elias's book provides many insightful illustrations of this mentality; students might present sections of the book to the class and compare the rules of courtly decorum with our own social codes.

The sensitivity to social interaction strikes the reader immediately in the vocabulary of *La Princesse de Clèves*. The author's use of verbs of perception evokes the myriad functions of observation, voyeurism, and self-contemplation in the creation of courtly knowledge or "worldliness." The recurrence of verbs such as *paraître* ("to appear"), *sembler* ("to seem"), *cacher* ("to hide"), *voir clair* ("to see clearly"), and *aveugler* ("to blind") underlines the problematic nature of communication at court. Occurring 419 times in the text, *voir* ("to see") is the fourth most frequently used verb (after the commonplace verbs *être* ["to be"], *avoir* ["to have"], and *faire* ["to do" or "to make"]). *Exposer* ("to expose") and its cognates, such as *ne se pas exposer à être vue* ("not to expose oneself to being seen"), also appear frequently and convey an even more potent sense of the dangers and vulnerability associated with public sight—witness this comment on the newly wed princess: "Elle était néanmoins exposée au milieu de la cour" (89) ("She was none the less in an exposed position in the midst of the court" [22]). Moreover, the author often employs these visual terms to cast an ironic commentary on the characters' perceptions or to emphasize the uncertainty of their feelings. *Voir* is used to represent the characters' intellectual processes and their appeals to others' understanding; it smoothes over the transitions into internal narratives, as when the vidame, before recounting his liaison with the queen, declares, "[I]l faut vous raconter tout ce qui s'est passé, pour vous faire voir tout ce que j'ai à craindre" (149) ("I shall have to tell you the whole story to bring the extent of my danger home to you" [75]). Just as the verb's literal meaning (suggesting the fallibility of individual vision) is never entirely absent from such locutions, the trustworthiness of the characters' narratives is never certain.

This literal and metaphoric usage of *voir* recalls a technique commonly found in seventeenth-century aesthetics, notably baroque painting, as Helen Karen Kaps explains: "As a baroque painter might use a mirror to introduce otherwise extraneous objects into a picture, and to give their reflected, stylized presence a certain necessity, which a direct representation would not have, Mme de Lafayette often shows us extraneous material refracted through the intellect of another character" (72). One might show a slide of Velázquez's *Las meninas* (1656) to illustrate this technique. The mirror in the background of Velázquez's painting reflects the faces of two people absent from the painted scene and makes the image — of a complex of frames within frames — even more ambiguous and compelling.

Visual terms serve many functions in *La Princesse de Clèves*: they advance the primary plot by integrating internal narratives into the princess's story, they underline the heroine's vulnerability in the vicious circle of courtly life, they cast an ironic commentary on the characters' feelings, and they evoke the distorting mirror effect of court intrigues — the way trivial comments and surreptitious glances become refracted, distorted, and exaggerated in the incessant gossip of the courtiers. Students could be given this brief summary of sight imagery and asked to provide examples from their reading or to discern other functions of visual language in the novel.

Given the author's predilection for verbs of perception and visual metaphors, it seems odd that Lafayette relies on formulaic hyperboles and clichéd adjectives in describing the characters of *La Princesse de Clèves*. The "portrait gallery" in the first pages of the book offers us ample social information on the characters (titles, genealogies, places in the hierarchy) but scant physical details. The duc de Nemours is described simply as "un chef d'œuvre de la nature" ("nature's masterpiece"), "l'homme du monde le mieux fait et le plus beau" (71–72) ("the most handsome and most nobly built man in the world" [5]). We know little about the heroine's appearance; her descriptions are couched in the hyperbolic language standard for classical images of female beauty, such as, "La blancheur de son teint et ses cheveux blonds lui donnaient un éclat que l'on n'a jamais vu qu'à elle; tous ses traits étaient réguliers, et son visage et sa personne étaient pleins de grâce et de charmes" (77) ("Her white skin and fair hair gave her a lustre no other girl could equal; all her features were regular, and her face, her figure, were full of grace and charm" [10]). This mode of description emphasizes the social effects of appearances rather than the physical features themselves (Kusch 315). Alongside the principals' many virtues (beauty, wit, bravery, and military glory) the narrative lists certain character flaws (the king's penchant for adultery and the queen's hypocrisy) in an equally admiring tone ("[la reine] n'en témoignait aucune jalousie; mais elle avait une si profonde dissimulation qu'il était difficile de juger de ses sentiments" (70) ("[the queen] never showed any jealousy, but she had such a profound capacity for dissimulation that it was difficult to guess her true feelings" [3]). Indeed, the king's moral laxity and the queen's skillful dissimulation (synonymous here with self-control) set the standard for social conduct in this world and prompt the heroine's mother to proffer her most valuable piece of advice: "Si vous jugez sur les apparences en ce lieu-ci [. . .] vous serez souvent trompée: ce qui paraît n'est presque jamais la vérité" (94) ("If you judge by appearances in this place, [. . .] you will frequently be deceived: what you see is almost never the truth" [26]). This warning foreshadows the princess's central dilemmas: her frustrated attempts to see behind the different façades of her beloved duc de Nemours and her eventual refusal to trust what she does see.

But the heroine's first role in the novel is that of an object—observed, coveted, and scrutinized by others. Her entrance into the fictional universe is depicted in passive terms: "Il parut alors une beauté à la cour, qui attira les yeux de tout le monde" (76) ("There appeared at court in those days a young woman so beautiful that all eyes turned to gaze upon her" [9]). A day later, while visiting a jeweler's shop, she is again described in a passive, reactive mode:

> [Le Prince de Clèves] fut tellement surpris de sa beauté qu'il ne put cacher sa surprise; et Mlle de Chartres ne put s'empêcher de rougir en voyant l'étonnement qu'elle lui avait donné. [. . .] [I]l la regardait toujours avec étonnement. Il s'aperçut que ses regards l'embarrassaient, contre l'ordinaire des jeunes personnes, qui voient toujours avec plaisir l'effet de leur beauté.   (77)

> [The Prince de Clèves] was so taken aback by her beauty that he was unable to hide his astonishment, and Mlle de Chartres could not help blushing when she became aware of it. [. . .] [He] continued to regard her with amazement. He became aware that she was embarrassed by his stare, unlike most young girls, who are usually pleased to see the effect of their beauty on men.   (10–11)

Implicitly sanctioning the aggressive curiosity of this society, the narrator passes no judgment on the prince's prolonged, intrusive gaze but rather remarks on the heroine's ignorance: she is so naive she does not even know how to react to an amorous look!

When the king's sister arranges their meeting the next day, she asks the prince, "Venez [. . .] voyez si je ne vous tiens pas ma parole et si, en vous montrant Mlle de Chartres, je ne vous fais pas voir cette beauté que vous cherchiez" (79) ("Come and see [. . .] whether or not I have kept my promise. Let me show you Mlle de Chartres: do you not see in her the beauty you have been looking for?" [12]). These characters look at the heroine and discuss her as if she were a finely chiseled statue, a precious vase, or some other prize luxury object. And apart from the blushing noted above, she does not seem to mind the attention. When the marriage negotiations are complete, she accepts the loveless union with the prince—whom she regards with indifference—as a necessary business transaction, her service to the family fortune. This image of the noble young woman as the necessary guarantor of her family's wealth, with all the emotional conflicts it implies, is a historically accurate assessment of upper-class women's lives in seventeenth-century France (see the section on marriage in *Histoire des femmes en Occident* [Davis and Farge 38–46]). One might use this historical context to help students perceive the gradual change in the heroine's character: from the naive young girl—a passive object in others' eyes—to the unhappily married woman who becomes an increasingly insightful participant in the action.

It is not until the scene at the ball when the heroine sees the duc de Nemours for the first time that she takes on an active, observant, and self-conscious role in the plot. The duke's effect on the princess is described as "surprising"; the sight of him seems to shake her out of her torpor and reveal the vast array of feelings and visual signals that were whizzing by her all along unnoticed. Where she previously seemed to exist only in the eyes or plans of others, her interest in M. de Nemours provokes the princess to draw on her own powers of observation and analysis. The narration emphasizes this change in a series of clauses that repeat the verb *to see* to suggest the heroine's realization of M. de Nemours's prestigious place at court and her fascination with his person: "Les jours suivants, elle le vit chez la reine dauphine, elle le vit jouer à la paume avec le roi, elle le vit courre la bague, elle l'entendit parler; mais elle le vit toujours surpasser de si loin tous les autres [. . .] qu'il fit, en peu de temps, une grande impression dans son cœur" (92) ("On the days that followed, she saw him in the company of the Reine Dauphine, she watched him playing tennis with the King, she saw him tilt at the ring, she heard him speak; but, whenever and wherever she saw him, he so surpassed all others [. . .] that he soon made a deep impression on her heart" [25]). At first the heroine's passion seems like an exciting initiation into the clandestine pleasures of court life: although the princess meets the duke frequently at the dauphine's apartments, only she is privy to his guarded signs of love. Her sense of safety proves illusory, however, when she blushes furiously (and dangerously) on overhearing a casual comment about the duke. Her love, she realizes, is not just a thrilling secret diversion but also an issue of public interest, and it could lead to terrible consequences for her marriage, her reputation, and her family's place at court. And so she resolves to quell her feelings by actively avoiding M. de Nemours, as if the mere sight of him were enough to draw her in against her will: "Elle ne pouvait s'empêcher d'être troublée de sa vue, et d'avoir pourtant du plaisir à le voir" (107) ("She could not help being disturbed at the sight of him, and yet taking pleasure in seeing him" [39]).

This notion of sight as an irresistible agent of passion is a familiar topos in *La Princesse de Clèves*. The Prince de Clèves, the chevalier de Guise, and the duc de Nemours all fall in love with the heroine at first sight and all three suffer as a result. The involuntary, irrevocable nature of these passions recalls Renaissance and baroque myths on the causal interdependence of love and vision. The passions, according to early modern theorists, penetrate one's blood through the eyes, the windows of the soul, and are then carried throughout the body by "animal spirits" heated by the heart and stomach. Although caused by a "passive" physiological reaction, they nevertheless provoke disturbing effects on the intellect and will. Hence passionate love was seen as a "sort of mental disease interfering with the free exercise of reason, and paralyzing the will: a communicable illness, transmitted from eye to eye" (Weinberg 308). The tragic destiny of sentimental Châtelart epitomizes the dire consequences of passionate sight. We are told that his frequent contact with the dauphine (as a go-between for his friend d'Anville) proved fatal: "ce fut en la [la dauphine] voyant souvent qu'il prit le commencement de cette malheureuse passion qui lui ôta la raison et qui lui coûta enfin la vie" (84) ("it was in seeing her [the reine dauphine] frequently that he began to fall prey to the ill-fated passion that deprived him of his reason and finally cost him his life" [17]). The princess's passion conjures a life-threatening impulse as well, thanks to her mother's deathbed warning: "vous êtes sur le bord du précipice: il faut de grands efforts et de grandes violences pour vous retenir" (108) ("you are on the edge of a precipice. You will have to make great efforts and do yourself great violence to hold yourself back" [39–40]). The worst that can possibly happen, her mother tells her, would be for her to "tomber comme les autres femmes" (108) ("fall like other women" [40]), to let passion contaminate her will and destroy her virtue.

Once aware of the danger of seeing M. de Nemours and of being seen by him and others, the princess tries to break away from court life. She avoids his visits, refuses invitations, and withdraws to her country home at Coulommiers. But these decisions are difficult because they demand false pretenses and lies and because their results are often worthless. Sometimes she avoids M. de Nemours's presence only to find images of him invading her thoughts and fantasies. Sometimes her husband forces her to resume public appearances for the sake of their social position. Most often she is betrayed by her youthful candor. Try as she might, she cannot master presenting the artful façades that are second nature to her companions at court. The notion of social life as a "perpetual carnival" of masked hypocrites was well-known to Lafayette's readers. I like to show students the satirical emblem "Mascarade universelle" ("Universal Masquerade"), engraved by Nicolas Guérard, which depicts a man and a woman who face each other but cannot see beyond the numerous masks (of sincerity, justice, generosity, compassion, etc.) that cover their faces until Time (a winged monkey) lifts the masks off, for as the legend tells us, "Le Temps découvre tout" ("Time discovers all"). (For a reproduction of this seventeenth-century emblem, see Davis and Farge 241.) A master of worldly deception, the duke easily sees through the princess's attempted disguises. Her transparency betrays her feelings at the same time that it suggests her essential difference from the duke's culture: her inability to master the masquerade of courtly society eventually translates into her refusal of its dangerous hypocrisy.

The duke exploits the princess's inexperience and fear of exposure on several occasions. In the midst of one social gathering, he deftly pockets a miniature portrait that the prince had made of his wife, only to look up and find her watching him. Realizing that any attention might prove disastrous, the princess remains mute and allows his theft to remain secret. The two characters' reactions reveal their different senses of power and self-control. M. de Nemours leaves the crowd, shuts himself in his room with the princess's image, and dreams of overcoming her virtue with passion: "il aimait la plus aimable personne de la cour; il s'en faisait aimer malgré elle" (137) ("he was in love with the person at court most worthy of love; he was making her love him despite herself" [64]). The princess remains in public and watches him leave in great agitation and embarrassment. It is not until later when she is alone that she realizes that her silent inaction might be read as tacit consent: she is filled with remorse and dread at the very thought.

This alternance between public confusion and private lucidity runs throughout the novel and allows the reader to see the heroine gradually emerge as an autonomous individual who has her own, decidedly uncourtly, principles. In her remorse over the stolen portrait she makes the momentous decision to admit her passion to her husband. Unaware of the pain it will cause him, she merely hopes to enlist his support for her absence from M. de Nemours and *le monde*. But the duke invades the poignant scene of her confession as well, watching with avid interest from a nearby window. To demonstrate the tension generated by this complex of seeing and unseeing glances, one might show slides of the scene: particularly evocative illustrations can be found in the 1891 English translation (2: 73) and in the 1864 edition of *Œuvres de Madame de Lafayette* (front.). Even the princess's most intimate moment in the novel, when she indulges in a sensuous reverie in the pavilion at Coulommiers, is broken open by the spying eyes of M. de Nemours, who looks on from behind a French window. This famous scene of voyeurism underlines the intensity and complexity of the gaze in *La Princesse de Clèves*. In the heroine's self-imposed refuge from the duke, she cannot help seeing him in her thoughts, especially since she has taken care to fill the pavilion with objects that remind her of him—his cane and a painting depicting his exploits on the battlefield. As she thinks of him, her body and face express an intense passion and happiness she will never experience in his presence. The desire to gaze on the beloved haunts both characters like a forbidden erotic temptation—tantalizing yet fraught with guilt and anxiety. M. de Nemours can scarcely control his rapture at the sight of the blissful princess, and he plots the best means to approach her, as though mesmerized by an irresistible force. When he suddenly awakens from this dream, however, his rational mind warns that visibility means danger—not a tangible threat to his person, but a more powerful menace to his emotions and social position. The princess goes through a similar conflict of temptation and resistance when she glimpses, or thinks she glimpses, the duke in the garden. The sight of her beloved arouses private longings she hardly dares admit; only by joining her maids can she repress these troubling sensations and assume the dignified air demanded of someone of her rank. To further complicate the issue of seen and unseen gazes, during the same episode a spy sent by the prince to trail M. de Nemours hides behind a fence and thus sees the duke enter the garden but does not see that he remains in hiding. The spy's resulting report unleashes the violent jealousy that ultimately causes the prince's death. In sad irony the prince admits on his deathbed that he would rather have remained *blind* to the whole episode.

The two portrait scenes illuminate the lovers' different attitudes toward representation and possession and help explain the heroine's final renunciation of M. de Nemours. Thanks to the rumors and intrigues that he has inspired at court, the duke's name is synonymous with skillful seduction. While he is tactful and subtle in his advances toward the princess, his actions nevertheless destroy her peace of mind, rob her husband of his security, and stoke the fires of jealousy. When the duke beholds the stolen portrait of the princess alone in his room, he rejoices in the thought of her imminent seduction. However, apart from the passionate gestures he glimpses during the night at Coulommiers, he looks in vain for an expression of love when the princess is in his presence. Indeed, he ultimately envies his portrait, exclaiming, "Laissez-moi voir que vous m'aimez, belle princesse [. . .] laissez-moi voir vos sentiments. [. . .] Regardez-moi du moins avec ces mêmes yeux dont je vous ai vue cette nuit regarder mon portrait" (211) ("Allow me to see that you love me, my beautiful princess [. . .] show me your feelings. [. . .] At least look at me as I saw you look last night at my portrait" [131]). It seems the heroine's sense of vulnerability and guilt far outweighs the pleasures she finds in loving the duke. While she gazes on his portrait with longing and rapture, she regards the actual man with fear and apprehension. It is as if she prefers the representation to the original, the dream of perfect love to the reality of what seems destined to become a common, sordid courtly passion.

The gaze — and its corollaries, vision and sight — constitute a number of metaphorical traps and prisons in the fictional universe of *La Princesse de Clèves*. Whether it be the gaze of others, an external observation, or even an imaginary vision, sight captures the individual and locks him or her into an inescapable labyrinth of trompe l'oeil appearances, illusions that oppose reality and truth. Although M. de Nemours appears to be a loyal and attentive lover, the princess is long in doubt over the real man behind the mask—all the more so because of his well-known reputation as the court Don Juan. Remembering her mother's admonition about the dangers of passion, she refuses him but for a time seems to waver on the brink of submitting to desire. It is not until the princess confronts the death of her husband that she finds the strength to reject the dangerous powers of the duke's sight and the vicious cycles of court intrigue for the wisdom of her own insight.

Ultimately, the heroine abandons the tempting illusion of reciprocal love and, under the figurative gaze of her dead husband and mother, prepares an alternative future free of M. de Nemours and *le monde*. She renounces all possibility of encountering the duke in person by withdrawing from the court, far from places that remind her of him and from windows that "see" (e.g., the episode of M. de Nemours's voyeurism from a neighboring apartment). Unlike the other courtiers, she feels no need to live in the public eye or to use her visibility to protect her social rank. Instead she flees to the calm pleasures of religion and solitude, seeking lasting contentment in the light of a clear conscience. Living outside the court in the end, the princess leaves examples of virtue that are "inimitable" because they remain invisible, except to the wise reader's admiring gaze.

NOTE

I would like to thank the students of my seminars on women writers of the ancien régime, especially Odette Menyard, for their ideas and conversations on *La Princesse de Clèves*.

Truly Inimitable?
Repetition in *La Princesse de Clèves*

Louise K. Horowitz

The indeterminate source of the lost letter that circulates through the Valois court, distributing along with the question of the letter's origin a fair measure of promiscuous passion, emblematically marks *La Princesse de Clèves*. The episode of the misplaced missive occurs midway through Lafayette's novel, and thematically and structurally it conditions the entire work. An inscribed sign of infidelity, the letter, addressed to the vidame de Chartres by one of his mistresses and lost by him during a tennis match, is initially and confusedly attributed by some members of the court to the duc de Nemours. Sowing anxiety concerning both its origin and its destination and making a clear display of unfaithful sexual activity, the letter worries not only the vidame (who fears that it will alienate the queen, to whom he has pledged exclusive faithfulness) but also Mme de Clèves, who readily believes its attribution to the duc de Nemours, and the duke himself, who anxiously and accurately fears the princess's reaction if the correct "destinataire" ("recipient") is not quickly determined.

In fact, the lost letter's circuitous path, occupying several dense pages of the second and third parts of the novel, generates considerable concern among many characters. Initiated by Mme de Thémines and destined for the vidame de Chartres, the missive is additionally read and handled by Chastelart, who passes it on to the reine dauphine, who gives it to her friend Mme de Clèves, who, on hearing Nemours's entreaty and his description of its intended receiver, delivers it to Nemours, who returns it to the vidame. An articulation of the genuine but deceived passion of its original sender, the letter is subsequently doubled by another written message to the vidame, from Mme d'Amboise, Thémines's close friend, who demands that Thémines's letter be returned to its source. The original letter, itself nothing more than the written and therefore mediated transcription of *un*mediated desire, is then hurriedly and unsuccessfully copied by the princess and the duc de Nemours to fool the queen and protect the vidame from her angry recriminations. Preoccupied with the charms of this singular moment of intimacy, they fail miserably in their goal and end not by sheltering the vidame but rather by exposing him to the queen's wrath. Concerning the future of the friendship between Catherine de Médicis and the vidame de Chartres, Lafayette succinctly concludes, "Leur liaison se rompit, et elle le perdit ensuite à la conjuration d'Amboise où il se trouva embarrassé" (166) ("Their liaison came to an end, and she eventually brought about his ruin at the time of the Amboise conspiracy, in which he was involved" [90]).

The letter and the complicated turns of the episode that textually envelops it also engender curiosity and anxiety in the reader. Such concern, however, may ultimately be only the displacement of another source of anxiety. At a less visible level, indeed, almost subliminally, Lafayette structures the episode by invoking a repeated name — Amboise — that, despite the complicated textual apparatus surrounding the elusive letter, succinctly captures a simultaneous inscription of love and death. This procedure is then textually magnified when the novelist has the princess copy the lost letter, signaling again the consuming passage from life to death, as originary passion enters, through the written media, not once, but twice, the deadening status of reproduction.

Lafayette uses a recurring device, extending the same name to a fictitious, imaginary character and to a historical one, the former a signifier of passion, the latter, of death. For example, the same appellation joins the force of life to that of death when Mme de Tournon, quintessential but wholly fictitious lover, is linked by a shared nomenclature to Tournon, the place where François I's eldest son, the dauphin, dies, in the redundant Oedipal pattern of *La Princesse de Clèves*. And in the episode of the lost letter Lafayette scatters the name Amboise, that is, as the name of Mme d'Amboise, fictitious friend of the letter's originator and accomplice in the ceaseless circulation of the vidame's desire, and, simultaneously, as an emblem of death, since the vidame's demise is preannounced at the end of the episode as resulting from the historical Amboise conspiracy, a failed 1560 effort by the Protestant faction to counter the increasing power of the Guise family.

The anxiety of origin thus quickly becomes the apprehension of death, in Lafayette's novelistic pattern, wherein reiterated names convey simultaneously creation and termination, love (life) and death, while the artifice of reproduction cancels and denies the moment of originary, spontaneous passion.

This pattern should cause no surprise, however, for the entire "story" of Mlle de Chartres, wife to the Prince de Clèves and would-be lover to the duc de Nemours, is itself markedly *unoriginal*, the surface manifestation of preexisting names and characters that signal its initiatory (in a nonpejorative sense) production. Enmeshed in a prestory, a prehistory of preexisting sources, the trajectory from the moment of love to the time of retreat, to the naming of death, is entirely prefigured by the buried names of Coulommiers, the country estate under construction by M. and Mme de Clèves.

Itself the polyvalent locus of the inscription of the princess's passion for Nemours (the château is the site of their mutually erotic reveries) and of death (Coulommiers is the site of the confession to the prince, which leads to his subsequent fatal illness and, ultimately, her own), the country retreat bears within its walls a fascinating testimony of origin and termination, in a history that is virtually closed off to us now, for lack of a familiar genealogical base, but that was no doubt eminently accessible to Lafayette's original audience.

As Micheline Cuénin (in her section of an article written with Chantal Morlet-Chantalat) and Faith Beasley (*Revising Memory*) have shown, Coulommiers is historically anachronistic in the novel, for the château did not yet exist in 1558–59, when most of the events of *La Princesse de Clèves* take place. This makes Lafayette's choice that much richer, as the name was bound to generate for the seventeenth-century audience powerfully reverberating echoes of more recent French history. Coulommiers, preeminent novelistic locus of creation and curtailment, of passion and denial, of love and death, contained within its walls an entire past of the complex intertwining of the Clèves and Nemours clans. Cuénin's study significantly returns Coulommiers to its source:

> Celle qui commanda à Salmon de Brosse cette somptueuse demeure est une Clèves par sa mère: il s'agit en effet de Catherine de Gonzague, fille d'Henriette de Clèves [. . .] veuve à vingt-cinq ans d'Henri Ier de Longueville. [. . .] Or, l'on sait que Jacques de Savoie, duc de Nemours, descendait des premiers Longueville, sa mère étant née Charlotte d'Orléans.   (118, 121)

> The woman who ordered Salmon de Brosse to construct this sumptuous residence is descended from the Clèves family on her mother's side. She was Catherine de Gonzague, the daughter of Henriette de Clèves [. . .] a widow at twenty-five when her husband Henri I of Longueville died. [. . .] Jacques de Savoie, the duc de Nemours, was a descendent of the first Longueville, his mother being Charlotte d'Orléans.

In 1678, at the moment of publication of *La Princesse de Clèves*, the château's occupant was Marie de Longueville, duchesse de Nemours and Catherine de Gonzague's granddaughter, who had quit the court and retreated to her country estate following the failure of the Fronde (119).

Thus Coulommiers's embedded names offer a clandestine source for the ostensibly fictional story shrouded in the history of the Valois monarchy. In truth, as Lafayette indicated she knew, openly labeling her novel an "imitation" in a letter to the chevalier de Lescheraine (*Correspondance* 2: 63–64), the fictional story of the seemingly imaginary princess is a decidedly unoriginal production, born of preceding scripts and historical and genealogical codes that not only condition and model but in fact entirely create and sustain it and, in the end, consign it to the same redundant history that the princess had seemingly eluded by virtue of her fictitious status. Existing ostensibly "outside" these codes, the princess is wholly inscribed and contained in them. Despite the ironic claims of "inimitability," she, along with everything and everyone else (for how would any escape?), is consigned the identity of "copy" that completely structures Lafayette's novel. For nothing and no one in this universe is "original." The factitious is its hallmark, whether one focuses on portraits of herself that the princess is having touched up or on the central painting of the siege of Metz that decorates the pavilion at Coulommiers (itself, as we have seen, emblem of the very unoriginality of the Clèves-Nemours interrelation, emblem of death and early widowhood, and emblem of ultimate retreat).

Concerning the painting of the siege of Metz, which prominently highlights

Nemours's triumph over the Holy Roman Emperor Charles V, we are told that this work, like several others the princess brings to Coulommiers, has been copied from an original that Mme de Valentinois had had made for her own country estate of Anet. Although space does not permit a full analysis here, Mme de Valentinois forms with that other elusive figure, the vidame de Chartres, a fundamental and "originary" couple for the novel, distributing desire, along with multiple partners, throughout the text. Yet they too are mere productions of earlier sources, succinctly detailed by Lafayette, both the mid-sixteenth-century progeny of the oldest noble families: the vidame is from the glorious house of Vendôme; and Diane de Poitiers, born into a family whose roots are traced to the "anciens ducs d'Aquitaine," is also linked to Louis XI, traditionally viewed as the first "modern" French king. For not the least of Lafayette's goals is the evocation of an entire civilization and culture, from its moments of origin to the time of its demise in the religious warfare about to erupt as the events of Lafayette's novel unfold. The painting depicting the siege of Metz, a copy (what else?) of the original that hung at Mme de Valentinois's country estate, is an extraordinary emblem of that culture's apotheosis. It is also by virtue of its status as copy, as reproduction, the ultimate bearer of death, the death of the passion that surfaces dramatically during the eventful love scene at Coulommiers and perhaps, too, the death of the culture that precedes the schism born of intense religious struggle and that Lafayette portrays as ineluctably doomed.

The constant tension between creation and reproduction, source and imitation, becomes, then, emblematic of a structure of repetition that obsessively conditions Lafayette's novel and that is so artfully concealed we are scarcely aware, as we read, of its predominance. From the originary couple of the vidame de Chartres and Mme de Valentinois emanate endless replications of each and both. I have discussed elsewhere the unremitting lack of individuation among the courtiers: if Nemours and the vidame are both targeted as the recipient of the lost letter, it is because these best friends are so remarkably similar, virtually interchangeable, cohabiting (like their promiscuous siblings, the French and English kings) an identical universe of freewheeling sexuality and compulsive infidelity. Even the duc de Nemours and the Prince de Clèves, whom we have traditionally been taught to view as profoundly "different," share controlling attitudes and interrogating postures that mark them as one. Both named Jacques, they testify to the confused status of husband and lover that informs the novel and to an undifferentiated duplication of function. In unvaryingly parallel fashion, the prince and the duc—Jacques de Nevers and Jacques de Savoie—mutually institute the reign of desire and the kingdom of death. In this strange world an "original" is instantly contaminated by its ceaselessly referring imitation. But who is the original?

Both Michel Butor and Peggy Kamuf ("Mother's Will") in their studies of *La Princesse de Clèves* have focused on this underlying structure of repetition. Butor refers primarily to the double scenes at Coulommiers—the confession by the princess to her husband and the "apparition" scene, in which Nemours, hiding outside the pavilion, gazes on the princess tying silk ribbons on his India cane, as she, simultaneously, is transfixed by the copy of the painting of the siege of Metz—and concludes that these moments are compulsively played and replayed in the novel. "They cannot help but try to play it again, always looking for summer houses, windows, silk shops" (159). Kamuf details further the replaying of "original" scenes, focusing on the first encounter between Nemours and Mlle de Chartres at the ball, when a noise signals his arrival; a noise that is then echoed at Coulommiers, as his scarf catches in a window. The original meeting, the moment of the birth of their mutual desire, is, we know, abruptly curtailed by the king—the very source of the command that they dance together—as he and the queens deny further intimacy in favor of a formal introduction. And this denial, this blocking of desire, will repeatedly replay throughout Lafayette's novel. "The suspension," writes Kamuf, "of certain knowledge sets up the patterns for the missed encounters which proliferate in the later section of the narrative—at the silk merchant's shop, in the public garden, and finally, in the most explicit repetition of the scene at the pavilion, across the courtyard, when the lovers furtively catch sight of one another" (228). The book's penultimate scenes rapidly replicate, yet once more, the hallmarks of the traumatic and imprinting earliest moments. The silk merchant's shop, from which Nemours may gaze on and contemplate the now-widowed Mme de Clèves, replays the very stuff of the book's most haunting passages. It is silk that marks the capital scene of the tournament in which the king is fatally wounded, as each courtier displays through that fabric the encoded colors of his beloved; and it is with silk ribbons that the princess dreamily decorates Nemours's India cane at Coulommiers. So too the very physical structure of the country estate, of the pavilion in the forest, is duplicated in the urban setting of the end: the silk shop's windows and doors, either open or closed, refigure the identical paradox of desire and repression marked by the same apertures at Coulommiers. (And the shop itself, from which Nemours gazes on Mme de Clèves, is yet one more replica of an earlier source, the jewelry store where that other Jacques, the Prince de Clèves, first encountered and desired Mlle de Chartres.)

We should not be surprised, therefore, given this spiraling structure of imitation, that the silk artisan's production gives rise to a desire on the part of the princess to re-create his work. "Le lendemain, cette princesse, qui cherchait des occupations conformes à l'état où elle était, alla proche de chez elle voir un homme qui faisait des ouvrages de soie d'une façon particulière; et elle y fut dans le dessein d'en faire de semblables" (222) ("The next day, Mme de Clèves, wanting to find an occupation appropriate to her present state, went to see a man whose house was close to hers and who did a special kind of work in silk; she was thinking she might do something similar herself" [140]). In fact, the entire landscape of the book's last scenes before the ultimate retreat dramatically reproduces the earlier ones of the "cabinet" and the gardens at Coulommiers: "Après avoir traversé un petit bois, elle aperçut au bout d'une allée, dans l'endroit le plus reculé du jardin, une manière de cabinet ouvert de tous côtés, où elle adressa ses pas. Comme elle en fut proche, elle vit un homme couché sur des bancs, qui paraissait enseveli dans une rêverie profonde, et elle reconnut que c'était M. de Nemours" (222–23) ("As she came out of a little wood, she noticed, at the end of an avenue in the most remote part of the garden, a kind of summer-house open at the sides, to which she directed her steps. As she drew near, she saw a man reclining on some benches, deeply absorbed as it seemed in reverie, and she recognized that it was M. de Nemours" [141]). And by now we should not be astonished that this final erotic reverie is interrupted, and therefore repressed, by a sudden noise made by her servants.

For the scenes at Coulommiers are the "origins" of those that surface at the end. Silk, gardens, courtyards, alleys, windows and doors (open and closed), sudden noises, desire and denial, love and death—all are inscribed reiterations of an earlier moment, productions of buried memory, all too readily *imitable* examples, like the princess herself. Is it any wonder that, in a desperate effort to re-create, however unconsciously, the initial paradisiacal moments, Nemours takes up residence at the Parisian silk shop as a "painter," there to capture "de belles maisons et des jardins que l'on voyait de ses fenêtres" (222) ("the fine houses and gardens that could be seen from the windows" [140]), the very image of Coulommiers? But imagination—as Rousseau and Derrida have signaled—the faculty that allows the representation of desire, is also that which permits the apprehension of death. Encased in spiraling images and structures of redundancy and repetition, much like the imitations of art that decorate Coulommiers, Nemours's efforts at creation are doomed unto death.

And it is this hailing of the "imaginaire" as agent of representation of love and death that finally structures the whole of *La Princesse de Clèves*. Not knowing who the Sunday painter installed in the shop across from her window is, Mme de Clèves nonetheless "creates" and fashions Nemours, the *image* of Nemours, from the hazy indeterminate account of the silk man and that of Mme de Martigues: "Mme de Clèves écoutait ce discours avec une grande attention. Ce que lui avait dit Mme de Martigues, que M. de Nemours était quelquefois à Paris, se joignit *dans son imagination* à cet homme bien fait qui venait proche de chez elle, et lui fit une idée de M. de Nemours [. . .]" (222; my emphasis) ("Mme de Clèves listened to these remarks with the closest attention. What Mme de Martigues had said to her about M. de Nemours's visits to Paris became connected *in her imagination* with this handsome man who came to a house so close to hers; it brought to her mind's eye a picture of M. de Nemours [. . .]" [140–41; my emphasis]). Running back and forth to the windows, promenading along the paths of the public garden, discovering there "une manière de cabinet ouvert de tous côtés" (223) ("a kind of summer-house open at the sides" [141]), Mme de Clèves feverishly works to re-create, along with the painter Nemours, the time and space of Coulommiers. But only for the briefest of moments, for she is hampered by another controlling image: "Elle sentait néanmoins une douleur vive de *s'imaginer* qu'il [Nemours] était cause de la mort de son mari" (221; my emphasis) ("It was none the less deeply painful to her *to imagine* that he was the cause of her husband's death" [139; my emphasis]). Originary source of love and death, of creation and end, the image of Nemours dies in the silence that alone may halt his ceaseless reproduction in the text, if not, finally, in life.

SPECIFIC TEACHING CONTEXTS

Teaching *La Princesse de Clèves* in Translation

Faith E. Beasley

While teaching *La Princesse de Clèves* in a "great works of Western civiliza-tion" course, I was struck by the students' scorn for and dislike of the princess. I had taught the novel in French for years and never encountered such hostility toward the protagonist. As we analyzed the confession scene, one student's question identified what I now believe to be the root of the problem. "Why is the princess so tired all the time? How old is she anyway?" he queried. I real-ized that the animosity was due, at least in part, to translation. In the translation we were using, *repos* had frequently been translated as *rest*, which did not con-vey the more important sense of "peace of mind" inherent in the French. The rift between my perception of the novel and my students' emerged because we were quite simply not reading the same text.

In recent years a number of new translations of this masterpiece have ap-peared. I have now used most of them in the classroom and have found that the translation chosen can radically alter and determine the students' comprehen-sion as well as appreciation of the text. In what follows I discuss some of the difficulties of translating *La Princesse de Clèves* and teaching it in translation. I analyze the four translations professors most frequently choose: Terence Cave's, Walter Cobb's, Robin Buss's, and John D. Lyons's edition of the 1892 translation by Thomas Sergeant Perry. I focus on specific terms that cannot be readily translated into English — such as *repos* and *aveu* — and some of the confusing and unfamiliar aspects of the text that identify it as a product of its literary, historical, and cultural milieu.

While my comments are mainly for non-French-speaking professors with little or no knowledge of seventeenth-century France or French, I believe that those who usually teach the novel in French will find much of the discussion useful when they have occasion to teach the text in English. An interpretation that they or the critics they use have developed using the French text may not be clear or even possible to teach when they use certain English translations.

"Une Agitation sans Désordre" ("A Kind of Orderly Unrest")

In many classrooms the opening pages of the novel can inspire an "unrest" bordering on rebellion. Whether in English or in French, the terms Lafayette chooses to set the scene and describe the characters can be as foreign to twentieth-century students as Sanskrit. *Galanterie, esprit,* and *amant,* for example, all have meanings specific to Lafayette's seventeenth-century context. Because the complex interplay between the princess and her social setting creates much of the powerful meaning of the text, students' understanding of this historical and cultural context is crucial. The novel opens with a multifaceted term describing the court, which reappears throughout the novel: "La magnificence et la *galanterie* n'ont jamais paru en France avec tant d'éclat que dans les dernières années du règne de Henri second" (69; my emphasis) ("Never has France seen such a display of courtly magnificence and manners as in the last years of the reign of Henri II" [3]). Students often associate *gallantry* only with love, which is perhaps why Cave opts for "manners" and Buss for "refinement," which convey its other senses. Similarly, the adjective attributed to Henri II, "galant," when translated as "gallant" can mean little to twentieth-century readers. Cave and Cobb opt for "chivalrous" and Buss for "courteous." Later one finds another example of the term when Mme de Chartres instructs her daughter to "lui faire confidence de toutes les galanteries" (82) ("to tell her if anyone ever talked to her of love" [15]); the translators render the term as "love" (Cave 15), "affairs of heart" (Cobb 13), "amorous remark" (Buss 34), and "sweet speeches" (Lyons 11). *Galanterie* was an important concept in seventeenth-century French literature, connoting the social decorum of which Lafayette's heroine is so acutely aware. It is important to underscore its various uses as one explains the particularities of the historical setting, especially when using the Lyons translation, which generally uses "gallantry" and "gallant," a move that does not confine *galanterie*'s meaning to either politeness or love.

A second word that is imprinted on the whole novel and appears in this first line is *jamais.* It can be translated in a variety of ways—as *ever,* or *never,* for example—but whenever it appears, it draws attention to the uniqueness of the person or action it modifies. For certain key scenes, one might find it useful to go back to the French to get a sense of Lafayette's use of the term, if only to count the number of times it appears. Lafayette uses *jamais* to distinguish the court and her protagonists from everything and everyone else, fictional or real.

She valorizes the court, saying, "Jamais cour n'a eu tant de belles personnes" (70) ("No court has ever brought together so many beautiful women and wonderfully handsome men" (Cave 4; Cobb 2, Buss 24, Lyons 3).[1] Lyons's substitution of the pluperfect tense here—"At no court had there ever been gathered together" (3)—changes the meaning. It allows for the possibility that later courts could have surpassed Henri II's. The simple past of the French places Henri's court above any other, past or present. Seventeenth-century readers recognized this valorization of a past court, and Valincour even found it subversive. He criticized the author for not acknowledging Louis XIV's court as the best. *Jamais* also qualifies the principal characters. Nemours has exceptional looks "que l'on n'a jamais vu qu'à lui seul" (72) ("the like of which has never been seen" [Cave 5]). Cobb eliminates *jamais* here: "that were his own special hallmark" (4), as does Buss: "that belonged only to him" (25). Similarly Lyons compares Nemours to others at court—"such as no other showed" (5)—but does not elevate him over all others past and present, as *jamais* does. The terms of Nemours's description are echoed in that of the princess, who possesses "un éclat que l'on n'a jamais vu qu'à elle" (77) ("a lustre no other girl could equal" [Cave 10]). None of the translations maintains the important linguistic parallel between the two principal characters. Cobb eliminates *jamais* entirely: "all radiated grace and charm" (9).

In the confession scene *jamais* appears with almost annoying regularity: for example, "un aveu que l'on n'a jamais fait à son mari"; "jamais donné nulle marque de faiblesse"; "je ne vous déplairai jamais par mes actions"; "plus d'estime pour un mari que l'on n'en a jamais eu" (171) ("no woman has ever made to her husband"; "never shown any sign of weakness"; "I shall never displease you by my actions"; "greater affection and esteem for one's husband than any wife has ever had" [Cave 95; Cobb 97, Buss 113, Lyons 66]). The exceptional and original nature of the action, like that of Henri's court and the two protagonists, is highlighted through Lafayette's use of *jamais*. In general the translators convey "jamais" using "never" and "ever." Cobb eliminates it once, stating "profound esteem for you" (114).

I emphasize the necessity of translating *jamais* as literally as possible when it occurs because it becomes a hallmark of the novel. It is essential to impart this characteristic because it elicited such critical fire in the seventeenth century. The concept of *vraisemblance* is complex and essential for an appreciation of *La Princesse de Clèves*. The historical novels that developed after 1660 had to be *vraisemblable* to be acceptable, that is, they had to adhere to accepted notions of plausibility and propriety (see Coulet, *Roman*; Showalter; Beasley, *Revising*). *Vraisemblance* thus refers to things not only as they are but also as they should be. *Bienséance*, or propriety, is often implicit in its usage. The primary way of ensuring *vraisemblance* was to ground the fiction in history. Novelists exploited the fact that in French only one word, *histoire*, designates both story and history. Lafayette seems to provoke the charge of being *invraisemblable*, or implausible, through her use of *jamais*, which highlights her fiction's difference. In addition, Lafayette comments on her novel's plausibility and propriety. When the terms *vraisemblance* or *vraisemblable* actually occur in *La Princesse de Clèves*, translators use a variety of words, such as "propriety," "convention," "decorum," "civility," and "courtesy." Given the association of the princess with *bienséance*, her constructed sense of propriety, it seems important to choose an English word such as *propriety* that is equally polysemous, as in the following example. In her lessons to her daughter, Mme de Chartres "joignait à la sagesse de sa fille une conduite si exacte pour toutes les bienséances" (89) ("reinforced her daughter's own good behaviour with such an exact respect for all the proprieties" [Cave 22; Cobb 21, Buss 42, Lyons 16]). It is especially important to transmit this atmosphere of *bienséance* when it is directly mentioned, as when the princess answers her husband's complaint that she does not have strong feelings for him after their marriage: She responds, "[I]l me semble que la bienséance ne permet pas que j'en fasse davantage" (87) ("It seems to me that propriety does not permit me to do much more" [Cobb 19]). Buss keeps "propriety" (40), while Cave opts for "decorum" (20). Lyons, however, eliminates the term: "it seems to me that you have no right to demand anything more" (15). This translation, without the reference to social conventions, could appear incomprehensible to readers, who might respond that a husband not only could demand more but also could justifiably expect it.

The concept of *vraisemblance* at the heart of novelistic composition is equally essential for understanding the confession scene. As we have seen in the use of *jamais*, Lafayette underscores this scene as exceptional. In the novel she explicitly undermines the concept of *vraisemblance* and in so doing transgresses the principal rule of the genre. After overhearing the confession, Lafayette writes, Nemours "ne savait quasi si ce qu'il avait entendu n'était point un songe, tant il y trouvait peu de vraisemblance" (178) ("was no longer certain whether what he had heard was not a dream, so implausible did it seem to him" [Cave 101]). Cobb translates the phrase containing *vraisemblance* as "unbelievable" (104) whereas Buss and Lyons choose "unlikely" (120; 70), which makes the connection with the rule of *vraisemblance* less possible. Lafayette seems to choose *vraisemblance* deliberately to make this connection both here and when the princess responds to the dauphine's retelling of the princess's confession. She responds defensively, "Cette histoire ne me paraît guère vraisemblable" (183) ("The story hardly sounds plausible to me" [Cave 106]). Cobb chooses "possible" (109) and Lyons "probable" (74). Buss mistranslates "guère," which means "not at all" or "hardly," as "somewhat": "seems somewhat improbable" (124).

A few other important concepts in the novel are difficult to convey in English or are especially perplexing for twentieth-century readers. The first is the complex notion of politics, a sphere that combines public and private in the novel. Thus in the opening, when the narrator states that "la politique" made it necessary for Catherine de Médicis to accept the constant presence of her husband's mistress (70), "political self-interest" (Cave 3) is a better choice than Cobb's "strategy" (2) or Buss's and Lyons's "policy" (23; 3), which makes students think that the French court had an official policy about mistresses. The activities of this court as depicted by Lafayette underscore the intersection of public and private. Every day Henri II attends the queen's "cercle" (70), which is a gathering for conversation that could be interpreted as being similar to seventeenth-century salons. Cave maintains "circle" (4), and Cobb translates it as "that hour" (2). Buss and Lyons make the meeting seem more formal and official by referring to it as "the hour when she received" (24) and "her audience" (3). It has often been remarked that Lafayette makes sixteenth-century court society resemble that of her own time. Portraying the queen's and the reine dauphine's gatherings as salon-type "circles" strengthens the affiliation between the two centuries.

The concept of marriage at the foundation of *La Princesse de Clèves* is frequently a stumbling block for twentieth-century students who do not realize that the union based on mutual passionate love is a relatively recent development (see Jensen in this volume). One must thus explain arranged marriages, especially those in aristocratic circles and those contracted specifically for political reasons. Many students tend to believe that the princess must love M. de Clèves at least a little since she did agree to marry him; they do not see that the marriage was arranged by her mother as a last resort when other, more advantageous partners fell through. It is important to stress that Lafayette creates a historical anomaly in M. de Clèves, for he is passionately in love with his wife.

This concept of marriage helps explain the equally confusing concept of *amant*. I have often heard students remark condescendingly that they thought France was a Catholic country. That the novel contains so many lovers and mistresses leads them to conclude either that the French have a different brand of Catholicism or that they are hypocritical and fundamentally immoral. It is important to explain that, given the accepted practice of arranged marriages, often between partners of substantially different ages, it was not uncommon for a partner to seek companionship outside marriage. In addition, in the seventeenth-century French lexicon, *amant* ("lover") does not always imply a sexual relationship. Similarly *maîtresse* ("mistress") does not always refer to a woman who has intimate relations with a man. Thus when Lafayette states that Nemours "avait plusieurs maîtresses, mais il était difficile de deviner celle qu'il aimait véritablement" (72) ("had several mistresses, but it was difficult to guess which one he really loved"; my trans.), she is stressing his desirability but not necessarily implying that he is some kind of gigolo. None of the translations keeps the singular "celle" ("the one"), although Cave does provide an explanatory note warning that *maîtresse* "should be taken in its older, less explicitly sexual sense" (206). Buss's translation could even compound the perception of Nemours as immoral. She writes that "it was hard to discern which of *them* he truly loved" (26; my emphasis), instead of at least limiting his love to one person.

Throughout the novel Lafayette frequently uses *maîtresse* to mean someone in an amorous relationship and to refer to a powerful person who controls or dominates, the linguistically feminine equivalent of "master." The English translations often vary the terminology, thus losing the particular style and meaning found in the repetition of the term. For instance, Lafayette describes Diane de Poitiers as "maîtresse de sa [Henri II's] personne et de l'Etat" (72) ("mistress both of his person and of the State" [Cave 6]). In reference to the princess Lafayette plays on the two meanings of the term to depict the princess's dilemma over whether to become Nemours's mistress or to remain her own mistress, that is, to control her life and sentiments. Most of the translators do not translate the term literally, making it impossible to draw connections between the application of the word to the princess and the many other uses and incarnations of the word in the novel. As we have seen with *jamais*, it is advisable to return to the French to get a sense of Lafayette's meticulous use of the term.

In the end the princess does appear to be her own mistress, for she rejects Nemours and spends "une partie de l'année dans cette maison religieuse et l'autre chez elle" (239) ("part of the year in the convent; the rest she spent at home" [Cave 156]). All the translators with one exception translate "maison religieuse" as "convent." Lyons chooses "religious house." The princess's relation to this convent is often problematical for students. Many leave the novel believing she has become a nun. It is important to underscore that Lafayette does not opt for this more conventional ending for novels about a woman in love. The princess remains between the two spaces. One must explain how such religious houses operated in the early modern period. It was not uncommon for women, especially aristocrats, to retire to a convent at the end of their lives, but this act did not entail taking the veil. Many women also went to convents for short periods and then returned to secular life.

In addition to conceptual problems of translations, there are two especially important words that defy any literal, single translation into English: *repos* and *aveu*. The *aveu*, or confession, scene, arguably the central scene of the novel and certainly the most controversial when it first appeared, in fact transpires out of the princess's desire to find *repos*. Furetière defines *repos* as the "état de ce qui est sans mouvement" ("the state of that which is motionless") and as "une quiétude d'esprit et de corps qui les met hors de trouble, de crainte et de soins" ("a calm of the spirit and of the body that frees them from trouble, fear, and cares"). Just before the confession scene, the princess begs her husband to allow her to remain at Coulommiers in order to avoid Nemours and the feelings he evokes in her. She explains that there is so much commotion at court and at M. de Clèves's that "il est impossible que le corps et l'esprit ne se lassent, et que l'on ne cherche du repos" (170). Cave conveys both senses of *repos* by translating with two nouns, "rest" and "tranquillity": "that body and mind inevitably become tired and one longs for rest and tranquillity" (94). This is a much better solution than simply choosing "rest," as the other translators do (Cobb 96; Buss 112, Lyons 65). Students not given both senses cannot help but agree with M. de Clèves when he responds, "Le repos [. . .] n'est guère propre pour une personne de votre âge" (170) ("Rest [. . .] is scarcely for a person of your age" [Cobb 96]). Cave's "Rest and tranquillity [. . .] are hardly what a woman of your age needs most" (94) is the most faithful and comprehensible translation. The princess's struggle between her *repos* and her love for Nemours is a constant theme of the novel. The translations vary among "peace," "peace of mind," "repose," "tranquillity," "tranquil mood," and "calm," as in the following instances: "Au nom de Dieu, lui [Nemours] dit-elle, laissez-moi en repos!"(179) ("In God's name, leave me in peace!" [Cave 103; Cobb 106, Buss 121]). In this instance Lyons simply uses "leave me alone" (71). When the princess does not see Nemours as often, "elle s'en trouvait dans quelque sorte de repos" (181) ("this gave her something resembling peace of mind" [Cave 104]). Cobb writes "some respite from her inner turmoil" (107; Buss 123, Lyons 72). The princess says, "[C]'est pour éviter ces malheurs que j'ai hasardé tout mon repos et même ma vie" (191) ("[I]t was in order to avoid these very misfortunes that I risked my peace of mind and even my life" [Cave 113]). (Cobb uses "repose" [117; Buss 132, Lyons 79]). When she finds Nemours has been watching her, "elle ne se trouva plus dans un certain triste repos" (222) ("the melancholy yet tranquil mood [. . .] gave way" [Cave 141]). Cobb uses "state of sad repose" (146), Buss "sort of sadness and calm" (160), and Lyons "sad tranquillity" (98). Her desire for *repos* figures as a key reason for her rejection of Nemours. She tells him, "Ce que je crois devoir à la mémoire de M. de Clèves serait faible s'il n'était soutenu par l'intérêt de mon repos" (232) ("What I believe I owe to the memory of M. de Clèves would be a feeble resource were it not sustained by self-interest, namely my desire for tranquillity of mind" [Cave 150]). Cobb (156), Buss (170), and Lyons (104) all opt for "peace of mind" in this instance. These reasons are reiterated by the narrator: "Les raisons qu'elle avait de ne point épouser M. de Nemours lui paraissaient fortes du côté de son devoir and insurmontables du côté de son repos" (236) ("Duty seemed to her a powerful reason for not marrying M. de Nemours, her peace of mind an insurmountable one" [Cave 153; Cobb 159, Buss 173, Lyons 107]).

Like *repos, aveu* has more than one meaning and plays a central role in two key scenes. The princess says to her husband, "[J]e vais vous faire un aveu que l'on n'a jamais fait à son mari" (171) ("I will make you a confession that no woman has ever made to her husband" [Cave 95; Cobb 97, Buss 113, Lyons 66]). The term reoccurs to refer to her conversation with Nemours at the end of the novel: "Je vous fais cet aveu [. . .] cet aveu n'aura point de suite" (228) ("I make this confession [. . .] my confession will have no consequences" [Cave 146; Cobb 151–52, Buss 165–66, Lyons 102]). Most translators and critics use "confession" for these two scenes. Lyons sometimes uses "avowal." However, in an article reprinted in the Norton Critical Edition, Joan DeJean calls attention to a second meaning, that of a loyalty oath, which the term still carried in the seventeenth-century lexicon ("Lafayette's Ellipses"). "Confession" has the disadvantage of making the princess appear guilty and the *aveu* appear a last resort taken out of weakness. When the connotation of fidelity oath is restored, these scenes become more suggestive and significant. In the *aveu* to her husband, the princess in fact does not appear weak or guilty. She does not admit directly to doing anything, and stresses to Clèves, "L'aveu que je vous ai fait n'a pas été par faiblesse" (172) ("It was not weakness that made me confess" [Cave 96; Cobb 99, Buss 115, Lyons 67]). Both M. de Clèves and Mme de Clèves associate the action directly with fidelity. M. de Clèves says, "Vous me rendez malheureux par la plus grande marque de fidelité que jamais une femme ait donnée à son mari" (172) ("You have made me unhappy by the greatest proof of fidelity that a woman has ever given her husband" [Cave 96; Cobb 99, Buss 114, Lyons 66]). (There is an error in the Lyons translation. It reads "happy" instead of "unhappy" [66].) After the *aveu* the princess "trouva même de la douceur à avoir donné ce témoignage de fidelité à un mari qui le méritait si bien" (175) ("even felt a certain sweetness in the idea that she had given such a token of fidelity to a husband who deserved it so much" [Cave 98; Cobb 101, Buss 117, Lyons 68]). *Avowal* or *declaration* might indeed be better terms.

Variations on a Text

Occasionally the four translations vary significantly enough to influence the interpretation of key points of the novel. A few such instances can be grouped under the heading "dealing with Diane de Poitiers." This duchess, a pivotal court figure, pervades the whole novel. Some critics view her relationship with the king as an important influence on the princess's conception of love and marriage. She is one of the first people introduced, and this description begins to create the image of the character on which Lafayette will continue to build. She states that Diane de Poitiers "paraissait elle-même avec tous les ajustements que pouvait avoir Mlle de la Marck, sa petite-fille, qui était alors à marier" (69) ("took care to adorn herself no less brilliantly than Mlle de la Marck, her granddaughter, who was at that time of an age to be married" [Cave 3]). This statement seems consistent with the insistence throughout the novel that the duchess's power has remained unaffected by time, a remarkable feat given that female power was usually associated with ephemeral beauty. Cobb and Buss interpret the phrase as a derogatory comment on Diane's defiance of time. Cobb states, "She herself was present too, dressed in finery, which would have been more appropriate to the tastes of her young granddaughter" (1), even adding "young" to make the transgression more apparent. Buss more subtly opts for "attired in a manner that might have befitted her granddaughter" (23).

The translators also contend with Diane's power differently. Mme de Chartres gives Diane's background, stating that, when Henri II became king, "Son pouvoir parut plus absolu sur l'esprit du roi qu'il ne paraissait encore pendant qu'il était dauphin" (98) ("Her power over the King's mind appeared more absolute than it had been while he was the Dauphin" [Cave 30]); Cobb (29) and Buss (49) are similar. In contrast, Lyons diminishes Diane's power: "Her power over the king seemed the greater because it had not appeared while he was dauphin" (22). This phrasing is inconsistent with the rest of this internal narrative, which describes Diane's power over the dauphin. In addition, "seemed great" gives the impression that this power is an illusion.

This "absolute" power in fact echoes the description we have already seen of Diane's relationship to Henri: "elle le [Henri] gouvernait avec un empire si absolu que l'on peut dire qu'elle était maîtresse de sa personne et de l'État" (72) ("she governed the king with a power so absolute that one may say she was mistress both of his person and of the State" [Cave 6]). Lyons chooses to depict this power negatively by adding "despotically": "ruled him so despotically" (5). Cobb too seems to have trouble with this absolute power. Diane's position as mistress of the state reappears as the king lies dying. The queen demands the return of the royal jewels. Learning that Henri is not yet dead, Diane replies proudly, "Je n'ai donc point encore de maître" (197) ("[T]hen no one is yet master over me" [Buss 137; Cave 199, Lyons 83]), thus maintaining her position as the king's mistress and indeed *maître*. Cobb takes away her absolute power over the king by making him the master when he adds "other": "Then I have no other master yet" (123).

A second set of influential translation variations occurs in the depiction of the princess's struggle for self-determination in the face of passion and society's expectations. Mme de Chartres warns her daughter that to remain a virtuous woman at court one must exercise an "extreme défiance de soi-même" (76) ("extreme mistrust of one's own powers" [Cave 10; Buss 30]). Lyons effaces the sense of self-determination, using "extreme care" (8), as does Cobb in choosing "extreme wariness" (8). It is important to maintain the sense of inner struggle and self-determination because it figures in two other key scenes. As Mme de Chartres lies dying, she urges her daughter to resist Nemours, calling on her daughter's self-control. Mme de Chartres leaves her with the following words: "Songez ce que vous devez à votre mari; songez ce que vous vous devez à vous même. [. . .] Ayez de la force et du courage" (108) ("Remember what you owe to your husband; remember what you owe yourself. [. . .] Have strength and courage" [Cave 40; Cobb 38–39, Buss 59, Lyons 28]). The mother beseeches the daughter to control her own destiny through self-control. This inner struggle resurfaces in the princess's interior monologue after she has experienced the pain of jealousy caused by the love letter destined for the vidame but mistakenly attributed to Nemours. The princess queries, "Veux-je manquer à Monsieur de Clèves? Veux-je me manquer à moi-même? (167) ("[Do I want] to be unfaithful to M. de Clèves? to be unfaithful to myself? [Cave 91–92; Cobb 94, Buss 110]). Curiously, Lyons translates only the first question—"Do I wish to fail in my duty to M. de Clèves?" (64), not the princess's consideration of her duty to herself. It is important to maintain both considerations in the princess's reasoning because both figure in her final rejection of Nemours. The princess refuses to marry him not only out of duty to her husband but also because she wants to retain control over her emotions and her life. She explains, "Ce que je crois devoir à la mémoire de M. de Clèves serait faible s'il n'était soutenu par l'intérêt de mon repos; et les raisons de mon repos ont besoin d'être soutenues de celles de mon devoir" (232) ("What I believe I owe to the memory of M. de Clèves would be a feeble resource were it not sustained by self-interest, namely my desire for tranquillity of mind; likewise, the reasons that speak in favor of tranquillity need to be supported by those that duty prescribes" [Cave 150; Cobb 156, Buss 169–70, Lyons 104]).

A few other differences are worth mentioning. First, the pavilion where the *aveu* takes place is translated with one exception as "pavilion"; Lyons opts for "summer-house." Since all critical commentary uses "pavilion," "summer-house" can be confusing. A second and more important difference is found in the translation of a defining characteristic of the court in which Lafayette conflates the traditional spheres of public and private by describing a court where love and politics are inseparable and where women play a central role: "Il y avait tant d'intérêts et tant de cabales différentes, et les dames y avaient tant de part que l'amour était toujours mêlé aux affaires et les affaires à l'amour" (81) ("There were countless interests at stake, countless different factions, and women played such a central part in them that love was always entangled with politics and politics with love" [Cave 14]). Cobb incorrectly substitutes "often" for "always": "love was often mixed with politics" (12). The Lyons translation seems to limit women's roles to intrigues instead of portraying them as a dominating presence: "there were so many interests and so many different intrigues in which women took part" (10).

Another significant variation occurs in the translation of the princess's feelings when she is faced with the prospect of marrying M. de Clèves. The French text makes clear that she is indifferent to him, in stark contrast to his passion for her. She tells her mother "qu'elle l'épouserait même avec moins de répugnance qu'un autre, mais qu'elle n'avait aucune inclination particulière pour sa personne" (87). I would translate this literally as "that she would feel less repugnance in marrying him than someone else but that she felt no particular attraction to his person." This is a strong statement that, given M. de Clèves's infatuation with the princess, creates an inequitable marriage. None of the translations convey the meaning of this statement as strongly as the French does. Cave substitutes "reluctance" for "répugnance" (20). Cobb renders the comparative as "than [. . .] anyone else," which makes it seem that she has compared him favorably with everyone else (18), as does "than any other man." In addition Buss uses "disinclination" for "répugnance" and chooses "not particularly attracted to him" instead of "no particular attraction" (39). The Lyons translation is the least literal and the most misleading: "that she would rather marry him than any one else, but that she had no special love for him" (14). In this version the princess seems to choose Clèves. "No special love for him" leaves open the possibility that she might feel something for him, whereas "no particular attraction" makes clear that she does not. The great difference in the feelings of the marriage partners, which is so important for understanding events of the novel, disappears.

Finally, instructors who are comparing the English with the French text as it exists in the 1996 Garnier-Flammarion edition will be surprised by a significant difference common to all the English translations. When Lafayette describes the decoration of Coloummiers for the reverie scene, we read in this new edition established by Mesnard, which replaces all previous Flammarion editions, that when the princess went to Coloummiers "elle eut soin d'y faire porter de grands tableaux que M. de Clèves avait fait copier sur des originaux qu'avait fait faire Mme de Valentinois pour sa belle maison d'Anet" (205). All other French editions state that the princess had the paintings copied: "elle eut soin d'y faire porter de grands tableaux qu'elle avait fait copier" ("these were copies she had had made" [Cave 125]). English translations rely on the previous French versions of this important passage that has elicited much critical commentary. Mesnard provides no explanation for his decision to alter the French text.

L'Embarras du Choix: *Which Translation?*

Given the plethora of new translations, how does an instructor choose the one best suited to the English-speaking classroom? Ultimately, the choice is a subjective one, for each edition has its relative merits. When I teach *La Princesse de Clèves* in English, I am always very conscious of the French behind the translation. Many of my own interpretations of the novel are founded on close textual readings that particularly emphasize Lafayette's specific vocabulary. For me it is essential that the English translation be as literal as possible. Lafayette's prose is often elliptical. She does not give us one way to interpret events, which is perhaps why the novel has continually inspired interpretations for over three hundred years. I believe the best translation is one that maintains the text's ellipses and ambiguities and not one in which the translator interprets as she or he translates, because such renderings often preclude the interpretation that the reader has derived from Lafayette's carefully constructed French prose. I also consider the "packaging" of the translation, that is, the explanatory notes and the introduction, important, for they can improve or detract from the English reader's experience and equally help or hinder the professor.

For these reasons, I consider Terence Cave's translation the best. Cave's text is the closest to the original French, and it reads smoothly—a difficult achievement indeed. Of the four translators analyzed here, he seems the most aware of his task, rendering a seventeenth-century French text accessible and enjoyable to a twentieth-century public whom he assumes to be unfamiliar with the French language and the novel's historical and literary context. He guides the reader with an excellent introduction and with numerous useful notes throughout the text that provide historical information and vocabulary explanations. Such information facilitates the transition from a seventeenth-century French context to a twentieth-century English one without overburdening the text. To judge by my students' reactions and my own experience in the classroom, reading Cave's translation is the closest one can come to experiencing *La Princesse de Clèves* as the reader of French does.

NOTE

[1]Here and throughout this essay the first page reference, preceding the semicolon, identifies the translation being quoted. The other page references, following the semicolon, locate the corresponding passages in other translations, which may be worded differently.

What's Love Got to Do with It?
The Issue of Vulnerability
in an Anthological Approach

James F. Gaines

In teaching *La Princesse de Clèves* from an anthology, especially one that focuses on the *scène de l'aveu*, or avowal scene (as they almost always do), one is drawn irresistibly to examining issues of morality, which has been one of the principal approaches to the novel since Valincour's first criticism on it (Williams 98–120; Beasley, *Revising* 234–38). Taken by itself, a moral analysis of the single passage might produce a reductive, relatively useless reading of the text. For instance, it certainly would seem to preclude making immediate use of such analytical breakthroughs as Laurence Gregorio's narratological-historical analysis in *Order in the Court*. But the environment of the anthology itself offers some help, for the avowal scene can take on special meaning in the context of other classic seventeenth-century scenes that the contemporary reading public knew by heart and with which the neophyte literary student also soon becomes familiar. In particular, such anthologies as the ones edited by Robert Leggewie and Morris Bishop often contain passages of other avowals or near avowals, including key scenes from masterpieces by Corneille, Molière, and Racine. I would argue that using such scenes as a matrix for evaluating the avowal scene in *La Princesse de Clèves* is not at all irrelevant or impertinent, since it involves a set of references very close to those of the novel's first readers.

By happy circumstance the placement of texts in modern anthologies often reproduces the chronological occurrence of avowal scenes, so that seventeenth- and twentieth-century readers alike would very likely have encountered *Le Cid*, *Le misanthrope*, *Le bourgeois gentilhomme*, *Andromaque*, and *Phèdre* before reading *La Princesse de Clèves*. The above-mentioned plays, the most widely available in print to North American audiences, contain avowal or near-avowal scenes that emphasize the critical element of moral as well as physical vulnerability in all admissions of love in the seventeenth century. Moreover, they present the scenes in a particularly visual, dramatic way that is extremely accessible to students, especially if videos are used in class to supplement the text.

Le Cid's first avowal scene (3.2) was originally judged as no less shocking or less logically acceptable (*vraisemblable*) than the one in *La Princesse*. Rodrigue dares to appear before the object of his passion without a supervisory escort and armed with the very sword that has taken the life of Chimène's father, the count. However, although Rodrigue's action is unmistakably bold, it is Chimène who manifests the sheer vulnerability of the situation, since Rodrigue makes no further secret of his passion and no longer has anything to lose. The wrenching decision between lineage and self, between duty and feeling that he underwent in the final scene of act 1 is over, and he can give full vent to his emotion with the reckless abandon of one who is doomed to pay for his actions. Chimène, in contrast, is hemmed in by the possible consequences of exposing her emotions. Having declined to express her longing for Rodrigue in act 1 out of pride, she now finds herself a prisoner of convention, constrained by the codes of propriety surrounding mourning and revenge for homicide. Although she senses that she loves the young man, she *can't* love him. She stands to lose not only a sort of generally revered Hispanic honor but also a more typically Gallic notion of superiority through worthiness of affection. Better to be worthy of Rodrigue's devotion and enjoy none of its rewards than to grasp at gratification that must be begged of a "superior." Instead of measuring feelings by their manifestations, which is the modern norm, people in the classical age tended to measure them by their presuppositions. Prevented by her sex from taking action through confronting death, at least in most imaginable circumstances, Chimène is permitted to admit her true feelings only after death has already swept the stage clear of all propriety, a fact that explains her vacillation in the final act, in which Don Fernand traps her in an unintentional avowal by making it seem that Rodrigue has been killed in a duel. (Niderst [103–11] points out an interesting parallel with the reversal in the denouement of *La Princesse de Clèves*, when the protagonist holds Nemours responsible for her husband's death, though, of course, in this case it is the object of passion who is blamed for the blocking character's demise, as if Chimène were to punish Rodrigue for killing Don Sanche.)

Le misanthrope is constructed around the very principle that an avowal scene is impossible in mid-seventeenth-century France. Célimène's vulnerability is much more problematical than Chimène's, and her reluctance to make an avowal of love may seem puzzling to a generation steeped in *Beverly Hills 90210*. First, Célimène is a widow, hence not subject to the constraint of virginal innocence attributed to a maiden like Chimène. Second, she has openly encouraged suitors. If Arsinoé is credible at all, we can even assume she has earned a reputation as a flirt. Thus she has already publicly declared her temperament, if not her specific intentions. Finally, an avowal made to Alceste or any of the other men who cluster about her need not carry any hint of dishonor, especially if she were to make the admission in private. In fact, a negative admission, either of nonlove or of love for another, could rid her of burdensome company without positively engaging her with any single man. Obviously, Célimène's dilemma and her persistent stalling show that, even for a sexually experienced, openly playful, and gregarious woman, the admission of passion must be avoided at all costs.

The key to Célimène's vulnerability is that passion implies a lack of control, a submission of will and personal glory to the dictates of an appetite that lies beyond or below logic or reason. If will is an essential component of selfhood, social armor aplenty is necessary to keep it intact, and worldly ladies can gratify their own desires only under the veil of providing charitable relief to their heartsick suitors. Célimène's very existence in the time and place of mid-seventeenth-century Paris, on the perimeter of the world's most brilliant court, is inseparable from her ability to attract and maintain a showy retinue of suitors, who constitute her own "royal" circle. In this sense she is striving to realize something akin to what Faith Beasley, in her analysis of *La Princesse de Clèves*, calls a "feminocentric history," consciously or unconsciously emulating figures such as Mary Stuart, Diane de Poitiers, and Catherine de Médicis (Beasley, *Revising* 195–222). If her irrepressible flirtatiousness exacerbates Alceste's misanthropy, his tendency to posit romance in terms of extreme dependency, having one partner to whom one owes every scrap of happiness and at whose feet one begs for pleasure, only stiffens her resistance more.

As early as the first scene of act 2 Alceste invites Célimène to make an avowal: "Parlons à cœur ouvert" ("Let's speak with open hearts"; 2.1.531; my trans.). The coxcombs Acaste and Clitandre actually show themselves to be more prudent than the misanthrope when they seek to avoid a direct confrontation and to ascertain their standing with Célimène indirectly in their carefully coded exchanges (3.1). Not only does Alceste fail time and again to extract his desired vow of passion (most notably in 4.3 and 5.2), but the supposedly revealing scene of the letters (5.4) produces only an illusion of certainty, since it is still unclear whether Célimène is affectively attracted to anyone. Both Alceste and Célimène couch their "proposals" in language that is virtually guaranteed to fail, and the only successful avowal in the play involves the deflected, curiously commonplace revelation that Philinte and Eliante share (4.1 and 5.4; see Gaines 78–82).

The vulnerability and danger of the avowal are depicted in a more overtly humorous way in the *dépit amoureux* (lovers' spite) confrontations in *Tartuffe* (2.4) and *Le bourgeois gentilhomme* (3.10). Though these scenes are not true avowals, since the characters involved have already revealed their emotions to their erstwhile partners, they do emphasize the fragility of one who admits dependence on the affective reciprocation of another. Misinterpreted signals and messages can draw even a mutually satisfactory relationship, such as that between Lucile and Cléonte or Covielle and Nicole, to the edge of disaster. The worst-case scenarios, those of being "Tartuffified" or turned over to the future Grand Turk, represent a form of physical and mental enslavement akin to that which threatens Mme de Clèves. They also demonstrate the real possibility in such situations that inner factors, such as the imperative of guarding one's social face and self-esteem, may pose just as much danger of unleashing evil consequences as external reactions involving the interlocutor's interpretation or manipulation. Mme de Clèves has no guardian angel such as Dorine or Nicole to rectify unbalanced disclosures, for her avowal takes place only after the only possible mediator, her mother, has passed away.

Andromaque is similar to *Le misanthrope* not only because Pyrrhus is a kind of natural-born misanthrope who apparently takes pleasure in obstructing the common will and flouting the powers that be but also because his desire restructures the play into a continual effort to provoke his "beloved" into an admission of passion. The fantasy of such an avowal is horribly distorted since Pyrrhus has murdered Andromaque's cherished husband, Hector, and poses a constant threat to the survival of her last treasure, their son, Astyanax. The Greeks cannot comprehend why Pyrrhus, alone among the victorious warlords, is not content simply to violate the captive queen, as his counterparts had done with their prisoners, but instead makes a mockery of their brute superiority by courting his own thrall. Students need to understand that Pyrrhus represents a skewed but very pure expression of French classical aristocratic values, while the Greeks are closer to modern totalitarians, concerned only with state power. It is true that Andromaque, still and forever wedded to the defunct Hector, is no flirtatious Célimène, but then again her sheer contrariness to Molière's female lead allows for contrasting observations and new insights into the theme of vulnerability. For Andromaque and all other women in Pyrrhus's vicinity, the avowal is a mechanism of psychic blackmail, a form of torture backed by the threat of death. Even Hermione, who has few scruples about sincerity, is exceedingly careful in her scenes with the besotted Oreste (2.2.519–36 and 5.3.1147–57 and 1188–1200) to stop short of a full-scale avowal of love for him, allowing his diseased mind to fill in with fantasy or fear what rational dialogue or logical reflection would deny him.

Phèdre's confession (2.4) may not reflect the major oppositions of classicism as clearly as the scenes in *Andromaque* do, because of its impromptu nature and its shockingly incestuous content, but it does embody the transgressive potential of such face-to-face confrontations, as well as the way they can rapidly go out of control. The utilitarian Œnone urges Phèdre to plead for the safety of her royal children, whom they presume to be threatened by the dynastic rivalry of their half-brother, but Phèdre finds that in Hippolyte's presence she cannot restrain the tide of her irresistable passion. In the face of this disclosure, Hippolyte's rationalism gives way to equivocation and self-pity, foreshadowing the Prince de Clèves's inability to pursue logical intentions following his wife's confidences. Phèdre's seizure of her stepson's sword, prompted by a desperate desire for self-annihilation, dramatically reverses the situation in Rodrigue's confrontation with Chimène, while paving the way for the princess's pleas to her husband for a different degree of self-effacement, letting herself and her crime be swallowed up in the solitude of the provinces.

The examples of Rodrigue and Chimène, Alceste and Célimène, Pyrrhus and Andromaque, and the others set the stage for the avowal in *La Princesse de Clèves* by identifying passionate love as a type of loss of control and direction. Excerpts from Descartes's *Discours de la méthode*, available in many anthologies, will help remind a class how horrifying disorientation was for the seventeenth-century mind and how much the philosopher preferred the rigors of rectilinear progression, no matter how hard, to the possibility of endless wandering on unguided headings:

[. . .] comme un homme qui marche seul et dans les ténèbres, je me réso-
lus d'aller si lentement et d'user de tant de circonspection en toutes
choses, que, si je n'avançais que fort peu, je me garderais bien au moins
de tomber.   (Bishop 1:128)

[. . .] like a man who walks alone and in the shadows, I resolved to go so
slowly and to use such circumspection in all things, that, even if I were
not to advance very far, I would at least keep myself from falling.
                                                         (my trans.)

Better to find one's way out of an unknown forest by walking a straight (if
longer) line than to be fooled by subtle, curving shortcuts, as Descartes states
in the second maxim in part 3 of the *Discours*.

The avowal was especially frightening for a woman because any man was capable of taking advantage of a woman who admitted she was smitten (Haase-
Dubosc 432–36). He could consider her his by right of "conquest" and
subsequently reject her as unworthy of him, since he had held out longer and
dissimulated better. It is important to inform students that during the classical
era dissimulation was considered a virtue by many (and some of them far more
nefarious than Philinte). So strong was this conviction that, before the Enlight-
enment and the cultivation of a sometimes specious sincerity by the likes of
Rousseau, it was automatically assumed that everyone was dissimulating to
some degree almost all the time. It was Mme de Lafayette's transgression
against this zeitgeist of falsehood, embodied in M. de Clèves's promise to pardon and respect a lady's perfectly honest avowal of attraction elsewhere, as well
as the princess's invocation of that doctrine of honesty in association with her
own determination to be different from other women—rather than any contradiction of internal fictional values—that provoked Valincour to charge that
Lafayette's novel lacks verisimilitude.

The avowal scene is especially comparable to the foregoing confrontations
because, unlike much of *La Princesse de Clèves*, which takes place in a third-
person narration that constantly intrudes into first-person consciousness, it involves a scene with dialogue, in which virtually the entire truth value of the
discourse is conveyed directly in the spoken words as they are exchanged. Furthermore, this dialogue serves as a nexus for other uttered commitments and
opinions expressed in previous sections of the novel, especially the prince's
claim, in the tale about Mme de Tournon (117; 46), that he would meet a sincere admission of adulterous inclination with sorrowful but detached counsel
rather than outraged anger. In fact, his ultimate response, morbid jealousy, is
neither sorrowful nor detached, but students might discuss and even anticipate
this very reaction if they are familiar with Alceste's obsessive jealousy, or even
Chimène's reproachful outburst against Don Sanche in the final act of *Le Cid*.

The princess's avowal deserves to be compared with Cornelian rhetoric on
another count, for it is also a kind of declamatory narration, or *récit* (not of

deeds but of the soul), and one delivered by the party of the first part, like Rodrigue's account of his victory over the invading Moors. Although the traditional *récit* was a tale of offstage action narrated by a confidant or other near-neutral party, Rodrigue is allowed by force of circumstance and royal indulgence to deliver his own stirring account of his exploits against the invaders who had sought to surprise Seville (4.3.1243–1329). The princess's *récit* of inner turmoil rather than bodily prowess is just as deserving of the classification, and perhaps even more so, since she reveals both weaknesses and strengths of character of which her husband never dreamed, whereas Rodrigue had already elicited expectations of his heroic character first by being the son of brave Don Diègue and then by vanquishing the count in single combat. This comparison with Rodrigue brings out the true nature of the princess's claims to extraordinary status, made first in her name by her mother, Mme de Chartres, who emphasized "combien la vertu donnait d'éclat et d'élévation" ("how much brilliance and distinction virtue bestows") and who "ne trouvait presque rien digne de sa fille" (76–77) ("considered almost nothing worthy of her daughter" [10]), evoking on her very deathbed the importance of "cette réputation que vous vous êtes acquise et que je vous ai tant souhaitée" (108) ("the reputation you have earned for yourself and I so much desired for you" [40]). This quest for superiority to other women, often reiterated in the novel, is even acknowledged somewhat ironically by M. de Clèves: "les femmes sont incompréhensibles; et, quand je les vois toutes, je me trouve si heureux de vous avoir que je ne saurais assez admirer mon bonheur" (110) ("women are incomprehensible and, when I look at them all, I consider myself so fortunate to have you as my wife that I cannot but be amazed at my good luck" [41–42]). It is again explicitly restated in the avowal scene, where the princess declares, "Songez que pour faire ce que je fais, il faut avoir plus d'amitié et plus d'estime pour un mari que l'on en a jamais eu" (171) ("Reflect that, in order to do what I am doing, it is necessary to have a greater affection and esteem for one's husband than any wife has ever had before" [95]). In this sense the work certainly embodies (and at the same time problematizes) the type of exemplary teaching of moral conduct discussed by Harriet Stone (see "Exemplary").

Obviously, the avowal scene deserves to be considered in some textual depth, even when it is taught as an excerpt from an anthology. To understand it fully, one needs some familiarity not only with the princess's austere upbringing, her mother's teachings, the circumstances at her marriage, and her acquaintance with Nemours at the ball (all of which happen before the avowal) but also with the duke's Peeping Tomism at Coulommiers and with the eventual downfall of the prince, events from the latter part of the story. The instructor might assign these passages to individual students for reports to accompany the general discussion of the avowal scene. Seen in the light of the total development of the text, the scene can still be appreciated from a variety of perspectives, since it can be seen as sadistic and cruel by critics, such as Danielle Haase-Dubosc, who interpret it as the product of psychoanalytic, deterministic forces that orient the heroine toward an inevitable showdown with death; as the product of skeptical confusion (Force); or even as assertive or optimistic by those who see it as a triumph of self-possession (Sweetser, "In Search") or female power (DeJean, "Lafayette's Ellipses"; Miller, "Emphasis").

Besides being studied for the elements within it that are typical, the avowal scene can be examined in its atypical aspects. Gregorio's emphasis on the dichotomy between speech and sight, which he developed on the basis of earlier insights by Claude Vigée, is significant here. We have noted that the scene involves an unusually dense concentration of spoken, direct dialogue. Such vision as takes place, namely, the eavesdropping of Nemours, results only in confusion, for the duke cannot satisfactorily identify the man to whom the princess says she is attracted. It is worth pointing out that in this sense the avowal reveals its own equivocal quality and functions in counterpoint to heroic *récits*, such as that of Rodrigue in *Le Cid*, for the princess obscures the key element of identity both from her known audience, the prince, and from Nemours, who is hiding in the greenery outside and would presumably derive the main glory from the disclosure. This equivocation, of course, places the burden of vulnerability henceforth on the men, forcing the prince into error and remorseful death and Nemours into voyeuristic impotence. The irony is underlined by the parallels between the duke's flawed eavesdropping and earlier and later events. Before the avowal scene there is the duke's first instance of combined subterfuge and psychic displacement, when he is able to steal the princess's miniature portrait only because she pretends to look the other way, being "bien aise de lui accorder une faveur qu'elle lui pouvait faire sans qu'il sût même qu'elle la lui faisait" (137) ("quite content to be able to grant him a favour without his knowledge" [64]). Afterward, there is his spying on the princess as she gazes on his image in the painting of the siege of Metz, where, though he learns that he is apparently the object of desire, he fails to assert himself as a flesh-and-blood equivalent of the princess's phantasm (209–10; 128–30). Both short passages make excellent report topics for students to set the avowal in context.

Gregorio is right to point out that the rest of the text privileges sight over sound; the visual imagery provides a much more reliable gauge of reality than courtly speech. The same critic hints that it represents a deceptive peak of optimism in a text steeped in quasi-Jansenistic gloom. Indeed, students can appreciate the princess's position as a would-be heroine hoping to strike a powerful blow against the murky order of playful infidelity by her exemplary, humanistic stand. I use the term *humanistic* here in a way that looks back toward the Renaissance, since it adheres to the stoical humanism of Montaigne's age rather than the nascent Lockean humanism of the eighteenth century.

Like Montaigne, Mme de Clèves is able to cultivate the self and its potential power as a bulwark against the instability, or *branlement*, that her restive emotions represent. (Marie-Odile Sweetser's "In Search of Selfhood" is a masterly summary of a number of excellent readings that emphasize the avowal as a key step in the evolution of the princess's character toward the realization of orthodox humanistic and spiritual goals.) The avowal thus functions as a first instance of stoical deadening of human sensitivity, fighting vulnerability from within in a way that Mme de Chartres, with her emphasis on avoiding the "occasions of sin" and maintaining the spirit intact, could never have anticipated. Ultimately, the most vulnerable parties are shown to be the mother, who wasted her efforts on the useless precautions of social armor, and the two adoring men, who were too weak to carry the burden of sincerity or to mortify their desires. Those who might be tempted to see the princess's ultimate withdrawal from society as an instance of victimization or a denial of her sexual role would do well to remember that she fares better than the men who precede her in death or abandon faith in their sexual "superiority" as a result of the affair. In Lafayette's novel vulnerability resides not so much in the conventions of passivity assigned to the feminine condition as in the inability to detach the self, male or female, from conventional roles or social poses in order to resolve the emotional contradictions that underlie them.

Finally, it bears mention that one of the greatest disservices that one can do to students through an anthological approach, no matter how well intentioned, is to convey the impression that all has been studied, all is in order, and nothing more remains to be said on a given work or its relation to that rather mythical collectivity called the canon. As a remedy against such platitudes, there is nothing better than the spice of polemical disagreement, and every decade seems to offer a renewal of the polemical skirmishes that started with Valincour. Perhaps each course covering great snippets from the classical age should include student reports on such stridently diverging interpretations, to encourage creative, critical readings of texts like *La Princesse de Clèves*, which began challenging the placid order of literature as soon as it appeared. Like the woman faced with the prospect of an avowal, the scholar is always vulnerable.

Romance and Novel in *La Princesse de Clèves*

Kathleen Wine

To describe *La Princesse de Clèves* as the first French novel is a crude oversimplification that one hesitates to pass on to undergraduates. Yet justice to Lafayette's text surely obliges us to convey that it somehow stands apart, as the narrative that has come to define a literary sea change. Once we determine how to nuance our account of the work's place in literary history, a thornier problem arises: how to make any such account meaningful to undergraduates who have little experience of the narrative traditions out of which it emerged.

The question of how to deal with literary context can of course be raised with regard to any text. It takes on particular urgency for me whenever I teach *La Princesse de Clèves* because of my predilection for the baroque romances that constituted an indispensable point of reference for Lafayette and her contemporaries. For me, Lafayette's masterpiece is closely bound up — through appropriation, parody, and nostalgic complicity — with this outmoded but still very much present genre. I resist reducing this tradition, as literary historians have tended to do, to a congeries of formal and thematic absurdities over which *La Princesse de Clèves* represents positive and unilinear progress. *Enfin Lafayette vint.* Rather, I would like my students to gain a sense of the dynamic relation with earlier genres that so often characterizes the most brilliant literary innovation.

But can students perceive such a dynamic if they have not experienced the earlier genre as an autonomous aesthetic phenomenon? Ideally, a course devoted to seventeenth-century or early modern fiction would give students a rich background against which to read not only *La Princesse de Clèves* but also the French novel in general. Year in and year out, however, I most frequently find myself, as, I imagine, do many colleagues, teaching *La Princesse de Clèves* in multigenre survey courses ill-adapted to consideration of problems peculiar to a single genre. I offer the following, then, as an approach that aims at integrating some basic considerations on Lafayette's contributions to narrative history into less specialized treatments of her masterpiece.

Studies of the seventeenth-century novel (see Lever for a useful survey and Mueller for plot summaries) often divide the fiction of the first half of the century into such categories as pastoral (Honoré d'Urfé's *L'Astrée*), heroic (Marin Le Roy de Gomberville's *Polexandre*), and *précieux* (Madeleine de Scudéry's *Clélie*). Contemporaries, however, usually grouped these works together as *romans*, stressing their underlying similarities. I employ the English *romance* here, pointing as well to the works' affinities with a recurring fictional mode that includes Greek "romances" like Heliodorus's *Ethiopica*, the courtly romances of the Middle Ages, and the "romantic" epics of Ariosto and Tasso.

The typical seventeenth-century romance was characterized by formal intricacy, ingenious plotting, and a happy ending featuring the marriage of the long-suffering principal characters. Beginning in medias res, it employed internal narratives to recount earlier events in the characters' lives as well as to introduce multiple subplots. Although these works were set in remote historical periods and regularly featured court intrigues and battle scenes, their great subject was aristocratic love as it was understood in the seventeenth century. For seventeenth-century readers, *roman* and *galanterie* went hand in hand.

By the 1660s the very word *roman* had come to connote a preposterously untruthful narrative. The genre's formal complexity and its recourse to chance struck classical sensibilities as irrational. "Dans un roman frivole aisément tout s'excuse" ("We pardon anything in a frivolous romance"), states Boileau, dismissing the genre as lacking the "exacte raison" ("L'art" 174) ("rigorous reason") required of the stage.[1] Nevertheless, a modern reader unfamiliar with their divergent critical fates might notice many similarities between *La Princesse de Clèves* and its predecessors. The noble protagonists of romance possess that same uniform brilliance that leads Antoine Adam to complain in his preface to the novel that Lafayette's characters are all "galants, bien faits et amoureux" (9) ("chivalrous, nobly built, and amorously inclined"). When M. de Nemours expounds on whether a man should wish his mistress to attend a ball, he is exploring a *question d'amour* of the sort popularized by the debates on the psychology of love featured in the *romans*. And throughout their courtship he and Mme de Clèves experience the passions and observe the decorum that the lovers of romance had conditioned readers to expect. These continuities are not surprising in the light of the romances' considerable influence over contemporary sociability. According to Marie de Gournay, indeed, *L'Astrée* had once served as "bréviaire" to an early generation of courtiers (Adam 1: 133).

When teaching students who have little experience of the earlier tradition, I find it best to stress these continuities, while limiting the analysis of formal differences. Students who last week were struggling to distinguish Racine from Corneille are ill-prepared for a discussion of how Lafayette modifies the internal narratives of romance. I therefore limit my prefatory remarks to a general discussion of the term *roman*. (For an excellent brief history, see the definition in Robert's *Dictionnaire historique*.) Like the English *romance*, it hearkens back to the chivalric romances of the Middle Ages and the romance vernacular in which they were written. Although the seventeenth-century romances differed in some respects from the Arthurian tradition with which students are usually familiar, they had come to seem just as unlikely to classical readers. Among the terms used by authors wishing to distinguish their works from the romance was *nouvelle*, resulting in an opposition similar to the one we make in English between *romance* and *novel*. The French, however, eventually restored the term *roman*, which now designates any moderately lengthy work of fiction. I ask students to discuss the implications of the two terminologies, one of which establishes a fundamental distinction between a traditional type of narrative and a new, or "novel," one while the other obliges us to see even the most radically innovative narratives as rooted in practices originating with the language itself. This discussion lays the ground for me to argue that *La Princesse de Clèves* can be better looked on as incorporating rather than breaking with romance.

Even such an argument, however, will not enable me to do justice to seventeenth-century romance, as I learned from my early attempts to present minilectures on the genre. Lugging stacks of weighty volumes into class, I fell afoul of a little-known generic law: all brief descriptions of romance are parodic. Playing to my audience, I found myself producing accounts of hyperventilating heroes and outlandish plots very like the dismissive treatments in literary histories. The introduction of textual excerpts does little to ameliorate this effect. The first chapter of *Clélie* and the opening pages of Lafayette's own belated romance *Zaïde*, for example, display some of the representative features of romance plotting: in the first, the principal characters are separated when an earthquake cleaves the ground between them on the eve of their wedding; in the second, a hero fleeing love and human society becomes enamored of the exotic shipwreck victim fate obligingly washes onto the shore of his isolated retreat (25–31). On the basis of these initial accidents, students can speculate fairly cogently on the course of the plots. This exercise, however, when performed by students who have not experienced the intricate unfolding of a romance plot, is invariably reductive.

When time does not permit longer readings, therefore, I have come to prefer authentic parodies to inadvertent ones. The famous speech in scene 4 of Molière's *Les précieuses ridicules*, in which Magdelon objects to her father's attempt to take "le roman par la queue" ("the romance by the tail") by arranging her marriage before any courtship (268–69), is a brilliant pastiche of precisely those features of romance that will be relevant to my discussion. In a single paragraph, it details not only the fateful accidents typical of romance plotting but also the gallant conventions still fully in evidence in the later novel. I do not, however, introduce this parody or my own account of romance immediately. Rather, I attempt to develop a context in which both the social meaningfulness of romance and its echoes in *La Princesse de Clèves* can come alive for students. Lafayette's own evocation of court society supplies that context.

In introducing the novel I therefore emphasize features of court life that will help students appreciate how the two types of fiction addressed social tensions. I stress that aspects of court life we may find superficial were deeply meaningful to seventeenth-century elites. Drawing loosely on Norbert Elias's *The Court Society* (41–65), I point out that for kings and princes, *magnificence*— the ostentatious display of status and wealth—was not a matter of choice but a mandatory expression of the grandeur of their lineage as compelling as professional duties are for us today. The size of Mlle de Chartres's retinue (77; 11) and the "magnificence admirable" of the supper at which her mother entertains the court after her wedding (89; 21) reveal the excellence of their *maison*. Likewise, marriage served primarily to enhance and display the prestige of the princely house. Mme de Chartres's reaction when two prospective matches for her daughter fall through offers a useful example: "elle fut bien étonnée que la maison de Clèves et celle de Guise craignissent son alliance" (83) ("she was astonished that the houses of Clèves and Guise should fear an alliance with her own" [16]). The mother is rejected as well as the daughter, and they are rejected not by mere individuals but by transcendent *maisons*.

The link between this sociological preamble and my generic problem is provided by an examination of the ambiguous role that love and gallantry play in court society. In principle love is a private matter, which cannot be allowed to intrude on the public problem of illustrating noble lineages. Thus although Mme de Chartres considers love for one's husband to be indispensable to a woman's happiness (76; 10), she does not permit its mere absence to overcome the dynastic considerations that dictate her daughter's marriage to the Prince de Clèves. Nevertheless, at court, love and gallantry are omnipresent, as this celebrated passage attests:

> L'ambition et la galanterie étaient l'âme de cette cour [. . .]. Il y avait tant d'intérêts et tant de cabales différentes, et les dames avaient tant de part que l'amour était toujours lié aux affaires et les affaires à l'amour.
> (80–81)

> Ambition and love affairs were the life-blood of the court [. . .]. There were countless interests at stake, countless different factions, and women played such a central part in them that love was always entangled with politics and politics with love.
> (14)

Students can readily imagine the conflicts that must result when *ambition* and *affaires*, the natural allies of marriage, are coupled with *amour* and *galanterie*. The question thus arises of why the court should have accorded such a public role to a gallantry that appears to undermine the court's values. The answer, I suggest, is bound up with romance.

Although this once-popular genre featured characters who strongly resembled those of *La Princesse de Clèves* in values and aspirations, its plots diverged in two important respects. First, although they too placed a premium on rank, the characters of romance usually managed in the end to achieve marriages that fulfilled their desires as well as their public obligations. Second, these unions were initially thwarted and finally achieved by means of a plotting that I summarize as based on *aventure*, a word whose double set of meanings takes us back to the chivalric romances that lie at the origins of the *roman* (see Coulet, *Le roman* 21–22, and the definition in Robert's *Dictionnaire historique*). Adventures, then as now, were events like shipwrecks or kidnappings, associated with danger and the unknown. But because of the word's etymological link to *avenir* ("future"), *aventure* was originally associated with destiny and chance and came to designate any unexpected or accidental event. More fundamental to romance plotting than dangerous catastrophes were those events that came about *par aventure*: the chance encounter, the fortuitously misdirected communication, the conspiracy foiled by accident. The proclivity of romance heroes for both types of adventure tends to reinforce the word's original meaning, creating the sense that the heroes' lives express destiny at work.

These essential features of romance plotting are succinctly summarized by Magdelon's speech: "le mariage ne doit jamais arriver qu'après les autres aventures" (268; "marriage should never take place until after one's other adventures"). Magdelon, however, is an ignorant bourgeoise who grossly misreads both romance and social reality. Adventures for her thus include not only happenstance ("les enlèvements" ["abductions"]) but its contrary—events dictated by social and psychological constraints—"les persécutions des pères [. . .] les plaintes, les désespoirs" ("oppressive fathers [. . .] lovers' laments and tribulations"). And these various categories of "adventures" she transforms into rules of etiquette, "dont, en bonne galanterie, on ne saurait se dispenser" (269; "which, by the rules of gallantry, one can scarce do without"), imagining that her father has committed a social solecism by arranging her marriage to a highborn suitor. Through Magdelon's misguided attempts at codification, Molière skewers the formulas of contemporary romance, whose underlying "rules" became increasingly apparent as the genre proliferated.

What accounted for the fascination this formula—marriage through adventure—had long held, not only for provincial adolescents but also for highborn courtiers? Students most readily see an element of universal wish fulfillment in the genre's use of chance to engineer a happy ending. By reminding them of the tension between *amour* and *affaires* we observed in *La Princesse de Clèves*, however, I can also lead them to think about the question in a more historically specific light. It then becomes apparent that romance resolves this contradiction. At the end of their travails, romance lovers discover that their seemingly individual desires have been serving their public obligations or vice versa. As Claudette Sarlet puts it, "le romanesque héroïque est fondé sur la coïncidence du corps fantasmé et du corps social. Une distorsion est posée au début, puis tout le récit mène à la fusion" (211) ("heroic romance is based on the identity of the body of erotic fantasy and the social body. The beginning of the romance posits a separation of these two bodies that the narrative will eventually reunite"). Students can speculate about why authors relied so heavily on chance adventures to bring about this fusion. Why not simply arrange for the protagonist to love his or her parentally designated spouse from the beginning? One obvious answer, that such a story would seem improbable, offers an interesting perspective on the alleged implausibility of romance. Perhaps the unlikely turns of fate were actually necessary in order to motivate the final reconciliation of desire and dynasty.

The elaborate plots of romance, then, supply a reassuring vision of individual and social integrity. Social institutions do not, in the end, conflict with human nature. The seemingly dangerous desires of the great turn out to be the authentic expressions of their public identities. However reassuring the romance plot, though, its popularity must have exacerbated existing tensions in court society. For the gallant demeanor affected by romance heroes preoccupied with love became integral to the noble public image, as Molière's play indirectly attests. Students often indignantly observe that Magdelon cares nothing for love, only for appearances. I suggest, however, that her concerns are less superficial than they might appear. Well aware that her public identity is bound up with her spouse's, Magdelon rejects the suitor her father has chosen because he offends her sense of self-worth. Although this seigneur La Grange outranks her, his failure to affect the gallant manners she has read about in romance persuades her he is a man of little consequence: "quelle estime, mon père, voulez-vous que nous fassions du procédé irrégulier de ces gens-là?" (267) ("can you really expect us, father, to respect the unseemly conduct of these personages?").

La Princesse de Clèves provides evidence that romance similarly affected the perceptions of more astute readers. The work's first sentence—"La magnificence et la galanterie n'ont jamais paru en France avec tant d'éclat que dans les dernières années du règne de Henri second" (69) ("Never has France seen such a display of courtly magnificence and manners as in the last years of the reign of Henri II" [3])—is commonly held to represent a break with romance, known for its historically remote settings. But equally striking is the singling out of a gallantry proper to romance as a distinguishing trait of the sixteenth-century French court. La Calprenède, one of the most prolific and successful romancers, actually anticipated Lafayette's phrase in his *Cléopâtre*: "Tout était galant à Rome, et magnifique" (qtd in Adam 2: 128) ("Everything in Rome was gallant and magnificent"). These repeated couplings of gallantry with the public virtue *magnificence* help explain why gallantry so preoccupied Lafayette's courtiers. For nourished by its alluring portrayal in romance, gallantry, as Magdelon perceived, had become a means for displaying the intrinsic merit of the noble and his lineage. It shines, in Lafayette's formulation, with the same dazzling "éclat" ("brilliance") as *magnificence*. By publicly displaying the colors and initials of Mme de Valentinois, the king transforms his faithful passion of twenty years into an expression of the excellence of the House of France on the same plane as his displays of *magnificence*.

For the king, this public exhibition of gallantry seems unproblematic. Mme de Valentinois appears alongside the queen as a supplemental sign of his grandeur. For the women of his court, however, the transformation of gallantry into a status symbol will prove more troublesome. As Mme de Chartres instructs her daughter, virtue is the public sign whereby highborn women achieve a comparable "éclat" (76; 10). Seventeenth-century romance deals with this imperative of feminine virtue by cloaking courtship in secrecy. Far from publicly displaying his lady's initials, the romance lover approaches even the private declaration of love with great delicacy, as Magdelon indicates:

Il cache, un temps, sa passion à l'objet aimé, et cependant lui rend plusieurs visites, où l'on ne manque jamais de mettre sur le tapis une question galante qui exerce les esprits de l'assemblée. Le jour de la déclaration arrive [. . .] et cette déclaration est suivie d'un prompt courroux, qui paraît à notre rougeur, et qui, pour un temps, bannit l'amant de notre présence. Ensuite il trouve moyen de nous apaiser, de nous accoutumer insensiblement au discours de sa passion et de tirer de nous cet aveu qui fait tant de peine.   (268)

At first, he hides his passion from his beloved, even as he pays her numerous calls, during which the company will sharpen its wits on the problem of gallantry that never fails to arise. The day of his declaration arrives at last [. . .] and this declaration prompts our outraged blushes and leads us, for a time, to banish our lover from our presence. Then he manages to pacify us, to accustom us imperceptibly to hear him discourse on his passion and to draw from us that most distressing of avowals.

As students read *La Princesse de Clèves*, I ask them to notice how closely M. de Nemours and the princess adhere to these procedures. Nemours, indeed, suffers banishment despite his forgoing of an explicit declaration, and Mme de Clèves endures agonies of humiliation for inadvertent revelations far short of an avowal. For all their punctilious discretion, however, their story takes a turn that confirms Magdelon's protest that to put marriage before love is to take romance "by the tail." For gallant courtship presupposes the benevolent universe of romance. The reader expects that the protagonists' desires have in fact led them to publicly acceptable spouses, and this expectation prospectively condones the lover's manipulation in extracting an avowal and the lady's concession in granting it. I propose to students that we view the story of the duc de Nemours and the Princesse de Clèves as a romance inserted into a novel of dynastic alliance. Not only is this story a typical example of romance courtship, but, as our discussion will make clear, it is also punctuated at significant intervals by the telltale signs of romance plotting. By incorporating a romance, as romance was actually practiced by French courtiers, Lafayette explores the consequences of the court's co-optation of a romantic gallantry whose implications it is ill-prepared to accept.

The meeting between Mme de Clèves and M. de Nemours clearly takes place under the sign of romance. Students easily perceive, along with Nemours's rival, the chevalier de Guise, the marks of the *aventure* in the accident that brings two beautiful strangers to dance together at a royal ball. Guise takes this "aventure qui avait quelque chose de galant et d'extraordinaire" (92) ("incident that had something so romantic and remarkable about it" [25]) as "un présage que la fortune destinait M. de Nemours à être amoureux de Mme de Clèves" (92) ("an omen that fate meant M. de Nemours to fall in love with

Mme de Clèves" [24]). What requires some elucidation is the complicity of the court in contriving and magnifying the adventure. Mme de Clèves and Nemours were bound to meet soon after the duke's arrival, and each instantly divines the other's identity; court gossip has indeed for days whetted the young woman's curiosity about the distinguished courtier. The coincidental character of the encounter is thus limited. Yet romance has so shaped erotic sensibilities in this court, where, generally speaking, everyone knows everyone, that the circumstance becomes a portentous event:

> Le roi et les reines se souvinrent qu'ils ne s'étaient jamais vus, et trouvèrent quelque chose de singulier de les voir danser ensemble sans se connaître. Ils les appelèrent quand ils eurent fini, sans leur donner le loisir de parler à personne, et leur demandèrent s'ils n'avaient pas bien envie de savoir qui ils étaient, et s'ils ne s'en doutaient point.   (91)

> The King and the Queens recalled that the couple had never seen one another before and found it somewhat strange to see them dancing together without being acquainted. They called them as soon as they had finished dancing, without giving them time to talk to anyone else, and asked whether each was not eager to know who the other was and whether they had not already guessed.   (24)

A reader of romance might here expect the king to command the gentleman to become the lady's *serviteur*. That is how *L'Astrée*'s King Torrismond, for example, sanctions the accident that leads the two handsomest dancers at his ball to dress in white: "[je] ne sçay qui a assemblé ce couple, mais si c'est la Fortune, elle montre en cela qu'elle n'est pas tant aveugle qu'on la dit" (3.3.86) ("I don't know who brought this couple together, but if it is Fortune, she must not be as blind as people think"). Since Mme de Clèves is married, however, such a gesture is clearly impossible. Why, then, do the monarchs so publicly proclaim that they think, along with the chevalier de Guise, that she and Nemours are predestined to love? Are they merely calling attention to one more superfluous sign of the court's gallantry, or are they conveying a hidden message? Students can discuss at length what the monarchs might be inadvertently saying to Nemours and the princess. The essential point is that the monarchs have no official plot to offer the couple.

I linger over this meeting because it displays so clearly two characteristics of the court's appropriation of romance: first, the contrived character of its adventures, which, unlike the adventures of romance, are arranged by the characters rather than by chance; and, second, the problematic character of gallantry as a very public status symbol that, outside its romance context, has no avowable purpose. I then propose that we analyze two subsequent episodes in the light of these characteristics. In the first, the vidame de Chartres loses a letter from his estranged mistress, Mme de Thémines. Now the accidentally misdirected letter was a common device for initiating the romance complications that Magdelon describes as "les jalousies conçues sur de fausses apparences" (269; "fits of jealousy based on false appearances"). Lafayette's contemporary Valincour criticized the letter and the resulting imbroglio as displaying the arbitrary plotting that readers had come to associate with romance: "il fallait que le génie qui préside aux aventures eût disposé les choses bien juste, pour faire que cette lettre produisît tous les événements qui arrivèrent dans la suite" *Lettres* 103) ("the genius who presides over adventures must certainly have arranged things very neatly in order to get this letter to produce all the events that followed from it"). I ask students, however, to consider the circumstances in which the vidame discovers its loss. At a large dinner party "le hasard" ("fate") turns the conversation to "jolies lettres" ("cleverly written letters"), prompting him to boast "qu'il en avait une sur lui, plus jolie que toutes celles qui avaient jamais été écrites" (146–47); "he had on his person the cleverest [letter] anyone had ever seen" (73). Despite the discretion he owes Mme de Thémines, the vidame leaps at the opportunity offered by chance to enhance his reputation for gallantry. His careless loss of the letter appears less as a coincidence than as a revealing slip by a courtier compelled to make public capital of his private *amours*.

What we subsequently learn about the vidame's relationship to his patroness, Catherine de Médicis, further associates this ostensible accident with the disastrous logic of courtly gallantry. In principle, few members of the court should be more adept at maintaining the separation between *amour* and *affaires* than the vidame and the queen. The queen treats her husband's gallant liaison with cool indifference (70; 3); the vidame confidently maintains his private liaisons while pursuing his political advancement with the queen. Yet both find this separation untenable. As if to compensate for her public indifference to love, Catherine de Médicis demands the fidelity of a lover from the man she appoints her political confidant. Conversely, the vidame feels no compunction in courting these political favors with the rhetoric of the gallant lover: "je la rassurai enfin à force de soins, de soumissions et de faux serments" (155) ("I finally reassured her by plying her with attentions, protestations of obedience, and false vows" [80]). It is no more than poetic justice that the queen should employ an affair of state — the *conjuration d'Amboise* — to wreak a private vengeance on her two-faced lover.

The case of the vidame provides students with a means of evaluating the more complex behavior of the duc de Nemours. From the outset, Lafayette pairs the two men: the narrator tells us that only the vidame is worthy of comparison with the duke (71; 5); Mme de Clèves concludes from her uncle's indiscretions that his friend must also be incapable of fidelity (167; 91). On one point, though, the two men differ. For rather than concurrently pursue *amour* and *affaires*, the duke abandons his ambition to wed Queen Elizabeth of England to devote himself entirely to Mme de Clèves, whom he courts with exemplary discretion. He therefore appears as a potentially authentic hero of romance, single-mindedly following the dictates of passion, while leaving his public advancement to destiny.

This identification is confirmed by another *aventure*: the coincidence that places him in the pavilion at Coulommiers just in time to overhear Mme de Clèves's fateful *aveu* to her husband. Like the letter that falls into the wrong hands, this conversation overheard by ears it was not intended for has provoked unfavorable comparisons with the devices of romance. If, however, Lafayette had simply fallen prey to lazy plotting, why would she so conspicuously evoke romance tradition in motivating the duke's presence? Hoping for an encounter with the princess, Nemours pays a visit to his sister's nearby estate. While stag hunting there, he "s'égara dans la forêt" (169) ("lost his way in the forest" [93]). Students do not require lengthy exposure to seventeenth-century romance to recognize this generic signal: the stag hunt and the moody lover, lost in the depths of the forest, point unmistakably to the chivalric origins of a tradition they know without knowing they know it. Lafayette none too subtly announces the beginning of an adventure while leaving it to the reader to notice the discordant notes. When the duke learns he has strayed near to Coulommiers,

> sans faire aucune réflexion et sans savoir quel était son dessein, il alla à toute bride du côté qu'on le lui montrait. Il arriva dans la forêt et se laissa conduire au hasard par des routes faites avec soin, qu'il jugea bien qui conduisaient vers le château.   (169)

> without reflecting on what he was doing and with no precise intention, he went off at full gallop in the direction that was pointed out to him. He found himself in the forest and allowed himself to be guided at random by well-marked paths, guessing that they would lead him to the château.   (93)

Like the meeting at the ball and the incident of the lost letter, this seemingly spontaneous *égarement* betrays a disquieting element of premeditation. Only after he has placed himself in the vicinity of Mme de Clèves does Nemours happen to get lost. Once a passerby has shown him the way to Coulommiers, he passively submits to chance, allowing his horse to carry him along roads clearly designed to lead travelers to the estate.

Like the court as a whole, indeed, like Magdelon as she complacently anticipates her artless blush, Nemours is both the creature and the creator of romance. Hardly aware that he is playing a role, he is propelled less by passion itself than by the urge to play the impassioned lover of romance. If chance helps bring Nemours to an adventure different from the one he sought to contrive, he has been its eager accomplice nonetheless. However, the disastrous consequences of the avowal he overhears have nothing to do with chance and everything to do with the courtly appropriation of romance. When Nemours leaves Coulommiers, he carries with him a possession very like the vidame's "jolie lettre," an extraordinary proof of the love of a remarkable woman. And, like the vidame, he cannot resist publicizing this proof of his own worth: "il tomba dans une imprudence assez ordinaire, qui est de parler en termes généraux de ses sentiments particuliers et de conter ses propres aventures sous des noms empruntés" (175) ("he fell into an error of judgement which is common enough: he talked about his personal feelings in general terms and told his own story under assumed names" [99]). At this moment Nemours ceases to be a romance hero. No longer the incomparable (71–72; 5) duc de Nemours, he is, like the vidame, an "ordinary" courtier, compulsively polishing his gallant image. Little did Mme de Clèves imagine, when she admired the letter of Mme de Thémines, that her own singular proof of passion and resolve was soon to travel the same prefabricated route, making the rounds of the court until it finally returned to her as yet another of Nemours's gallant adventures (183; 105–06).

If we cannot say that the French novel begins with *La Princesse de Clèves*, we can safely say that *La Princesse de Clèves* begins where romance ends: with marriage. Strangely enough, although Lafayette's refusal to begin her novel like a romance is universally applauded, her heroine's refusal of a romance ending—love *and* marriage—remains controversial, for critics as for students. It is not for me to tell my students whether the princess should have declined this ending. I do ask them to consider her decision in the light of what they, and she, may have learned about romance at court. That Mme de Clèves finally hears M. de Nemours's declaration of love and proposal of marriage is due to a final "accident." The vidame asks his niece to pay him a visit, having previously arranged for the duke to enter by a hidden staircase, "comme si le hasard l'eût conduit" (225) ("as if by chance" [144]).

Romance dies when its contrivances come to seem all too apparent, its twists of fate inevitable, its endings predictable. Perhaps the fate of M. de Nemours is rather like that of the *romans* that shaped his real-life models. For all his considerable charm, he loses his power on the day the princess begins to anticipate what will happen next: "Vous avez déjà eu plusieurs passions; vous en auriez encore; je ne ferais plus votre bonheur [. . .]" (231) ("You have already had a number of passionate attachments; you would have others. I should no longer be able to make you happy [. . .]" [149]).

NOTE

[1]Except where otherwise indicated, all translations are mine.

Reading *La Princesse de Clèves* with the *Heptaméron*

John D. Lyons

In college many students discover a great source of intellectual excitement and delight: that texts are not monads but part of an energetic exchange of statement and response, question and answer, pattern and alternative. Entering college students are familiar, of course, with comparative readings. Any two texts can be compared—this is a standard composition assignment in which the text is passively located within a more or less arbitrarily chosen set. A major leap in sophistication occurs when students discover that many texts contain within themselves the clues to their place within a cultural and intellectual tradition, when students discover, in other words, the explicit and implicit intertextuality with which texts create a tradition retrospectively. In pointing out such clues teachers do not give students information that they can simply recall; instead we point them toward further reading and toward an open-ended interpretation.

I taught *La Princesse de Clèves* with the *Heptaméron* in an introductory comparative literature course that took as its guiding theme the experience of reading. This approach was meant to make students conscious of their own experience as readers while they read about literary characters who had been affected by books. The readings ranged from Augustine's *Confessions* to Nabokov's *Pale Fire*. Most of the students were freshmen or sophomores, and some had had introductory courses in English or another literature. The readings were in English. I did not ask the students to read works on modern narrative theory, since I preferred to have them discover and elaborate the relevant concepts by examining the narratives themselves.

The students read *La Princesse de Clèves* first and then selections from Marguerite de Navarre's *Heptaméron*. The connection between the two texts is based on a simple observation: the only explicit reference to another literary text in *La Princesse de Clèves* is to the *Heptaméron*. In telling the princess the story of Anne Boleyn and Henry VIII of England, the reine dauphine mentions Marguerite de Navarre, "dont vous avez vu les contes" (133) ("whose stories you will no doubt have seen" [61]). Since no other literary work is mentioned in Lafayette's book, this reference may very well strike an attentive reader even without historical background. Once we begin to explore the events mentioned in the novel and the context in which the novel was written, the reference to the *Heptaméron* becomes even more inviting. The events of Lafayette's novel take place primarily in 1558–59, precisely the moment of the posthumous publication of the first two editions of the *Heptaméron*. It is less obvious, but important, that Lafayette was connected with the milieu that produced "a collection of tales in open homage to the most illustrious French practitioner of the form, Marguerite de Navarre" (DeJean, *Tender Geographies* 53). This collection is the *Nouvelles françaises* (1657), published under the name of Segrais, but apparently the result of a collective effort inspired and directed by the duchesse de Montpensier, who is represented in the *Nouvelles* as the princesse Aurélie. Montpensier was the great-great-granddaughter of Marguerite de Navarre, and the princess Aurélie refers to the tales of the *Nouvelles françaises* as the stories (*contes*) of her grandmother. If Segrais functioned as literary secretary and public literary go-between for Montpensier, he served Lafayette in the same capacity when she issued her novel *Zaïde* (1670). Thus there is not only a textual but also a genealogical and social connection between Marguerite de Navarre and Lafayette. Over the past three centuries the kinship between these texts has often been recognized or suspected (e.g., Paulsen 16; Cholakian 100, 251, 254), but no one has yet given a systematic account of the relationship between Lafayette's text and Marguerite de Navarre's.

My approach to teaching this intertextual relation grows out of my view of the heroine's role in Lafayette's novel. Seeing the princess as a determined yet often frustrated interpreter of narratives, I have always invited students to think of her as like themselves. She is new to the court, overwhelmed with information about the courtiers' names, family alliances, ancient and largely concealed feuds, and shifting titles. She is also confronted with a series of stories that are designed, apparently, to fill her in on the court and on human nature but that also challenge her ability to fit it all together.

A course can include different formal and thematic links between *La Princesse de Clèves* and the *Heptaméron*, depending on the amount of reading assigned in Marguerite de Navarre's work, whether it be the prologue alone, a single substantial tale, many selected tales, or all of them. Marguerite de Navarre's work is available in the original sixteenth-century French (Classiques Garnier), in a modernized French version (Garnier-Flammarion), and in a complete and readable modern English translation by P. A. Chilton (Penguin). I have not yet had students read the whole of the *Heptaméron* along with *La Princesse de Clèves*. Instead, I have had them read the prologue and a selection of six to ten tales (the selection has varied from year to year).

On the basis of the prologue, we can explore the general concepts of generic tradition, narrative structure, and the gender of the narrator and the audience. The *Heptaméron* prologue introduces ten characters, five women and five men, trapped by a flood and looking for a way to pass the time. The oldest of the characters, Oisille, proposes religious activities, especially reading Holy Scripture and practicing attentive self-examination. The younger, more worldly characters include Hircan, who hints that his ideal pastime would be making love with one of the other characters. Storytelling is then suggested as a kind of compromise between Scripture and sex. Parlamente, a character often described by critics as representing Marguerite herself, proposes imitating two models: Boccaccio's *Decameron*, on the one hand, and, on the other, a new *Decameron*-like set of tales planned by King François I along with Marguerite de Navarre, the crown prince Henri, and the crown princess Catherine de Médicis. We can immediately recognize here not only the author of the *Heptaméron* itself but also the king and queen (Henri II and Catherine) of *La Princesse de Clèves*.

The prologue sets up an intertextual relation with the *Decameron* and announces the intention to produce a renewed, more truthful, French collection of tales, thus issuing a kind of challenge to the Boccaccian tradition within which the prologue sets the *Heptaméron*. Lafayette's mention of Marguerite's tales can be seen as a way of inscribing *La Princesse de Clèves* within a lengthy tradition of storytelling. This insight in itself can correct the tendency to isolate Lafayette's work, and French classicism generally, as if it sprang out of nowhere and did not situate itself with respect to generic markers.

Concepts of narrative structure arise in conjunction with this intertextual link to the novella tradition. At first glance, students do not see *La Princesse de Clèves* as having any structural similarity to the *Heptaméron*. The earlier work consists of a series of separate tales, each with a different set of characters. The only links appear to be the ten prologue characters (or, more accurately, frame characters) who tell one another the stories. Lafayette's work, in contrast, has only a small number of foreground characters (the princess, her mother, the prince, Nemours, the crown princess, and a few others). In fact, *La Princesse de Clèves* is usually—with the exception of Valincour's critique—described as founding a French tradition of spare, taut narrative that is deep and intense rather than sprawling and heavy with incidents. So at first glance the sixteenth-century work seems centrifugal or open-ended while the seventeenth-century one looks centripetal and carefully closed.

On further probing, however, we can see that this description of the narrative structure needs to be qualified. After all, one of the earliest features of Lafayette's text to be criticized is the presence of "digressive" episodic or internal narratives, stories told not by the general anonymous narrator of the novel but by characters themselves. The princess hears all these internal narratives and tries to fit them together into a pattern to provide a model of human conduct that she can use to guide her actions and to predict those of others. Although there are other brief narrations by characters in the novel, what are traditionally called the "internal tales" concern Diane de Poitiers, Anne Boleyn, Mme de Tournon, Marie de Lorraine, and the vidame de Chartres (Niderst 137).

This line of inquiry can lead to a vision of *La Princesse de Clèves* and the *Heptaméron* as having a structural similarity under an initially disorienting difference of proportion. Compared with the earlier work, Lafayette's novel has a greatly expanded frame narrative and considerably reduced internal narratives or tales. Yet in both texts there are characters who hear and interpret tales and who try to formulate general principles on the basis of them. The princess's immediate entourage — her mother, her husband, her uncle, and the crown princess — forms a storytelling group dispersed throughout the novel. Unlike the *Heptaméron* frame narrative, Lafayette's novel has one character whose special function is to listen to stories and interpret them, the princess herself, who does not tell any of the internal stories.

Reading *La Princesse de Clèves* with the *Heptaméron* can help bring out a third major issue: the gender of the narrators and its significance. Lafayette's novel is very often taught in the context of women's studies and valued as an affirmation of the woman writer. Yet, paradoxically, the gender and all other identity markings of the narrator are removed. Some readers assume that the narrator is a woman, since the author was a woman, while others do not — which leads to awkward pronominal choices, such as "when the narrator introduces the characters, she/he. . . ." Marguerite de Navarre's work, beginning with the prologue, gives us the opportunity to discuss the effacement of narrative identity as we turn from the sixteenth-century to the seventeenth-century text. The general narrator of the *Heptaméron*, like the narrator of *La Princesse de Clèves*, is barely identified, but most *Heptaméron* narrative is given by gendered, and otherwise characterized, frame characters. If we assume that the ideal form of Marguerite de Navarre's work would be one hundred tales, then fifty stories would be told by women and fifty by men. The arrangement permits the reader, and even the other frame characters, to weigh the subject position or gender perspective of each narrator in representing the "reality" that is so highly valued in the *Heptaméron* prologue. Lafayette's novel seems to participate in the construction of an abstract narrator who transcends gender, somewhat in the way La Rochefoucauld's *Maximes*, despite being the product of salon exchanges between men and women, is enunciated by a universal subject.

However, in Lafayette's work, the gendered narrator does remain apparent in a small, but not insignificant, portion of the overall text, the internal tales. The two stories told by the crown princess, one about her mother, Marie de Lorraine, and one about Anne Boleyn, and the stories told by Mme de Chartres about Diane de Poitiers, by M. de Clèves about Sancerre and Mme de Tournon, and by the vidame about his relationship with the queen are marked by the gender of their narrators. Moreover, the gender of the narrator is related, in *La Princesse de Clèves*, to the emphasized character of each internal narrative. Mme de Chartres, for example, clearly emphasizes Diane de Poitiers even though her story includes information about François I and Henri II, while M. de Clèves's story emphasizes Sancerre's perspective even though Mme de Tournon is the dominant, active character. One-on-one comparisons of Marguerite de Navarre's and Lafayette's internal narrators' practices raise many questions for discussion and writing: Who is telling the story? Who is listening? What is the effect of the story on the listening character? How does this effect differ from the effect on the reader of the novel?

If students have time to read one substantial tale from the *Heptaméron*, such as tale 10 (thirty-two pages in the English version), they can study thematic similarities between Lafayette's and Navarre's books. Tale 10, about Amadour and Floride, is the one most often compared with *La Princesse de Clèves*. In fact, it has been called "the prototype of *La Princesse de Clèves*" (François 312). This claim seems to me to be far-fetched and to isolate one tale from the whole (a procedure that is almost as absurd as publishing the story of Mme de Tournon separately from the rest of *La Princesse de Clèves* would be). Nonetheless, if we take the widely accepted view that the meaning of a literary work is generated in part by the history of its interpretation, then the story of Floride and Amadour has become part of the intertextual tradition of *La Princesse de Clèves*, and tale 10 is one of the most often studied tales in the *Heptaméron* (Conley; Kritzman).

Tale 10 has in common with Lafayette's story the intensity, length, and secrecy of the hero's courtship and the corresponding secret passion of the married woman he pursues. In both stories the heroine spends the last years of her life happy in a convent, having firmly decided not to grant her lover what he asks and what she herself may—or may not—also desire. Each heroine continues to love her suitor long after breaking off contact with him. Floride, like the Princesse de Clèves, attaches great importance to virtue and duty. In both stories the heroine's difficult situation comes about through unwise decisions by her mother: Mme de Chartres marries her daughter to a man her daughter does not love after other possible, highly glorious matches prove politically impossible, while Floride's mother champions Amadour's love for her daughter and places her daughter in a dangerous situation alone with the suitor. Like Amadour, Nemours violates certain limits he owes it to his beloved to respect (he reveals the astounding confession she makes to her husband, and he penetrates her private space several times under different pretexts), while the princess likewise exceeds conventional limitations (her unheard-of avowal to her husband) in her own defense.

If a course includes still more readings from the *Heptaméron*, broader thematic comparisons become available. I suggest here several that I have found useful.

First is the question of the degree to which human beings can reach their goals by taking appropriate steps with a knowledge of probabilities and patterns. Many of Lafayette's characters, including the heroine, see human emotion and conduct as falling into predictable patterns. Knowledge of these patterns can be used to control the outcome of events. Mme de Thémines's letter to the vidame tells how she both understood and exploited such patterns in his conduct. It is just such a rule of male emotion that the widowed princess invokes in deciding not to marry Nemours. Permanent fidelity from a satisfied male lover is so far beyond the rules of nature that the princess's only hope, she says, would be in a "miracle" (231; 148). Lafayette seems to contrast the plainly evident predictability of human conduct with the general unpredictability of history—Henri II denies any validity to an astrologer's prediction that he will die in a duel, but the prediction comes true in historical fact, as told in *La Princesse de Clèves*.

The *Heptaméron* as a whole is concerned precisely with the stable patterns of human conduct—the frame characters discuss at great length the relation between each tale and such generalizations. Although Marguerite de Navarre's storytellers disagree on the relative morality or immorality of men and women and on the extent to which conduct patterns are gender-specific, there is considerable agreement that a pattern does exist and that trying to locate and describe it is worthwhile. As in Lafayette's work, the characters who understand the normal course of behavior and who covertly and patiently adapt their conduct accordingly are able to achieve their aims, whether good or bad. The presiding judge from Grenoble, in tale 36, is similar to Mme de Thémines in manipulating appearances and carrying out a private vengeance without public revelation. Likewise the wise woman, the *saige dame* of tale 26, is able to guide the young man she secretly loves back to the path of virtue because she understands better than he that he is, as we say, just going through a phase.

A second important theme in both works is the issue of the relations between the sexes, a basis of much of the novella tradition and the nascent modern *roman*. Marital infidelity, rejected courtship, honor and its contrary, public disgrace—these are themes common to both Lafayette's and Marguerite de Navarre's stories. Here a major difference between the *Heptaméron* and *La Princesse de Clèves* is the latter's consistently disenchanted or pessimistic assessment of passionate love. For Lafayette, all amorous relationships seem doomed to brevity and instability. Although Lafayette's novel does offer one example of a permanent relationship (between Henri II and Diane de Poitiers), we can easily argue that Henri never fully "possessed" Diane. In the *Heptaméron*, in contrast, there are many tales of married couples that find great happiness in mutual love, despite a momentary infidelity on the part of the husband or the wife (e.g., tales 37, 38, and 59). The *Heptaméron* includes long-term adulterous relationships that do not fit the negative model that dominates Lafayette's work. For example, the queen of Naples, in tale 3, takes as lover a gentleman whose wife is the king's mistress: "This amicable arrangement permitted the continuation of their amours for many years to come, until at length old age brought them to order" (*Heptameron* 88). A third thematic pattern of both works is the relation of women to power, both to the politics of a monarchical and feudal state and to the micropolitical level of the family. In *La Princesse de Clèves* Diane de Poitiers, Catherine de Médicis, and the crown princess exercise varying degrees of control over treaties, appointments, and policies (for instance, the crown's treatment of Protestants). In the *Heptaméron* well-known women of the period appear as characters exercising benevolent authority, especially in the administration of criminal justice. In the very first tale Marguerite de Navarre's powerful mother, Louise de Savoie, initiates the judicial process that brings murderers to justice. Marguerite de Navarre herself appears frequently, for instance in tales 22 and 72, where she intervenes on behalf of women abused by confessors. In such instances the power of woman as storyteller and the power of woman as political figure are represented together. Tying the two books closely is the mention in both of women's role in the negotiations leading to the Peace of Cambrai. This reference to the "Paix des Dames," as it is traditionally known, "evokes for the reader women who replace men in traditional roles of power" (McKinley 153).

The last theme I mention is the relation between will and action. Both Marguerite de Navarre and Lafayette raise the question of self-control. In *La Princesse de Clèves*, many characters, particularly women, are presented as very successful in achieving their long-term aims because of a high degree of control over their spontaneous, short-term emotional reactions. In the *Heptaméron* such self-control is treated with great ambivalence. The virtuous lady of tale 26 does succeed in guiding the young sieur d'Avannes toward a better life by concealing her passion for him. However, the price she pays is death; her control over her emotions destroys her physically. In tale 30 a virtuous and deeply religious widow tries to keep her son from sinning sexually with the servant maid, but the mother ends up having sex with her son without his knowing it. This lurid tale seems quite remote from the glances and conversation of *La Princesse de Clèves*. Yet the limits of will do appear in Lafayette's work, in which physical self-control seems much more easily achieved, or, rather, the scale on which such control is measured is much more severely and minutely calibrated. Mme de Clèves discovers to her dismay, like the *Heptaméron's* widow, that she cannot fully control her sexual attraction: she betrays excessive concern for Nemours when he is hurt in a tournament. Although there may seem to be a great difference of scale between sexual intercourse and the simple expression of concern, both women discover that will alone cannot provide an absolute guarantee of conduct: at times one must retreat from the occasions of such conduct.

The comparative opportunities I mention are only a beginning. As with the *Heptaméron* itself, which stops abruptly at tale 72, the difficulty with studying the *Heptaméron* and *La Princesse de Clèves* together is concluding. For me this difficulty is itself a pedagogical opportunity. Although *La Princesse de Clèves* is a major text of French classical literature, it undoes any assumption that "classical" means simple, transparent, stable, or unproblematic. And while both Marguerite de Navarre's and Lafayette's works can be considered to be major texts in a tradition of writing by women and to aim at the empowerment of women, these works undo any assumption that such writing is one-sided or reductively didactic. Instead, the *Heptaméron* gives us new ways to reveal the richness and complexity of *La Princesse de Clèves* and to demonstrate that Lafayette demands an active, critical reading.

Mediation of Desire in *La Princesse de Clèves*

Anne Callahan

The theme of romantic love often initially attracts undergraduate nonmajors to my course French Masterpieces in Translation. The challenge is to capitalize on the desire to know about romantic love and to transform it into a desire to read literature. I make this goal explicit from the start; in fact, the pedagogy of the course is best described as mediation of desire.

To get the students' attention, I begin by suggesting that heterosexual romantic love must be one of the most unnatural relationships between human beings. It took a highly artificial and elaborate system of codes, rituals, and rules of conduct to introduce the notion that a man could love a woman to a society in which the ideal relationship was male friendship, *amitié virile* (Nelli).

The system was chivalry, and its philosophy of love, known today as *courtly love*, a term coined by Gaston Paris in 1896, was called *fin'amors*, refined love, in twelfth-century Provence, where the prototype of the modern Western ideal of romantic love was invented by the troubadours (Painter; Nelli; Rougemont). Tristan and Iseut, the first romantic lovers in Western literature, fall in love not because of a natural inclination but because they drink a love potion. One objective of the pedagogy in the course is that students come to recognize that the most powerful love potion is literature itself. Models of heterosexual romance in literature create a desire in the reader to imitate their roles and structures; these models recur sometimes explicitly and sometimes implicitly in a variety of related cultural forms, like popular film, music, fashion, and advertising, in which they mediate consumer desire. My role in the course can be compared to the one Mme de Chartres plays in *La Princesse de Clèves* when she warns her daughter against love; I mediate the desire to read literature by speaking of its dangers, minimizing none of its charms. When we read the novel four weeks into the course, students enjoy recognizing the mediation of desire in the mother's pedagogy.

At the first class meeting I introduce René Girard's thesis that desire does not originate with the individual desiring subject, that all desire is mediated (*Deceit*). Students have no trouble with this proposal if the instructor begins with the idea of mimetic rivalry, giving examples of how desire is mediated by another person—a rival or an idealized model—who desires or possesses the same object. Once students understand mimetic desire in its simplest manifestation, the instructor can present the idea that mimetic desire does not always have a distinct, individual rival or model as its mediator but that it can also be mediated through structural equivalents of rivals and models, such as obstacles.

The next move is to introduce the idea that literature itself is a mediator, a love potion or philter as it were. Romantic love is mediated within the narrative world by rivals and obstacles and from without by earlier narratives, which are cultural artifacts on the same order of significance as laws and religion. To make this point, I read a few lines from canto 5 of the *Inferno*, in which Dante tells how the fatal lovers, Paolo and Francesca, met their death because they shared a kiss they read about in a medieval romance: "One day, to pass the time away, we read of Lancelot—how love had overcome him. We were alone, and we suspected nothing. [. . .] When we had read how the desired smile was kissed by one who was so true a lover, this one, who never shall be parted from me, while all his body trembled, kissed my mouth" (5.127–36).

I teach *La Princesse de Clèves* as a version of the romantic love narrative tradition, which begins with medieval romance; we first read *Tristan et Iseut* and several of Chrétien de Troyes's Arthurian romances. In the *Heptaméron*, written between 1542 and 1549, Marguerite de Navarre questions the ideals of courtly love by stressing the impossibility of knowing the real motivations behind the performance of its rituals (Furber and Callahan 55). In preparation for *La Princesse de Clèves*, we read tale 10, the story of the lovers Amadour and Floride, whose names represent their functions in the tale. In their story, confusion about the meaning of the courtly love ritual, the *asag*, or love test, leads to attempted rape. That the fault lies in the courtly ritual is made clear by Amadour when he defends himself for having tried to force himself on Floride:

> My lady, for as long as I can remember I have longed to love a good and honourable woman. But I have found few who are truly virtuous, and that is why I wanted to test you out—to see if you were as worthy to be admired for your virtue, as you are to be loved for your other attributes. And now I know for certain that you are.   (143)

When Floride resolves that she can only pass the love test by giving no further sign of her love to Amadour, he sees this as a challenge to become more aggressive sexually, even cruel and abusive, and when the lovers meet for the last time it is as mortal enemies. Needless to say, both the popular-press and academic publications on "date rape" (Roiphe; MacKinnon) provide much material for class discussion.

The confrontation scene that leads to the permanent separation of the lovers in Marguerite's tale prepares students for a similar standoff in *La Princesse de Clèves*, a classic double bind generated by the paradoxical structure of the love test.

By the time they read *La Princesse de Clèves*, students are familiar with the myths, ideals, metaphors, symbols, rituals, images, and relationships that Mme de Lafayette evokes as she both represents her heroine in the tradition—and writes her out of it.

The elements of the structure of desire that are familiar to students from previous readings are:

1. the myth of androgynous fusion, which is the goal of the exchange of hearts in *fin'amors* and which produces the romantic hero as a feminine male;

2. the philter as a metaphor for desire that is mediated and not "natural";

3. the *asag* (love test), which establishes the heroine's worthiness to replace the *compagnon*, or male friend, as the significant other, creating the double bind of sexual desire and compulsory abstinence;

4. the triangle of the courtly lovers and the woman's husband, who is also the lover's friend and therefore model, rival, and obstacle at once—he occupies the traditional masculine position in the system, and under his gaze the lovers share the feminine position;

5. the inevitable rivalry between the lovers themselves because of the abstinence required by the *asag*, which forces the woman into a spurious masculine position in the triangle in which she often replaces the male rival or model, as in *La Princesse de Clèves*; and

6. the *Liebestod*, represented as either physical death or some version of definitive physical parting meant to produce the illusion of eternal desire.

This illusion is shattered by the ending of *La Princesse de Clèves*: the duke's desire dies away: "le temps et l'absence [. . .] éteignirent sa passion" (239) ("time and absence [. . .] quenched his passion" [156]). As for the princess, she withdraws from the world of desire to religious devotion and practice.

Before discussing how Mme de Lafayette writes her heroine out of the tradition, it is important in an undergraduate class to first discuss how the princess and M. de Nemours captivate the reader's attention as conventional romantic lovers. For this reason I focus attention on the elements listed above as thoroughly and as systematically as possible.

The femininity of the male lover is the first characteristic of the conventional representation of gender in romantic love that I bring up, beginning with Tristan's position as the object of Mark's gaze. Mark is fascinated by Tristan's beauty: "yet most he wondered at the stranger boy, and still gazed at him, troubled and wondering whence came his tenderness [. . .] it was blood that spoke, and the love he had long since borne his sister Blanchefleur" (Bédier 8). Tristan resembles his mother, Blanchefleur, Mark's sister; Tristan replaces Blanchefleur as the object of desire lost to Mark's rival, whose name, Rivalen, defines his function in the narrative. The courtly lover in medieval romance occupies a feminine position vis-à-vis the traditional masculine figure in the conventional triangle of lord, lady, and knight. It helps to show students works of art depicting two romantic images: first, images of women as objects of the gaze, then images of romantic couples in poses suggesting androgynous fusion, where both sexes attract the gaze of the spectator, not individually but as a single figure for romantic love. Gustav Klimt's *The Kiss*, in which the lovers appear to be clothed in a single piece of elaborate fabric, brings the point home very well, as does a lot of advertising copy that celebrates the same sort of union. The feminine hero first appears as the courtly lover in medieval romance, then again in the Renaissance as the *galant*, a figure central to the depiction of courtly love in 1678, when *La Princesse de Clèves* was published.

M. de Nemours is established early in the novel as the romantic hero whose extraordinary beauty distinguishes him from his fellow *galants*: "un chef d'œuvre de la nature [. . .] il avait un enjouement qui plaisait également aux hommes et aux femmes [. . .]" (71–72) ("nature's masterpiece. [. . .] He had a light-hearted manner that was attractive to men and women alike [. . .]" [5]). His position as object of the gaze is established: "on ne pouvait regarder que lui dans tous les lieux où il paraissait" (72) ("it [was] impossible to look at anyone else when he was present" [5]). His beauty is rivaled only by that of Mlle de Chartres, the other spectacular beauty who "appeared" at court (76; 9). Neither is described as an individual, but each represents a certain type of beauty. The type of the feminine male hero reappeared in the next century as the rake, whose femininity is aptly evoked by the very name of Richardson's Lovelace; after the French Revolution decimated the social class to which rakes like Lovelace and Laclos's Valmont belonged, the feminine hero was reborn in Romanticism as the sensitive poet-lover in the image of the troubadour. Students enjoy coming up with examples of the prototype in popular culture, including actors famous for playing romantic leads and musicians who perform love songs — Rudolph Valentino, Errol Flynn, Tyrone Power, Elvis Presley, and Michael Bolton. Brad Pitt's re-creation of the Tristan figure in the film *Legends of the Fall* is a pertinent example. Students are fascinated by the idea that the sexual relation in heterosexual ideal love might be not sexual difference but a shared femininity. An example of this double feminine is the vision of M. de Nemours and the princess dancing together under the gaze of the entire court, including the king (91; 24).

The dancing couple is established in the reader's imagination as a figure of romantic love, a mediation echoed in the reaction of the chevalier de Guise, who witnessed the scene as if it were the operation of the philter:

> [C]e qui se venait de passer lui avait donné une douleur sensible. Il le prit comme un présage que la fortune destinait M. de Nemours à être amoureux de Mme de Clèves; et, soit qu'en effet il eût paru quelque trouble sur son visage, ou que la jalousie fît voir au chevalier de Guise au-delà de la vérité, il crut qu'elle avait été touchée de la vue de ce prince [. . .].   (92)

> [W]hat had just taken place caused him the sharpest pain. He took it as an omen that fate meant M. de Nemours to fall in love with Mme de Clèves. Whether her face had really betrayed some inner turmoil or whether jealousy had caused the Chevalier de Guise to see more

than was there, he believed she had been affected by the sight of the
prince [. . .].   (24)

The philter in this case is reputation and the stock roles to which it destines the
hero and heroine of the novel, and both lovers are seduced by its power:

> Ce prince était fait d'une sorte qu'il était difficile de n'être pas surprise
> de le voir quand on ne l'avait jamais vu, surtout ce soir-là, où le soin qu'il
> avait pris de se parer augmentait encore l'air brillant qui était dans sa per-
> sonne; mais il était difficile aussi de voir Mme de Clèves pour la première
> fois sans avoir un grand étonnement.   (91)

> He had such presence that it was difficult not to be taken aback on seeing
> him when one had never seen him before, especially that evening, when
> the care he had taken to dress elegantly added still more lustre to his ap-
> pearance; but it was also difficult to see Mme de Clèves for the first time
> without being amazed.   (23)

In fact both the princess and the duke take special care to adorn themselves for
the ball, and this scene of "love at first sight" is actually a setup mediated by the
roles assigned them by their culture, which is not different from ours in this
regard.

Iseut's mother prepares the fatal love potion; Mme de Chartres prepares a
version of the philter when she mediates her daughter's desire for romantic
love by representing its fatal attraction. She is also the agent of the love test,
setting it in motion through her deathbed wish that her daughter renounce her
feelings for M. de Nemours and remove herself from the temptations of the
court. In the definitive renunciation scene of the novel, the refusal is linked in
the language of the lovers to the paradoxical *asag*, the love test that places into
dialectical opposition sexual desire and sexual abstinence. M. de Nemours ac-
cuses the princess of fabricating the existence of an obstacle to the satisfaction
of his desire: "Il n'y a point d'obstacle. [. . .] Vous seule vous opposez à mon
bonheur; vous seule vous imposez une loi que la vertu et la raison ne vous
sauraient imposer" (233) ("There is no obstacle. [. . .] You alone stand in the
way of my happiness; you alone have made for yourself a law that virtue and
reason could never impose" [150–51]). Her response establishes that the representation of desire is its only reality and that desire is mediated by codes and
rituals: "Il est vrai [. . .] que je sacrifie beaucoup à un devoir qui ne subsiste que
dans mon imagination" (233) ("It is true [. . .] that I am sacrificing a great deal
to a duty that exists only in my imagination" [151]). She in turn confronts M. de
Nemours with the truth about his desire: it is not a natural inclination but one
mediated by obstacles: "les obstacles ont fait votre constance" (231) ("your con-
stancy has been sustained by the obstacles it has encountered" [148–49]).

In triangular desire the three players change positions constantly to create new couples—both homosexual and heterosexual. Two examples suffice: two men whose rivalry is represented by their mutual desire for a woman in which case homosexual identification is the key (Sedgwick 47), or a woman and a man who form a single figure of romantic love under the masculine gaze of the husband, who represents traditional masculinity. A version of this configuration appears in the scene in which Nemours and the princess copy Mme de Thémines's letter. The princess's husband has sent for M. de Nemours to help his wife recreate the dangerous letter, and all three shut themselves up to work on it:

> Cet air de mystère et de confidence n'était pas d'un médiocre charme pour ce prince et même pour Mme de Clèves. La présence de son mari [. . .] la rassur[ait] en quelque sorte sur ses scrupules; elle ne sentait que le plaisir de voir M. de Nemours, elle en avait une joie pure et sans mélange qu'elle n'avait jamais sentie. Cette joie lui donnait une liberté et un enjouement dans l'esprit [. . .].   (165)

> This atmosphere of mystery and secrecy had no small charm for Nemours and even for Mme de Clèves. The presence of her husband [. . .] helped to silence her scruples. She felt only the pleasure of seeing M. de Nemours, a pure, unmixed delight that was new to her, and from this delight came a mood of gaiety and freedom [. . .].   (89)

The eroticism of this scene of writing is created by its triangular structure, reminiscent—mimetic in fact—of the classic courtly triangle of lord, lady, knight. It favors the arousal of sexual desire through its representation in the replication of a love letter. Repetition and mimesis are essential here as they have been throughout the novel in the circulation of desire through stories and letters.

Only the pavilion scene is more erotic. Here, as in the writing scene, desire is mediated through representation. Readers witness desire not of the object but of an image of the object as constructed in the imagination. And the imagination is fired by the literature that has gone before. M. de Nemours spies on the princess through the wide open windows of the little summer house: "elle était seule; mais il la vit d'une si admirable beauté qu'à peine fut-il maître du transport que lui donna cette vue" (208) ("she was alone, and looked so wonderfully beautiful that he could scarcely control his rapture at the sight" [128]). I ask a student to read the scene aloud in class, which brings out its erotic allure; the reader and the duke are seduced together: "Il faisait chaud, et elle n'avait rien, sur sa tête et sa gorge, que ses cheveux confusément rattachés" (208) ("It was hot, and on her head and breast she wore nothing but her loosely gathered hair" [128]). The bizarre conventions of courtly love, which pretend that the lovers are one in spirit and body while insisting on the secrecy of their love and on their sexual abstinence, is perfectly captured in this scene. The lovers are together in

the frame: the open window and the light evoke a painting, an evocation inten-
sified by the presence of a painting in the scene. The mediation of desire
through representation is highlighted by the description of the princess's actions:

> Elle était sur un lit de repos, avec une table devant elle, où il y avait
> plusieurs corbeilles pleines de rubans; elle en choisit quelques-uns, et
> M. de Nemours remarqua que c'étaient des mêmes couleurs qu'il avait
> portées au tournoi [. . .] elle prit un flambeau et s'en alla proche d'une
> grande table, vis-à-vis du tableau du siège de Metz, où était le portrait de
> M. de Nemours; elle s'assit et se mit à regarder ce portrait avec une at-
> tention et une rêverie que la passion seule peut donner.   (208–09)

> She was reclining on a day-bed with a table in front of her on which
> there were several baskets full of ribbons. She picked out some of these,
> and M. de Nemours noticed that they were of the very colours he had
> worn at the tournament. [. . .] [S]he took a candlestick and went over to a
> large table in front of the painting of the siege of Metz that contained the
> likeness of M. de Nemours. She sat down and began to gaze at it with a
> musing fascination that could only have been inspired by true passion.
> (128)

The princess plays with fetishes (Butor) and gazes at an image of the duke
while he looks at what might be read as "the real thing." But the fetishes and
images recall the power of imagination governing M. de Nemours's desire as
he looks through the window framing her rapture. The heroine's body in this
scene is no more real than the representation of M. de Nemours as a hero at
the siege of Metz. What he sees is not only her but also his own image in her
gaze at his portrait: "On ne peut exprimer ce que sentit M. de Nemours dans ce
moment. Voir [. . .] une personne qu'il adorait [. . .] tout occupée de choses qui
avaient du rapport à lui et à la passion qu'elle lui cachait [. . .]." (209) ("It is
impossible to express what M. de Nemours felt at this moment. To see a
woman he adored [. . .] entirely absorbed in things connected with him and
with the passion she was hiding from him [. . .]" [128]).

Refined courtly love is evoked with the reference to colors, tournament, and
the hero in battle, and these conventional references might well draw our attention away from the irony of the scene. The exchange of identity essential to
romantic love is symbolized by the two stolen portraits in the novel; he steals an
image of her, beneath her gaze in her boudoir (136; 64), and she in turn steals
an image of him to take to her summer house. In conventional terms an image
is a substitute for real presence; this substitution is described in the medieval
codes as the source of the "lover's reverie" (as in Chrétien de Troyes's
"Lancelot"). Lafayette shows that the other's absence is preferable to his or her
presence, since it confirms that the androgynous fusion, the goal of the exchange of hearts, has been realized.

In addition to the theories of René Nelli and Girard, which I refer to constantly in the course, I try to analyze each text from a different perspective on issues surrounding desire, representation, and gender. Students come to understand that gender roles are positional, however much sexuality is biological.

Before we discuss the pavilion scene, I have the students read John Berger's chapter on woman as "the surveyed and the surveyor" from *Ways of Seeing*. The painting *The Reclining Baccante*, by Felix Trutat (1824–48), prefaces the chapter: a nude woman reclines on a daybed while a man looks at her through an open window.

> Men look at women. Women watch themselves being looked at. This determines not only most relations between men and women but also the relation of women to themselves. The surveyor of woman in herself is male: the surveyed female. Thus she turns herself into an object—and most particularly into an object of vision: a sight.   (47)

In the European tradition of writing and other forms of representation, the woman's body is the object of a single desire that is shared by both lovers; her body is viewed as the site of erotic pleasure. The woman writing heterosexual desire becomes a split subject just as the troubadour splits himself into the male writer, the desiring subject, and the feminine other. The difference for the woman writer is that she identifies with the women in the tradition at the same time that the very act of writing moves her into the subject position traditionally associated with the masculine. There is an inevitable double bind for a woman writing in a tradition in which the surveyor, or we might say the representer or the writer, occupies the masculine position. For the woman to represent the sexual difference, or the feminine difference that allows for the illusion of heterosexuality in romantic love, she has to make a double structural move. She first moves into the masculine position of the writer, or the lover: hence the princess is depicted as fetishizing M. de Nemours and gazing at his portrait; she is a desiring subject. However, the site of eroticism in this novel as in every novel in the tradition is the woman's body. There is no possibility of a "sexual relation" if the scene continues with the woman in the position of desiring subject who gazes at an object of desire; hence M. de Nemours's menacing presence in the pavilion scene. If Mme de Lafayette had said, for instance, "La Princesse de Clèves, c'est moi!" it would have made no impact. In fact, it would have made no sense, nor would it be possible, given the feminine and masculine positions in the writing process, for her to say, "Le duc de Nemours, c'est moi!" There is a structural impasse for a woman writing in a system in which the function of the feminine is to represent male self-difference (Johnson)—in which male identity is restructured into its masculine and feminine dimensions through writing the self as the feminine. Or, as has been suggested, in which the woman in the triangle is an illusory object of male desire, a third term, a figure of the male rivals' mutual desire or of their desire to occupy each other's place, to displace each other (Girard; Nelli; Sedgwick).

One of the most brilliant features of *La Princesse de Clèves* is that its action turns on the impossibility of either the characters' or the reader's distinguishing between representation and "the real thing." *Gallantry* is the term Mme de Lafayette uses to describe the code of behavior in love affairs, which are spreading during the last years of Henry II's reign and pandemic in the court of Louis XIV (80; 14). I define *gallantry* as the "performance" of courtly love, in the same way that *sprezzatura* describes the affectation of chivalric behavior among gentlemen of the aristocracy in Castiglione's *Book of the Courtier*. In other words, gallantry, like *sprezzatura*, is the calculated and deliberate performance of something that has come to be considered "the real thing," that is, courtly love and chivalry. This "real thing," however, was originally an elaborate system of representation, highly coded and ritualistic, such as the performance that created the illusion of heterosexual romance, of "true love" in the troubadour literature.

My approach to teaching *La Princesse de Clèves* is to focus on the princess as a "good reader." The novel is a critique of courtly love and is as ironic as *Madame Bovary*—also required reading—in its portrayal of literary seduction and of romantic love. In both novels the heroine falls prey to the representation of the role of the heroine in heterosexual romance; Lafayette gives the princess an awareness of the seduction of representation and mimesis and prepares the reader for her canny refusal to play the role written for her in the narrative tradition, in spite of—and this is important if the students are to understand the pleasure of reading—her strong desire to do so, a desire that has been mediated by the very representations that she refuses. Emma Bovary's tragedy is her lack of awareness of the dangers of representation and her desire to identify with the adulterous heroines in romantic love narratives, including Iseut, the heroine of the first book the students read.

The key scenes point to the mediation of desire through representation. Once the students have a sense of this aspect of the novel, they are able to discuss the role of each stolen portrait, of each internal narrative that replicates the princess's story in spite of her insistence that her story is original: "il n'y a pas dans le monde une autre aventure pareille à la mienne" (187) ("there could be no other story like mine in the world" [110]). They see that each tale of gallantry becomes a mirror that reflects the story we are reading. The princess's ultimate awareness that it is impossible to believe a lover who plays his role so expertly, to see beyond the veil of representation, is prefigured when she sees M. de Nemours steal her portrait. She knows that he in turn has seen her seeing him steal her image: "Mme de Clèves aperçut par un des rideaux, qui n'était qu'à demi fermé, M. de Nemours [. . .]" (136) ("Through one of the curtains, which was only half drawn, Mme de Clèves caught sight of M. de Nemours" [64]). In this play their gaze is never mutual, neither in the stolen portrait scene nor in the pavilion scene; androgynous fusion is an illusion created by the philter. At the novel's conclusion, the curtain is drawn open, and the princess decides to withdraw from the prison of representation to become one of those individuals "qui ont des vues plus grandes et plus éloignées" (237–38) ("who have a more elevated and more detached vision" [155]). The princess's consciousness, along with her ultimate choice of autonomy, offers an example not of inimitable virtue but of the certain knowledge that to learn the language of the recurring myths and narrative models of romantic love is to gain the ability to think critically about them, freeing a subject from identifying with representations of femininity and masculinity, from mistaking them for a lived or livable reality.

Teaching *La Princesse de Clèves* in a Women's Studies Course

Elizabeth J. MacArthur

I most often teach *La Princesse de Clèves* in a course on French women writers in translation, with a group of eighty to one hundred students. More accurately the course is a survey of French women novelists from the seventeenth century to the present in which we read *La Princesse de Clèves*, Staël's *Corinne*, Sand's *Indiana*, Colette's *La vagabonde*, and Marguerite Duras's *L'amant*. In 1995 for the first time I replaced *Corinne* with Graffigny's *Lettres d'une Péruvienne*, Charrière's *Mistriss Henley*, and Claire de Duras's *Ourika*, all now available from the MLA. I have chosen these novels for several reasons, including their availability in paperback in English, their interest and accessibility to under-graduate students, their shared themes, and my own taste. Like many courses, this one meets several agendas simultaneously: it fulfills requirements in for-eign literature in translation and in writing for students from a variety of de-partments, but it also attracts students majoring in French or women's studies. It will be many students' only exposure to French literature or to literature by women, and it will be most students' first exposure to a feminist perspective on literature.

I have organized the course around the notion of interpretive communities in which women play a central role. It is important to stress at the outset that I mean not communities of women but communities of both sexes in which women as well as men are seen to have power. Influenced by the work of Gér-ard Genette and Nancy K. Miller, I hypothesize that our conceptions of which books—and which lives—are plausible depend enormously on the communi-ties to which we belong. One purpose of the course, then, is to create an inter-pretive community within which students can read the novels as valuable and can broaden their ideas of what life choices and gender roles are possible. Ju-dith Butler proposes that "gender identity might be reconceived as a per-sonal/cultural history of received meanings subject to a set of imitative practices which refer laterally to other imitations and which, jointly, construct the illusion of a primary and interior gendered self or parody the mechanism of that construction" (138). Gender roles are stories we tell and perform, plots we learn from culture ("received meanings") and act out ("imitative practices") in our own ways. The more such stories students encounter and the greater the variety of such stories circulating in culture, the more likely it is that divergent performances of gender roles will be possible and accepted in the culture.

In presenting both the novel and the historical context in which it was writ-ten and received, I focus on the circulation and discussion of stories within communities. I suggest that *La Princesse de Clèves* is largely about the way the princess uses the stories she hears to shape her life; I also describe how the court and salon circles that were Lafayette's audience circulated and discussed the novel and how Lafayette capitalized on her readers' desire for the work. I then try to structure the class so that my twentieth-century California students can circulate and discuss stories in roughly analogous ways. Of course I encourage them to recognize the literary techniques in the novels we study, but in fact for most of the students the course serves above all as an opportunity to encounter and come to terms with stories very different from those they have previously read, heard, or seen on television. I like to think that even students who don't read all the novels on the syllabus are being exposed to a wider repertoire of stories and gender positions.

Interpretive Communities within the Novel

The first story that shapes the princess's life is not one she hears but one into which she is thrust at age sixteen: the story of the court of Henri II. Critics have demonstrated that Lafayette's depiction of the court grants powerful roles to women: Lafayette writes history as a story that has both female and male leading characters (see Beasley, *Revising*). Her narration consistently emphasizes the interconnections between political events and amorous intrigues, uncovering the hidden stories that motivate visible historical actions. "Il y avait tant d'intérêts et tant de cabales différentes, et les dames y avaient tant de part que l'amour était toujours mêlé aux affaires et les affaires à l'amour (81) ("There were countless interests at stake, countless different factions, and women played such a central part in them that love was always entangled with politics and politics with love" [14]), explains the narrator, and Mme de Chartres tells her daughter, "Depuis douze ans que ce prince règne, [Diane de Poitiers] est maîtresse absolue de toutes choses" (98) ("The King has been on the throne for twelve years now, and [Diane de Poitiers] has throughout that time had sovereign authority in all matters" [30]). The main historical event that occurs during the novel, the peace treaty, is represented primarily as two marriages. In Lafayette's rewriting of history, then, it is the interactions between women and men that determine the course of events; in a sense, Lafayette inserts her protagonist into a community that she as historian has already interpreted as allowing some power to women.

Yet despite Lafayette's focus on the role and power of women, the world the princess inhabits grants greater autonomy and authority to men. The princess spends much of her time in spaces dominated by women, such as the reine dauphine's apartments, but instead of making her satisfied with the power of women at court these experiences seem to make her wish for even more independence from men. In discussing Lafayette's use of history with the class, I ask whether the princess's decision to spend half of every year in a convent might not be connected with her previous positive experiences in communities of women, whether alone with her mother or in the reine dauphine's apartments. To what extent is the historical story Lafayette tells readers meant to explain the princess's ultimate refusal of court life?

Presenting the novel as a parable about the circulation of stories within interpretive communities allows me to address in a relatively coherent and time-efficient way two central sets of issues that perplex students: why the princess makes seemingly implausible decisions, notably to confess her love to her husband and to refuse Nemours at the end, and what role is played by the internal narratives, the seemingly digressive stories that many readers believe impede the progress of the princess's story. For it is the princess's "reading" of the stories she hears that leads her to shape her life as she does. I ask students to read the internal narratives especially carefully and to make lists of all the things the princess might learn from hearing them. We then discuss how what she has learned helps motivate the major decisions she makes. How do the stories circulating at court shape the story of her own life?

Male infidelity is a recurrent theme. The story of Anne Boleyn and Henry VIII (133–35; 60–63) provides one of many striking examples of men seducing and rejecting, even destroying, women; the story of Diane de Poitiers and the kings (93–99; 26–31), like the story of the vidame's relations with Mme de Thémines (149–59; 75–83), suggests that men are most likely to continue loving women if their love is not reciprocated (or does not appear to be). Such tales, combined with the princess's knowledge of Nemours's reputation, help explain her final decision not to marry him. One might also discuss the emphasis in many of the stories on control over one's passions. Mme de Thémines succeeds in reawakening the vidame's love by exercising such self-mastery that he thinks she no longer loves him (149; 75); the vidame's inability to stop pursuing love affairs despite the queen's warnings leads to his downfall (155, 166; 80, 90). The princess's desire to maintain control over her feelings for Nemours even when the rest of society would no longer consider them inappropriate might then be explained by the lessons she has learned from such tales, as well as from her mother's repeated advice.

The most important example of the circulation and interpretation of a story within the novel, however, is the princess's own confession to her husband. I ask students to point to the conversations and tales that prepare the way for this confession; in particular we analyze her husband's commentary on the Sancerre-Tournon story (116–17; 45–46) and the chain of reflections set in motion in the princess by his commentary (138, 146, 168; 65, 72, 92). We then examine the process by which this most intimate of scenes between husband and wife becomes a publicly circulated tale, passing from Nemours to the vidame to his mistress, Mme de Martigues, and thence to the dauphine, who promptly recounts it to the princess herself (175, 181–84; 99, 104–07]). Like Mme de Thémines's letter, this confession of female passion becomes the object of considerable fascination for its listeners. The princess might well conclude that the only passion safe from public exposure is a passion kept utterly to oneself; this would help explain the autoeroticism of the famous scene of the cane and ribbons (208; 128), as well as her final decision to refuse to allow her feelings to depend in any way on another person.

Because of the importance of judgments of *invraisemblance* ("implausibility") in the reception of the novel, I focus on the fact the characters within the novel, including the princess herself, recognize the implausibility of her actions. Throughout the book the princess is described as exceptional, unique, not conforming to society's expectations about female character or behavior. Mme de Chartres has educated her daughter to be exceptional, and her final deathbed torment is the fear that the princess might "tomber comme les autres femmes" (108) ("fall like other women" [40]). After her mother's death, the princess strives to be different as much as to be virtuous. The dauphine recognizes the princess's difference when she exclaims, "[I]l n'y a que vous de femme au monde qui fasse confidence à son mari de toutes les choses qu'elle sait" (164) ("[Y]ou are the only woman in the world who confides to her husband all the things she knows" [88]). The princess's sense of being extraordinary and the other characters' judgments of her as implausible crystallize around the princess's two most important actions, her confession to her husband and her ultimate refusal of Nemours. As soon as the prince has heard the confession, "à peine put-elle s'imaginer que ce fut une vérité" (174) ("she could hardly imagine [what she had done] was true" [98]. Nemours feels flattered to be loved by a woman "si différente de toutes celles de son sexe" (175) ("so different from all others of her sex" [99]), and "Il ne savait quasi si ce qu'il avait entendu n'était point un songe, tant il y trouvait peu de vraisemblance" (178) ("He was no longer certain whether what he had heard was not a dream, so implausible did it seem to him" [101]) (see also 174, 186; 98, 110). When the princess is forced to play the role of critic of her own story, in front of the dauphine and then Nemours, she twice questions its *vraisemblance*, saying, "Cette histoire ne me paraît guère vraisemblable" (183) ("The story hardly sounds plausible to me" [106]), and then, in response to the dauphine's allusion to "l'avis de Mme de Clèves, qui soutient que cette aventure ne peut être véritable" (186) ("Mme de Clèves's view that the story must be a fiction" [108]), she replies, "Je ne crois pas en effet qu'elle le puisse être" (186) ("That is indeed my view" [108]). Once the story is out, the princess's greatest regret seems to be that "[c]'est pourtant pour cet homme, que j'ai cru si différent du reste des hommes, que je me trouve comme les autres femmes" (190–91) ("it is for this man, whom I believed so different from other men, that I have become like other women" [113]). Similarly, when the prince has died, the princess tells Nemours she is sacrificing her love for him "à un devoir qui ne subsiste que dans mon imagination" (233) ("to a duty that exists only in my imagination" [151]), and the examples of virtue she leaves behind at the end of her life are "inimitable" (239; 156). Such passages make it clear that Lafayette was aware of how extraordinary the princess's behavior would appear to readers (see Miller, "Emphasis"; Laugaa).

The Reception of the Novel

Although most late seventeenth-century readers probably found the princess's actions extraordinary and implausible, members of at least one segment of Lafayette's public would have recognized themselves, or their aspirations, in her. The women who organized and frequented the salons seem to have shared the princess's desire to escape patriarchal control and create spaces in which women reign. I describe the seventeenth-century salons to the class (drawing on the work of critics such as Carolyn Lougee, Ian Maclean, Dorothy Backer, and Roger Picard) and explain that Lafayette spent much of her life in the salons. I stress two related characteristics of the salons: the governing role played by women and the critique of marriage. The salons allowed women to create and judge literary works, as well as to construct rules for social interaction; in the salons, women were relatively free from control by fathers, husbands, and the dictates of the male-dominated Académie Française. Some *précieuses*, such as the marquise de Rambouillet's daughter Julie d'Angennes, were celebrated for deferring marriage, postponing the moment when men would regain control of their lives. Maclean, Lougee, and others have argued that salon women wanted the freedom enjoyed by men, either to refuse marriage or to be married in such a way as not to lose autonomy. Lafayette's story of the princess's rejection of Nemours would have seemed eminently plausible to this particular interpretive community.

Readers who did not share the values of the salons were of course more critical. I outline for the students the quarrel between Valincour and Charnes, focusing on Valincour's attack on the novel's *invraisemblance* ("implausibility") and Nancy Miller's interpretation of the attack ("Emphasis"). I also describe the publicity campaign orchestrated by the *Mercure galant*. What I try to convey to the students is some sense of the popularity of the novel, the excitement it generated, the way "everyone" was talking about it. Lafayette's novel was a widely circulated story, and it generated avid interest even among those who never read it (see Goldsmith in this volume; DeJean, *Ancients*). In this way the story of the princess's confession to her husband moves beyond the reine dauphine's apartments within the novel, to the Parisian salons and even provincial homes of Lafayette's contemporaries. Within *La Princesse de Clèves* women such as Mme de Thémines and the princess herself lose control of the circulation of their stories of passion; outside the novel, though, Lafayette managed to capitalize on this desire-fueled circulation of a story of female passion. It is a wonderful paradox of Lafayette's triumph that she succeeded in arousing so much desire for a story about the renunciation of desire.

The Classroom as Interpretive Community

Unsurprisingly, my students never desire Lafayette's novel as avidly as her seventeenth-century readers did. Nonetheless, I try to design the assignments and class time in such a way as to enable students to form an interpretive community of their own. Thus I devote about half the class time to discussion, despite the great number of students. I forewarn students on the first day of class that I don't believe in lecturing about literature, and I ask them for suggestions on how to facilitate discussion in such a big class. One technique is to collect a question or comment from each student at each class. I can then open discussion by having two or three students read their questions. This exercise also encourages students to reflect on the novels at least briefly before class, and by reading all the questions between classes I get a better idea of the students' interests, abilities, and confusions. I also distribute lists of plot questions and interpretive questions on each novel to help students read more carefully. For example, I ask what the princess is doing when Nemours spies on her in the pavilion, why the ribbons are yellow, what other portraits appear in the novel, who is gazing at whom in this scene as compared with the rest of the novel, and so on. Students also give brief class presentations in groups of five or six. This time-consuming exercise has a multitude of benefits: it forces students to meet with me, however fleetingly; it forces students to get together in smaller "interpretive communities" outside class; and it forces every student to speak at least once in class and thus participate in the classroom community. I urge the groups to choose focused topics, such as references to the princess as exceptional or a comparison of the endings of *Lettres d'une Péruvienne* and *La Princesse de Clèves*.

I give greater weight to papers than to the final exam, since papers allow students to engage individually with the novels. The paper topics I propose are meant to facilitate the kind of weighing of stories and gender roles that occurs within the novel. The most successful topic over the years has been an analysis of the princess's decision to refuse Nemours and to withdraw from the court. I guide class discussion toward a number of possible explanations, focusing on Mme de Chartres's influence on her daughter, the relative importance of duty and *repos*, the representation of Nemours's character, and the princess's emphasis on control and mastery. Student papers necessarily grow out of the context of these discussions, the interpretive community of the classroom, but they also reveal the students' individual engagements with the novels.

Since *La Princesse de Clèves* is the first book we study, our discussions of it serve as an introduction to the primary issues of the course. For each novel we study, I give information on the context in which the author wrote, on the author's strategies for having her work taken seriously (anonymity, male pseudonyms, etc.), and on the novel's reception by contemporaries. As with Lafayette, each author's anxiety about her own exceptional life or about the reception of her work is also inscribed within the novel, in the conflicts between the protagonist's choices and the conventional plots she is expected to follow (see Miller, "Emphasis"). All the novels reveal a frustration with the gender roles offered by society and with the restrictions on women's — and men's — lives. In *Mistriss Henley* and *Ourika* the heroine dies or is silenced because she cannot conform to society's expectations. In *La Princesse de Clèves, Lettres d'une Péruvienne, Corinne, Indiana,* and *La vagabonde,* the heroine chooses to withdraw from society to pursue a goal whose realization would be impossible within society's constraints. These withdrawals too might be viewed as a kind of death: the Princess of Clèves has been very ill and becomes detached from earthly concerns; Zilia refuses Déterville's hand in marriage and lives in her country house, outside of French society; Corinne is considered dead by her English relatives when she moves to Italy to live as she wishes; Indiana and Ralph attempt suicide before they are reborn together into their island paradise; Renée breaks off her love affair with Max and becomes increasingly absorbed in writing. Yet this death to society also makes possible a perhaps utopian alternative, a rebirth into a better existence. What each novelist represents as "better" is, however, very different; for Sand, Indiana's new life resembles an improved version of familiar patriarchal structures, in which female happiness depends on but also allows for the love of men, whereas for Colette and perhaps Graffigny and Lafayette, the new life involves a rejection of such structures.

Another recurring topic of discussion is the role of mothers within patriarchal society. To what extent are the protagonists' choices prepared by their mothers' instructions, and do those instructions perpetuate the status quo or rather allow the daughters to envision alternative possibilities for women? None of the novels provide simple answers to these questions; the Princesse de Clèves, for example, can be seen as unduly controlled by her mother's lessons, playing a role prescribed by her mother, or as partially freed from society's controls by those lessons (see Kamuf, *Fictions;* Hirsch); Corinne's stepmother, Lady Edgermond, enforces society's laws more blindly even than the men do, but Corinne herself becomes a kind of idealized, liberatory mother to her half-sister, Lucile, and Lucile's daughter, Juliet, at the novel's end; the mother of Marguerite Duras's narrator alternately pushes her to sell her body to earn money for the family and punishes her violently for doing so, yet she also enables her daughter to escape familial and social constraints in a way neither of the brothers can. It is striking how few of these protagonists have—or become—biological mothers. Zilia, Mistriss Henley, Corinne, Ourika, Indiana, and Renée have lost their mothers, and Mistriss Henley, Corinne, Ourika, and Indiana find only partially satisfactory substitutes. Mistriss Henley is the only protagonist to become pregnant, and her pregnancy becomes the source of such tension and misery that it helps explain why the other characters, or their creators, should have wished to avoid having children.

The extent to which each protagonist escapes societal constraints and fashions her own life is correlated with her use of images and texts. Art historians and film theorists have shown that throughout Western civilization women have tended to be positioned as objects of a male gaze and that this positioning grants power to men while reinforcing women's powerlessness (see Mulvey; J. Berger). (I do not have students read these theoretical texts, but I summarize them and read excerpts aloud in class.) This familiar structure of the gaze is apparent in the novels in this course; there is, for example, the famous scene in *La Princesse de Clèves* where Nemours secretly watches the princess wrapping ribbons around a cane, as well as the many performance scenes of *Corinne* and *La vagabonde*, in which the heroines are the object of male gazes. However, even these scenes, which seem to reinscribe female powerlessness in traditional ways, resist simple interpretation. For Renée and Corinne derive much of their power as subjects from their performances, and they are described as controlling the reactions of their rather passive audiences rather than being appropriated by active gazes. And if the Princesse de Clèves is the object of Nemours's gaze, she is also the subject of her own gaze at him, in the painting she has transported with her to Coulommiers, and even the subject of a kind of masturbatory gaze at herself. Marguerite Duras's narrator too uses images (real and imagined photographs) in an active process of interpreting and shaping her own life. Zilia, Mistriss Henley, Corinne, Renée, and Marguerite Duras's narrator are also writers, creating images of the world or of themselves through their own texts. These representations of women as writers and performers can be juxtaposed with Butler's discussions of performing gender.

Professors of literature often bemoan contemporary students' incompetence at close reading of texts. I too attempt to make students more attentive interpreters, not only of the books we read but also of all the cultural texts around them. Focusing on the circulation of stories within interpretive communities has the advantage, however, of acknowledging that even stories that students do not read closely might play crucial roles in their lives. Just as some of Lafayette's contemporaries who never read *La Princesse de Clèves* surely offered opinions of the princess's conduct to their friends, so some students who do not read the novel surely participate in class discussions and even use the novel in reflecting on the construction of gender roles. David Kaufer and Kathleen Carley coined the term "reverse vicariousness" to describe the way communities circulate knowledge of texts by word of mouth. If vicarious pleasure and knowledge come from reading about acts rather than experiencing them oneself, then *reverse* vicariousness would be talking about a book rather than reading it oneself. Kaufer and Carley explain that "we normally think of immediate viewing or reading as vicarious experiences for face-to-face interaction. But, in this case, a viewer or reader uses face-to-face interaction to experience the viewer or reader role vicariously" (66). And in fact we all get much of our knowledge of literature just this way. I am not proposing that we tell students not to read the books we assign; I am proposing that we recognize the importance of hasty or "distant" reading, even of conversation alone, in circulating stories and thus in making students aware of the cultural construction of gender roles and of the possibility of performing gender in new ways.

APPENDIXES

APPENDIX 1
THE QUARREL OVER *LA PRINCESSE DE CLÈVES*: PASSAGES FROM VALINCOUR, *LETTRES*, AND CHARNES, *CONVERSATIONS*

As Valincour's *Lettres* and Charnes's *Conversations* are each a few hundred pages long, it is of course difficult to extract passages from the authors' complex arguments. All we can hope to do here is to highlight a few passages that give a sense of the issues the critics considered important to debate. Both texts are in dialogue form. Each author creates a cast of fictional characters who debate the merits of the novel, much as Lafayette's audience in the salons may have done. Thus the passages chosen are often attributed to a character and are not necessarily meant to represent the voice of the author. Charnes's text is a point-by-point response to Valincour's critique. We have modernized the spelling and accents of the French texts; the translations are ours.

1

As Elizabeth Goldsmith points out in her contribution to this volume, much of the debate turns on not just the novel itself but also the role of literature in society, the role of the critic, the status of the author, and the role of the reading public.

Valincour

Valincour asks who should judge and according to what standards.

> Je vous admire, lui dis-je en l'interrompant, et je pense que vous voulez examiner *La Princesse de Clèves* selon les règles du Poème Epique. Croyez-moi, mon cher Monsieur, vous êtes un juge trop sévère, et trop savant pour elle. Ces sortes de bagatelles ne sont point de votre compétence; il faut les renvoyer aux Dames, et aux Cavaliers, qui en jugeront mieux que vous. Je n'ai point d'autres règles, que celles du bon sens, me répondit-il, et je prétends que l'on est obligé de les garder aussi bien dans une petite nouvelle, que dans un plus grand Poème Epique.   (92)

> I admire you, I said, interrupting him, but I think you want to examine *La Princesse de Clèves* according to the rules for the Epic Poem. Believe me, my dear Sir, you are too severe a judge and too learned for [this *nouvelle*]. Your competence is not for these sorts of trifles; they must be sent to the Ladies and Gentlemen who will judge it better than you. I have no

other rules than those of common sense, he answered, and I maintain that one must keep to them as much in a small *nouvelle* as in a greater Epic Poem.

Charnes

Charnes returns consistently to his primary line of defense: the novel was a huge success, and thus it is a good book. The public should have the first and last word.

"Il n'y a guère d'apparence que s'il eut eu autant de défauts dans ce Livre, qu'il [Valincour] a cru y en voir, ce Livre eut été assez heureux pour éblouir un siècle aussi éclairé que le nôtre" (ix–x) ("It can scarcely seem, were there as many flaws in this Book as [Valincour] believed there to be, that this Book would have been fortunate enough to dazzle a century as enlightened as our own").

"Les personnes de bon sens qui ne se piquent point d'écrire, sont plus disposées à rendre justice au mérite. Ils ne sont guidés que par le plaisir qu'ils goûtent, ou par l'utilité qu'ils trouvent dans l'ouvrage qu'on leur présente. Ceux-ci ont sans doute remarqué que tout ce qui pouvait rendre un récit agréable, se trouve dans *La Princesse de Clèves*" (xv–xvi) ("People with common sense who do not pride themselves on writing are better disposed to give justice to merit. They are guided only by the pleasure they taste or by the usefulness they find in the work presented to them. These people have no doubt noticed that everything that could make a story agreeable is found in *La Princesse de Clèves*").

2

La Princesse de Clèves was viewed as an exceptional novel primarily because its heroine does exceptional things.

Valincour

Valincour critiques the princess's behavior and in so doing reveals the expectations concerning the comportment of women in society. In addition, according to Valincour, the novel is implausible because the hero does not act like a hero should.

On the Novel's Plausibility

"Quand ce n'eut été que pour la bienséance, j'eusse voulu que la passion de M. de Nemours eut commencé au moins quelques jours avant celle de Mme de Clèves. Cela eut été plus régulier" (138) ("If only for the sake of propriety, I would have preferred M. de Nemours's passion to have begun at least a few days before that of Mme de Clèves. That would have been more legitimate").

"Je suis fâché seulement que l'Auteur lui [la princesse] fasse faire toutes les avances; car cela se peut appeler ainsi dans un commerce comme le sien. [. . .] Mme de Clèves voit M. de Nemours; elle l'aime la première; elle ne peut cacher sa passion, ni à sa mère, ni au chevalier de Guise" (143–44) ("I am annoyed only because the Author has her make all the advances; that is what we could call dealings such as hers. [. . .] Mme de Clèves sees M. de Nemours; she loves him first; she can hide her passion neither from her mother nor from the chevalier de Guise").

On the Aveu ("Confession") Scene

"[Un] des plus extraordinaires événements dont on ait jamais ouï parler" (39) ("[O]ne of the most extraordinary events anyone has ever heard of").

"Se trouve-t-il souvent des femmes qui fassent à leurs maris des confidences de cette nature?" (215) ("Are there many women who would confide in their husbands in this manner?").

On the Reverie Scene

"Mais, Madame, que vous semble de Mme de Clèves, qui en s'en allant à Coulommiers, y fait porter de grands tableaux? [. . .] Je suis sûr que vous me répondrez d'abord que cela n'est pas excusable" (245–46) ("But, Madame, what do you think of Mme de Clèves, who when she goes to Coulommiers has some large paintings transported? [. . .] I am sure you will answer first that this is inexcusable").

"A vous parler franchement, l'action me paraît un peu inconsidérée. [. . .] [E]lle eut mieux fait de donner à sa passion quelque satisfaction plus sensible, pourvu qu'elle eut été plus secrète" (247) ("To tell you the truth, the act appears to be a bit rash. [. . .] She would have done better to give her passion greater satisfaction, as long as it was more secret").

"[C]ela n'est pas excusable; [. . .] s'en était déjà trop pour une femme qui se piquait de vertu, que d'avoir dans son cœur les sentiments qu'elle avait, [. . .] il ne fallait pas chercher encore les moyens de les entretenir, et même de les fortifier" (246) ("This is inexcusable; [. . .] it was already too much for a woman who prided herself on being virtuous to have such feelings in her heart, [. . .] she shouldn't have looked for ways to maintain them and even to make them stronger").

On the Ending

Mme de Clèves dit ici tout ce que devrait dire M. de Nemours. C'est elle qui lui parle de sa passion, qui lui découvre tous les sentiments de son cœur, et qui le fait avec un ordre et une tranquillité qui ne se ressent guère du trouble qu'un pareil aveu donne toujours aux femmes un peu retenues. L'on dirait qu'elle n'est venue là que pour parler, et M. de Nemours pour écouter, au lieu que ce devrait être tout le contraire. A peine en seize pages trouve-t-il le moyen de lui dire deux ou trois mots à la traverse. [. . .] D'ailleurs, ajouta-t-elle, à quoi bon faire une si longue déclaration à un homme qu'elle aimait, et qu'elle avait résolu de ne pas épouser? Si elle avait assez de force pour surmonter son inclination, pourquoi n'en avait-elle pas assez pour la cacher? [. . .] En vérité, il lui [Mme de Clèves] eut été bien plus glorieux de ne rien dire. (270–71)

Mme de Clèves says here everything that M. de Nemours should say. She's the one who speaks to him about her passion, who reveals to him all the feelings of her heart and who does it with an order and a tranquillity that do not reveal the uneasiness that such a declaration always gives women who are somewhat reserved. One would think that she only came to speak and the duc de Nemours to listen, whereas it should be just the opposite. In sixteen pages he is hardly able to say two or three words in response. [. . .] If she had enough strength to overcome her inclination, why didn't she have enough to hide it? [. . .] in truth, it would have been much more glorious for her to say nothing.

Elle avoue à cet homme qu'elle a de l'amour pour lui, mais qu'elle ne veut pas l'épouser: et cela par quelle raison? La raison me semble très belle, interrompis-je brusquement, et digne du courage, et de la vertu de Mme de Clèves. Elle s'imaginait que M. de Nemours était la cause de la mort de son mari. [. . .] Elle croyait devoir ce sacrifice à la mémoire de son mari. Cette action n'est-elle pas héroïque? Elle le serait peut-être, me répondit-elle, si Mme de Clèves n'avait point eu dans l'esprit d'autre motif que celui que vous venez de rapporter. Mais écoutez-la parler elle-même. "Ce que je crois devoir à la mémoire de M. de Clèves serait faible, s'il n'était soutenu par l'intérêt de mon repos." Et qu'est-ce que [l'intérêt de son repos]? C'est la crainte de n'être plus aimée de M. de Nemours après qu'elle l'aurait épousé. Cela "lui paraît un si horrible malheur," qu'elle emploie sept ou huit pages à le dépeindre avec des termes de la plus raffinée coquetterie. Voilà-t-il pas une belle raison pour ne pas épouser un homme? Et depuis la Sapho du *Grand Cyrus*, s'est-il rencontré une femme à qui cette vision soit tombée dans l'esprit?

(273–75)

She confesses to this man that she has love for him but that she doesn't want to marry him—and for what reason? The reason seems very beautiful to me, I interrupted brusquely, and worthy of Mme de Clèves's courage and virtue. She imagined that M. de Nemours was the cause of her husband's death. [. . .] She believed she owed this sacrifice to her husband's memory. Isn't this action heroic? It would be, perhaps, she answered, if Mme de Clèves didn't have in mind another motive than the one you have just reported. But listen to her speak herself: "What I believe I owe to the memory of M. de Clèves would be a feeble resource were it not sustained by self-interest, namely my desire for tranquillity of mind." And what is this desire for tranquillity of mind? It's the fear of no longer being loved by M. de Nemours after marrying him. This "seems to her to be such a terrible unhappiness" that she takes seven or eight pages to portray it in terms of the most refined coquetry. Isn't that a lovely reason not to marry a man! And not since Sapho of *Le Grand Cyrus* has anyone encountered a woman with such a vision in mind.

Charnes

Charnes justifies the princess's extraordinary actions by consistently underscoring how they are motivated by the story. In contrast to Valincour he does not view her as weak, and he views the end as a victory for the princess. It is interesting to note that until recently most criticism followed Valincour's interpretations, especially concerning the princess.

On the Princess's Inaction When Nemours Steals Her Portrait
    "C'est pour ces raisons qu'elle prit sagement le parti de ne rien dire, et non pas par faiblesse, ni par aucun désir qu'elle eut de voir son portrait entre les mains du duc de Nemours. [. . .] Enfin l'Historien même justifie assez bien par tout ce qu'il dit, qu'on doit louer la prudence de la Princesse de Clèves en cette occasion" (54–55) ("It's for these reasons that she decides wisely to say nothing, and not out of weakness nor out of any desire to see her portrait in M. de Nemours's hands. [. . .] In short, the Historian himself justifies this quite well by everything he says; one must praise the Princesse de Clèves on this occasion").

On the Princess's Character
    Que croyez-vous, dit Damon, de ces gens, qui conviennent si facilement avec le Critique, que Mme de Clèves n'a point d'esprit, et qui prétendent défendre ce caractère d'innocence, qu'ils supposent en elle, parce qu'il ne faut que cela pour intéresser le lecteur? Ils ne sont pas meilleurs juges que lui, répondit Cléante. Ce n'est pas la faiblesse qu'ils trouvent en Mme de Clèves, qui intéresse le lecteur: c'est cette vertu qui est toujours plus forte que les mouvements de la passion de cette princesse, et qui la fait enfin sortir victorieuse du combat où l'Historien l'avait ingénieusement engagée.   (156–57)

    What do you think, said Damon, of those people who agree so willingly with the Critic and say that Mme de Clèves has no spirit and claim to defend the innocent character they suppose she has because that's enough to interest the reader? They are no better judges than he is, answered Cléante. It's not the weakness they find in Mme de Clèves that interests the reader: it's that virtue that is always stronger than the princess's passions and that allows her in the end to emerge victorious from the battle in which the Historian/Novelist had ingeniously engaged her.

On the Ending

M. de Nemours y a dit tout ce qu'il y devait dire. Mais, Mme de Clèves devait enfin triompher de toutes ses faiblesses, c'était à elle à parler beaucoup, et non pas à M. de Nemours, dont la passion devait enfin céder au devoir austère et à la généreuse résolution de Mme de Clèves. [. . .] "Et les raisons de mon repos ont besoin d'être soutenues de celles de mon devoir." Et c'est même en cela qu'on peut reconnaître que le caractère de Mme de Clèves est admirablement bien soutenu jusques au point de sa victoire.   (261–63)

M. de Nemours said everything he had to say. But Mme de Clèves had to triumph finally over all her weaknesses; it was up to her to speak at length and not up to Nemours, whose passion had to yield in the end to Mme de Clèves's austere duty and generous resolve. [. . .] "And the reasons of my tranquillity of mind need to be supported by those of my duty." It is even in this that we can recognize how admirably well supported is Mme de Clèves's character up to her victory.

3

What kind of work is *La Princesse de Clèves*? Critics of the time believed that a novel had to appear above all *vraisemblable* and that novelists were to use history to instill this essential criterion into their fictions.

Valincour

Valincour criticizes *La Princesse de Clèves* because it is *invraisemblable*, even though the author uses history.

"[I]l n'y a rien de véritable, dans tout l'ouvrage, que quelques endroits de l'histoire de France, qui, à mon sens, devraient n'y être point" (88) ("There is no truth in the entire work, except for a few passages from French history that, in my opinion, should not be there at all").

"Car enfin il me semble que la marque d'un excellent ouvrage, c'est de n'avoir rien d'absolument inutile; et je ne puis concevoir de quoi servent ici l'histoire de Mme de Tournon, celle d'Anne de Boulen, et plusieurs autres traits de l'histoire de France qui y sont répandus" (22–23) ("It seems to me that the mark of an excellent work is to have nothing extraneous. I cannot conceive of a purpose for Mme de Tournon's story, that of Anne Boleyn, and many other elements of French history that are strewn throughout").

"J'ai eu peine à comprendre le rapport qu'il peut y avoir entre ce qu'elle lui conte de Mme de Valentinois, de Mme d'Estampes, de la mort du dauphin, et l'Histoire de la Princesse de Clèves. Cependant il me semble, que dans des ouvrages de cette nature l'on ne doit rien souffrir, qui ne soit nécessairement lié au sujet" (18–19) ("I had trouble understanding what relation there could be between what she tells her about Mme de Valentinois, Mme d'Estampes, and the dauphin's death and the History/Story of the Princesse de Clèves. It seems to me, however, that in works of this nature, we must not put up with anything that is not necessarily tied to the subject").

Charnes

Charnes devotes a large part of his response to Valincour to defending Lafayette's use of history. He stresses that the laws of the genre require the use of history because that is the best way to ensure *vraisemblance*. He hails *La Princesse de Clèves* as an example of a new vision of history as well as of a new type of fiction, a new genre that needs new rules, which Valincour refuses to recognize.

On the Introduction

Ces trente-six pages qui lui [Valincour] ont semblé si longues n'ont en-nuyé que lui. Plût-à-Dieu! que nous eussions notre histoire écrite de cette manière! Je suis assuré que ces trente-six pages ont coûté plus de trente-six heures à l'Auteur, et ceux qui s'y connaissent s'en sont bien aperçues. C'est le précis de plusieurs volumes, qu'il lui a fallu étudier. Ces portraits différents de personnes qui se ressemblent par la valeur, par la haute naissance, et par tant de grandes qualités, et qu'il faut néan-moins varier, sont des chef-d'oeuvres; et je ne crains pas de dire qu'ils ap-prochent de ceux des meilleurs auteurs de l'antiquité, et qu'à l'avenir ils pourront servir de modèle aux meilleurs Historiens.   (33)

These thirty-six pages that seemed to him [Valincour] so long were bor-ing only to him. Would to God that we had our history written this way! I am sure that those thirty-six pages cost their Author more than thirty-six hours, and specialists are well aware of that. The Author had to study sev-eral volumes to do the précis of them. Those different portraits of people who resemble one another through worth, high birth, and so many great qualities, yet that had, nonetheless, to be varied, are masterpieces; and I would have no qualms in saying that they come close to the portraits of the best authors of antiquity, and in the future, they will be able to serve as models for the best historians.

On the Necessity of the Internal Narratives

"Quand l'histoire de Mme de Tournon ne donnerait pas autant de plaisir qu'elle en donne [. . .] il faudrait convenir qu'elle est bonne à cent choses dans l'endroit où l'auteur l'a mise. [. . .] Elle sert à faire que Mme de Clèves réfléchisse sur elle-même, et à lui marquer les moyens qu'elle doit prendre, pour mériter l'estime de son mari [. . .] et la moitié de ces raisons me suffira à

l'égard de l'histoire d'Anne de Boulen, en dépit de la critique" (48–49) ("Even
if the story of Mme de Tournon didn't give as much pleasure as it does [. . .]
one would have to agree that it's good for a hundred things in the place where
the Author put it. [. . .] It makes Mme de Clèves reflect about herself, and
marks out for her the steps she must take to deserve her husband's esteem
[. . .] and half of these reasons would be enough for me as concerns the story of
Anne Boleyn in spite of the criticism of it").

On the Princess's Plausibility

"Que quand il [auteur] serait bien assuré, qu'il n'y a jamais eu de Mlle de
Chartres à la Cour de Henri II l'auteur aurait pu fort bien en inventer une, sans
sortir du vraisemblable; parce qu'il peut y avoir eu bien des dames à la cour de
Henri II dont l'histoire n'a point parlé" (114) ("Even if he [the author] were
sure that there had never been a Mlle de Chartres in Henri II's court, he could
very well have invented one without going beyond the plausible (*vraisemblable*) because there could have been many women in Henri II's court whom
history has never spoken of").

On La Princesse de Clèves *as an Example of a New Genre*

Mais je dois vous dire présentement, que les Histoires galantes, qu'on
fait aujourd'hui, ne sont ni dans l'une ni dans l'autre de ces deux es-
pèces. Ce ne sont pas de ces pures fictions, où l'imagination se donne
une libre étendue, sans égard à la vérité. Ce ne sont pas aussi de celles
où l'auteur prend un sujet de l'histoire, pour l'embellir et le rendre
agréable par ses inventions. C'en est une troisième espèce, dans la-
quelle, ou l'on invente un sujet, ou l'on en prend un qui ne soit pas uni-
versellement connu; et on l'orne de plusieurs traits d'histoire, qui en
appuient la vraisemblance, et réveillent la curiosité et l'attention du
lecteur. On pourrait dire, que j'invente la description que j'en donne. Je
ne fais pourtant que la tirer du sujet même, et je ne puis pas en aller
chercher une chez les anciens, puisque ces sortes d'ouvrages sont une
invention de nos jours.   (129–30)

But I must tell you presently that the *Histoires galantes* that are being
written today are neither of the one nor of the other of these two kinds
[of writing]. They are not pure fictions, where the imagination has free
range with no concern for the truth. Neither are they like those fictions
where the author takes a subject from history in order to embellish it and
make it pleasant through his inventions. They are a third kind, in which
one either invents a subject or takes one that is not universally known;
and one adorns it with several features from history that sustain plausibility [*vraisemblance*] and awaken the reader's curiosity and attention. One
could say that I'm inventing the description I'm giving of this genre.
However, I am only drawing it from the subject itself, and I can't go look-

ing for it among the ancients since these sorts of works are an invention of our day.

Enfin nos derniers auteurs ont pris une voie qui leur a semblé plus propre à s'attacher le lecteur, et à le divertir; et ils ont inventé les Histoires galantes. [. . .] Ce ne sont plus des poèmes ou des romans assujettis à l'unité de temps, de lieu, et d'action, et composés d'incidents merveilleux et mêlés les uns dans les autres: Ce sont des copies simples et fidèles de la véritable histoire, souvent si ressemblantes, qu'on les prend pour l'histoire même. Ce sont des actions particulières de personnes privées ou considérées dans un état privé, qu'on développe et qu'on expose à la vue du public dans une suite naturelle [. . .] on peut souvent considérer les actions qu'elles contiennent, comme les ressorts secrets des événements mémorables, que nous avons appris dans l'Histoire. [. . .] Il ne s'agit pas ici d'un poème épique, d'un roman, ni d'une tragédie. Il s'agit d'une Histoire suivie, et qui représente les choses de la manière qu'elles se passent dans le cours ordinaire du monde.   (134–36)

In short, our recent authors have taken a path that seems more likely to them to attract the reader and to divert him; and they have invented these *Histoires galantes*. [. . .] They are no longer Poems or novels subject to the unities of time, place, and action and composed of marvelous [fantastic] incidents mixed up together. These *Histoires galantes* are simple and true copies of real history, which they often resemble so closely that they are taken for history itself. These are particular actions of private people or considered private that are developed and exposed to the public view in a natural sequence [. . .] the actions they show can often be considered as the secret forces of the memorable events we have learned in History. [. . .] It is not a matter here of an epic poem, a novel, or a tragedy. It's a matter of a sustained History/Story that represents things in the way they take place in the ordinary course of the world.

Part 1

From the first sentence the court of Henri II is described in superlative terms like "n'ont jamais paru en France" ("never has France seen"). What is the effect of these superlatives?

Diane de Poitiers (Mme de Valentinois) was Henri II's mistress; Catherine de Médicis was his wife and the queen.

Throughout the descriptions of the courtiers, pay particular attention to the following characters: the Prince de Clèves; the duc de Nemours; Mme de Chartres; Mlle de Chartres, who will become the Princesse de Clèves.

Mlle de Chartres's upbringing is crucial to the novel. Read carefully the paragraph that begins, "Il parut alors . . ." (76) ("There appeared at court . . ." [9]). How does Mme de Chartres's education of her daughter differ from other mothers' education of their daughters? What value does Mme de Chartres give to virtue? Notice the importance she places on "tranquillité," which will be a key concept throughout the novel. To understand this concept better, read (several pages further) the last sentence of the paragraph that begins, "Les personnes galantes sont toujours bien aises . . ." (83) ("Women who enjoy affairs of the heart . . ." [16]).

When Mlle de Chartres visits the jewel merchant, she loses her tranquillity (77; 10). What words express her reaction when she notices that the Prince de Clèves is looking at her? Notice the repetition of the verb *admirer* and the adjective *admirable* ("amaze" and "amazing"); in the seventeenth century, *admirer* meant to see with surprise.

Pay close attention to the paragraph that begins, "Mme de Chartres, qui avait eu tant d'application . . ." (80) ("Mme de Chartres, who had made such efforts to instil . . ." [13–14]), in which Lafayette describes the dangers of love and of the court. An understanding of these intertwined dangers is important to an understanding of the novel.

Mary Stuart is the reine dauphine; she will become the queen of Scotland. Her father is James V and her husband will become the king of France, François II. Speaking with Mlle de Chartres, she introduces the notion of jealousy, another key notion in the novel (84–85; 17–18). Her story explaining why the queen and Mme de Valentinois hate her—because they were jealous of her mother, Marie de Guise — constitutes the first of the five internal narratives (sometimes called "digressions"). Each concerns verifiable historical characters whose actions or destinies relate to the story of the Princesse de Clèves.

In the paragraph beginning, "Le chevalier de Guise lui avait donné quelque sorte de jalousie . . ." (86) ("The Chevalier de Guise had to some extent provoked his jealousy . . ." [19]), M. de Clèves proposes marriage and foreshadows his own unhappiness by describing his feelings for Mlle de Chartres as "d'une nature qui le rendrait éternellement malheureux si elle n'obéissait que par devoir aux volontés de madame sa mère" (86) ("of a kind that would make him eternally unhappy if she obeyed her mother's wishes only out of duty" [19]). Pay close attention to the word *devoir* ("duty"); this word in all its forms (as noun and verb) is important throughout the novel.

Mme de Chartres is not able to arrange the advantageous marriage she wanted for her daughter. Why not?

At the ball celebrating the engagement of the duc de Lorraine, Mme de Clèves and Nemours fall in love at first sight. Pay close attention to the description of their meeting, starting with the paragraph that begins, "Elle passa tout le jour des fiançailles . . ." (90) ("She spent the whole of the day of the betrothal . . ." [23]).

After this first encounter Mme de Clèves sees Nemours everywhere. In the paragraph beginning, "Les jours suivants, elle le vit . . ." (92) ("On the days that followed, she saw him . . ." [25]), the connection between physical and psychological space is introduced. Nemours is everywhere, and Mme de Clèves cannot escape him; he is everywhere in her world, which becomes a closed space.

What follows (93–99; 26–31) is the second internal narrative about Mme de Valentinois. One of the novel's main themes is introduced here when Mme de Chartres says, "Si vous jugez sur les apparences en ce lieu-ci . . ." (94) ("If you judge by appearances in this place . . ." (26).

Read carefully Mme de Chartres's dying words to her daughter (108; 39–40); they are key to an understanding of the novel.

Part 2

This part of the novel begins with the third internal narrative, which introduces the idea of an *aveu*, an avowal or confession. Pay attention to the paragraph beginning, "Je vous donne, lui dis-je, le conseil que je prendrais pour moi-même . . ." (116) (" 'I am giving you,' I told him, 'the advice I would follow myself . . .' " [46]). You will see later how this statement foreshadows an important episode. This internal narrative also illustrates the theme of contradictory emotions (or the Pascalian notion of *contrariétés*). When Mme de Tournon dies, Estouteville feels two contradictory emotions.

Read carefully the scene of Nemours's visit to Mme de Clèves after his return from England (126–28; 55–56). He lets her know of his love indirectly. Note her reactions in the paragraph beginning, "Mme de Clèves entendait aisément la part qu'elle avait . . ." (127) ("Mme de Clèves had no difficulty in perceiving . . ." [56]). Subsequently, she tries to avoid Nemours but does not succeed; this is a development of the notion of a closed world from which there is no exit.

The fourth internal narrative begins, "Elle était d'une bonne maison d'Angleterre . . ." (133) ("She came from a good English house . . ." [61]), and is about Anne Boleyn, one of Henri VIII's wives. This story develops the theme of jealousy.

Immediately following this internal narrative is the scene in which Nemours steals a portrait of Mme de Clèves, who sees the theft but says nothing, while Nemours sees that she sees his theft. Notice the descriptions of the princess's turmoil, which develops the notion of contradictory emotions, or *contrariétés*. She is happy to be the accomplice of a man she loves but is also filled with remorse for loving a man who is not her husband. She remembers her husband's story about Mme de Tournon and thinks about confessing her love for Nemours to Clèves. This sets up the most famous scene in the novel.

Before getting to the confession scene, you will read the lost letter episode, which develops the themes of appearances and of male infidelity. The princess's reaction to the letter is key; she will continue to remember her feelings of jealousy.

The vidame de Chartres's story, explaining his own relationship to the love letter, constitutes the fifth internal narrative (149–57; 75–83).

Part 3

Notice how many women the vidame de Chartres is betraying.

In the scene in which Nemours explains the letter to the princess, note the shifts in her feelings for him. What does she feel after she and Nemours have sent the letter? What does she ask herself in her interior monologue (167–78; 91–92)?

The princess decides to go to the country — to Coulommiers — to avoid Nemours. Does she succeed in escaping him?

The confession scene starts with the paragraph beginning, "Il entendit que M. de Clèves disait à sa femme . . ." (169) ("He heard M. de Clèves saying to his wife . . ." [93–94]). Notice the reactions of each of the men and of the princess herself.

Part 4

When Nemours visits Mme de Clèves, who refuses to see him, you will find further development of the theme of contradictory emotions, or *contrariétés*. Notice the paragraph beginning, "M. de Nemours sut bientôt . . ." (201) ("M. de Nemours soon discovered . . ." [121]).

M. de Clèves also suffers from contradictory emotions that he is unable to control. Read carefully the paragraph beginning, "N'en doutez pas, madame . . ." (204) ("Have no doubts on that score, Madame . . . " [124]).

The princess flees once again to Coulommiers and is unable (again) to escape Nemours. Compare her reactions to the painting of Nemours and to the real man.

When the spy reports to M. de Clèves about Nemours's visit to Coulommiers, how does M. de Clèves react? Why does he believe the spy?

What is the princess's reaction to her husband's death?

The scene at the silk merchant develops the theme of closed space.

Mme de Clèves sees Nemours at the vidame de Chartres's and makes a second confession. What are her reasons for refusing Nemours?

At the end of the novel, does the princess manage to find tranquillity? How do you interpret the last line?

GENEALOGY, *LA PRINCESSE DE CLÈVES*

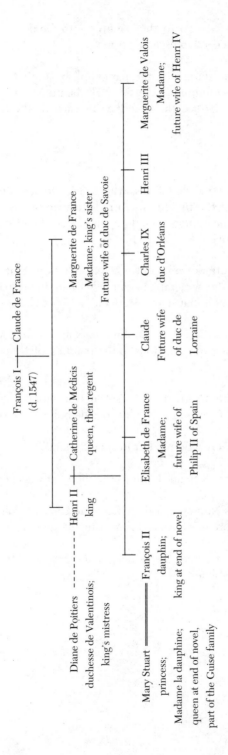

François I
(d. 1547) ⎯⎯ Claude de France

Diane de Poitiers
duchesse de Valentinois;
king's mistress

Henri II ⎯ Catherine de Médicis
king   queen, then regent

Marguerite de France
Madame; king's sister
Future wife of duc de Savoie

Mary Stuart ⎯⎯ François II
princess;   dauphin;
Madame la dauphine;   king at end of novel
queen at end of novel,
part of the Guise family

Elisabeth de France
Madame;
future wife of
Philip II of Spain

Claude
Future wife
of duc de
Lorraine

Charles IX
duc d'Orléans

Henri III

Marguerite de Valois
Madame;
future wife of Henri IV

The story takes place in 1558–59, the year of King Henri II's death and of the weddings of his daughter Elisabeth and of his sister Marguerite. Elizabeth I has just become queen of England, and Philip II, king of Spain.

There are several political factions at court. The principal oppositions are Catherine de Médicis versus Diane de Poitiers, Catherine and Diane versus Mary Stuart, and the Guise family (including Mary Stuart) versus the Montmorency family, protected by the king.

Note: *Dauphin* means heir to the throne. When François II becomes king, he is no longer the dauphin.

NOTES ON CONTRIBUTORS

Faith E. Beasley is associate professor of French at Dartmouth College. She is the author of *Revising Memory: Women's Fiction and Memoirs in Seventeenth-Century France* (1990) and of articles on seventeenth-century French women writers, the salons, and the development of literary taste during the seventeenth century. She is writing a book on the role of the seventeenth century in the creation of France's national identity.

Anne Callahan is professor of French at Loyola University, Chicago. She is the co-author of *Erotic Love in Literature: From Medieval Legend to Romantic Illusion* (1982) and has published articles on Rousseau, Sand, Colette, Duras, and the *trobairitz*. She is completing *The Voice of Pleasure: The Troubadour Effect in Fictions of Heterosexual Desire*, on the representation of "the feminine" as male self-difference in heterosexual romantic love narratives.

Julia V. Douthwaite is associate professor of French at the University of Notre Dame. She is the author of *Exotic Women: Literary Heroines and Cultural Strategies in Ancien Régime France* (1992) and of articles on topics such as monsters and feral children and on writers such as Graffigny, Prévost, and Rousseau. She is at work on *The "Wild Girl" and Natural Man: Literature, Science, and the Popular Imagination, 1724–1818*.

James F. Gaines is professor of French at Southeastern Louisiana University. He is the author of *Social Structures in Molière's Theater* (1984) and *Pierre Du Ryer and His Tragedies: From Envy to Liberation* (1987). He has edited, with Perry Gethner, Du Ryer's 1638 tragedy *Lucrèce* (1994) and, with Michael Koppisch, *Approaches to Teaching Molière's* Tartuffe *and Other Plays* (1995). He has written numerous essays devoted to the authors already cited as well as to Corneille, Boileau, Tallemant des Réaux, and La Bruyère and to issues of social, theatrical, and aesthetic values in the seventeenth century. He is working on a book tentatively entitled *Molière and Paradox*.

Elizabeth C. Goldsmith is associate professor of French at Boston University. Her publications include *Exclusive Conversations: The Art of Interaction in Seventeenth-Century France* (1988), *Writing the Female Voice: Essays in Epistolary Literature* (1989), and *Going Public: Women and Publishing in Early Modern France* (edited with Dena Goodman, 1995). She is working on a study of women's autobiography in the seventeenth century.

Rae Beth Gordon is associate professor of French literature at the University of Connecticut, Storrs. She is the author of *Ornament, Fantasy, and Desire in Nineteenth-Century French Literature* (1992). She has completed a book-length manuscript on cabaret and early cinema entitled *Why the French Love Jerry Lewis*. In addition to several essays on nineteenth-century French poetry, she has published a number of articles on the Parisian cabaret and early French cinema.

Louise K. Horowitz is professor of French at Rutgers University, Camden, and a member of the Rutgers University, New Brunswick, graduate faculty. She is the author of *Love and Language: A Study of the Classical French Moralist Writers* (1977) and of *Honoré d'Urfé* (1984). Her most recent publications have focused on patterns of origin, identity, and repetition in Racine's tragedies and Molière's comedies, as well as in *La Princesse de Clèves*.

Katharine Ann Jensen is associate professor of French and of women's and gender studies at Louisiana State University. She is the author of *Writing Love: Letters, Women, and the Novel in France, 1605–1776* (1995) and of various articles on women writers in ancien régime France. She is working on a book on famous women's accounts of mother-daughter relations in French literature from the seventeenth century to the early twentieth century.

Marie-Paule Laden is visiting scholar in the French department at the University of California, Berkeley. She is the author of *Self-Imitation in the Eighteenth-Century Novel* (1987). She is working on a book on Isabelle de Charrière.

Michèle Longino is associate professor of French at Duke University. She is the author of *Performing Motherhood: The Sévigné Correspondence* (1991) and numerous articles on seventeenth-century French literature. She is at work on a second book, tentatively entitled *The Staging of Exoticism in Seventeenth-Century France*.

John D. Lyons is Commonwealth Professor of French at the University of Virginia. He is the author of *The Tragedy of Origins: Pierre Corneille and Historical Perspective* (1996) and numerous articles on seventeenth-century French theater and narrative. He is writing a study of the theoretical discourse about tragedy in seventeenth-century France.

Elizabeth J. MacArthur is associate professor of French at the University of California, Santa Barbara. She is the author of *Extravagant Narratives: Closure and Dynamics in the Epistolary Form* (1990) and articles on epistolarity and on garden design from Versailles to Ermonville. She is writing a book on liberalism and reading publics in eighteenth-century France, provisionally entitled *Embodying the Public Sphere*.

Louis MacKenzie is associate professor of French and chair of Romance languages and literature at the University of Notre Dame. He is the author of *Strategies of Fragmentation in Pascal's* Lettres provinciales (1988). He has published on authors ranging from Du Bellay to Mallarmé and Gide, as well as Pascal, Racine, and La Bruyère. He is working on a study of poetry about poets.

Éva Pósfay is associate professor of French at Carleton College. She has published articles on Lafayette and Montpensier and coauthored the French reader *Vagabondages littéraires: Initiation à la littérature d'expression française* (1996).

Lewis C. Seifert is associate professor in the Department of French Studies at Brown University. He is the author of *Fairy Tales, Sexuality, and Gender in France, 1690–1715: Nostalgic Utopias* (1996). He has written articles on seventeenth-century literature and is currently working on a book on civility and masculinity in early modern France.

Harriet Stone is associate professor of Romance languages and literature and comparative literature at Washington University in Saint Louis. She is the author of *Royal Disclosure: Problematics of Representation in French Classical Tragedy* (1987), *The Classical Model: Literature and Knowledge in Seventeenth-Century France* (1996), and articles on Racine, Lafayette, and orientalism, among other subjects. She is editing an issue of *L'Esprit Créateur* entitled *Racine for the Next Millennium*.

Inge Crosman Wimmers is professor of French studies at Brown University. Her publications include *Metaphoric Narration in* A la recherche du temps perdu (1978), *Poetics of Reading: Approaches to the Novel* (1988), and *The Reader in the Text: Essays on Audience and Interpretation* (edited with Susan Suleiman, 1980). She is completing a book on rereading Proust from new critical perspectives.

Kathleen Wine is associate professor of French at Dartmouth College. She has published articles addressing the question of genre in d'Urfé, La Fontaine, and Lafayette. She has completed a book-length manuscript on the interrelations of genre and politics in *L'Astrée*.

SURVEY PARTICIPANTS

Mary McAleer Balkan, *Seton Hall University*
Richard Danner, *Ohio University*
Joan DeJean, *University of Pennsylvania*
Dean de la Motte, *Guilford College*
Ruth Essex, *Ben-Gurion University of the Negev*
Perry Gethner, *Oklahoma State University*
Timothy Hampton, *University of California, Berkeley*
Patrick Henry, *Whitman College*
Michael S. Koppisch, *Michigan State University*
David LaGuardia, *Dartmouth College*
Richard W. Lemp, *United States Air Force Academy*
Terese Lyons, New York, NY
Anne M. Menke, San Francisco, CA
David Mickelsen, *University of Utah*
Michael Paulson, *Kutztown University*
Gervais E. Reed, *Lawrence University*
Timothy J. Reiss, *New York University*
Jérôme de Romanet, *State University College of New York, Geneseo*
Sylvie Romanowski, *Northwestern University*
Shelley Sewall, *University of California, Davis*
Marie-Odile Sweetser, *University of Illinois, Chicago*
Eva Van Ginneken, *California State University, Fullerton*
Allen Wood, *Purdue University*

WORKS CITED

Adam, Antoine. *Histoire de la littérature française au XVIIe siècle*. 5 vols. Paris: Mondiales, 1962.

Albanese, Ralph, Jr. "Aristocratic Ethos and Ideological Codes." Henry 87–103.

Autour de Madame de La Fayette. Spec. issue of *Dix-septième siècle* 181.4 (1993): 607–746.

Backer, Dorothy. *Precious Women*. New York: Basic, 1974.

Beasley, Faith E. "Lafayette H/historienne: Rescripting Plausibility." Beasley, *Revising* 190–243.

———. "Marie-Madeleine Pioche de la Vergne, comtesse de Lafayette (1634–1693)." Sartori and Zimmerman 272–84.

———. "Le plaisir du public: Querelles critiques et littéraires." *Ordre et contestation au temps des classiques*. Paris: Biblio 17, 1992. 179–85.

———. *Revising Memory: Women's Fiction and Memoirs in Seventeenth-Century France*. New Brunswick: Rutgers UP, 1990.

Beaunier, André. *L'amie de la Rochefoucauld*. Paris: Flammarion, 1927.

———. *La jeunesse de Mme de Lafayette*. Paris: Flammarion, 1926.

Bédier, Joseph, ed. *The Romance of Tristan and Iseut*. New York: Pantheon, 1965.

Benjamin, Walter. "The Work of Art in the Age of Mechanical Reproduction." *Illuminations*. Trans. Harry Zohn. New York: Schocken, 1978. 217–51.

Berger, John. *Ways of Seeing*. London: BBC, 1972.

Berger, Robert W. *A Royal Passion: Louis XIV as Patron of Architecture*. Cambridge: Cambridge UP, 1994.

Biet, Christian. "Droit et fiction: La représentation du mariage dans *La Princesse de Clèves*." *Mme de Lafayette, La Princesse de Montpensier, La Princesse de Clèves*. Spec. issue of *Littératures classiques* (Supplément 1990): 33–54.

Bishop, Morris. *A Survey of French Literature: Volume One: The Middle Ages to 1800*. 2nd ed. Orlando: Harcourt, 1965.

Boileau-Despréaux, Nicolas. "L'art poétique." Boileau-Despréaux, *Œuvres* 159–88.

———. "Les héros de roman." Boileau-Despréaux, *Œuvres* 286–310.

———. *Œuvres*. Ed. G. Mongrédien. Paris: Garnier, 1961.

———. "Satire X." Boileau-Despréaux, *Œuvres* 67–88.

Bray, René. *Formation de la doctrine classique*. Paris: Nizet, 1927.

Brooks, Peter. *The Novel of Worldliness*. Princeton: Princeton UP, 1969.

Burke, Peter. *The Fabrication of Louis XIV*. New Haven: Yale UP, 1992.

Butler, Judith. *Gender Trouble: Feminism and the Subversion of Identity*. New York: Routledge, 1990.

Butor, Michel. "On *The Princess de Clèves*." Trans. P. Hapgood. Lyons 155–59. Rpt. of "Sur *La Princesse de Cleves*." *Répertoire I*. Paris: Minuit, 1960. 74–78.

Castiglione, Baldassare de. *Book of the Courtier*. New York: Penguin, 1976.

Chamard, Henri, and Gustave Rudler. "Les sources historiques de *La Princesse de Clèves*." *Revue du XVIe siècle* 1 (1914): 92–131, 289–321; 5 (1917): 1–20, 231–43.

Charnes, Jean-Antoine, Abbé de. *Conversations sur la critique de* La Princesse de Clèves. 1679. Ed. François Weil et al. Tours: U de Tours, 1973.

Chodorow, Nancy. *The Reproduction of Mothering: Psychoanalysis and the Sociology of Gender*. Berkeley: U of California Press, 1978.

Cholakian, Patricia F. *Rape and Writing in the* Heptaméron *of Marguerite de Navarre*. Carbondale: Southern Illinois UP, 1991.

Chrétien de Troyes. *Arthurian Romances*. New York: Penguin, 1991.

Cohn, Dorrit. *Transparent Minds: Narrative Modes for Presenting Consciousness in Fiction*. Princeton: Princeton UP, 1978.

Conley, Tom. "The Graphics of Dissimulation: Between *Heptaméron* 10 and *L'histoire tragique*." Lyons and McKinley 65–81.

Coulet, Henri. "Le roman héroïque." Coulet, *Le roman* 160–83.

———. *Le roman jusqu'à la révolution*. Paris: Colin, 1967.

———. "Les romans de Madame de Lafayette." Coulet, *Le roman* 252–62.

Cuénin, Micheline. *Roman et société sous Louis XIV: Mme de Villedieu*. 2 vols. Paris: Champion, 1979.

Cuénin, Micheline, and Chantal Morlet-Chantalat. "Châteaux et romans du XVIIᵉ siècle." *Dix-septième siècle* 118–19 (1978): 101–23.

Danahy, Michael. *The Feminization of the Novel*. Gainesville: U of Florida P, 1991.

———. "Le roman est-il chose femelle?" *Poétique* 25 (1976): 85–106.

———. "Social, Sexual and Human Spaces in *La Princesse de Clèves*." *French Forum* 6 (1981): 212–24.

Dante Alighieri. *The Divine Comedy*. 3 vols. New York: Bantam, 1980–84.

Davis, Natalie Zemon, and Arlette Farge, eds. *Histoire des femmes en Occident*. Vol. 3. Georges Duby and Michelle Perrot, gen. eds. Paris: Plon, 1991.

———, eds. *A History of Women in the West*. Vol. 3. Georges Duby and Michelle Perrot, gen. eds. Cambridge: Belknap–Harvard UP, 1992.

DeJean, Joan. *Ancients against Moderns: Culture Wars and the Making of a Fin de Siècle*. U of Chicago P, 1997.

———. "Female Voyeurism: Sappho and Lafayette." *Rivista di letterature moderne e comparate* 40.3 (1977): 201–15.

———. "Lafayette's Ellipses: The Privileges of Anonymity." *PMLA* 99 (1984): 884–900.

———. *Tender Geographies: Women and the Origins of the Novel in France*. New York: Columbia UP, 1991.

Derrida, Jacques. *Of Grammatology*. Trans. G. Spivak. Baltimore: Johns Hopkins UP, 1976.

Dictionnaire historique de la langue française. Paris: Dictionnaires le Robert, 1993.

Duchêne, Roger. *Mme de La Fayette, la romancière aux cent bras*. Paris: Fayard, 1988.

Elias, Norbert. *The Court Society*. Trans. Edmund Jephcott. New York: Pantheon, 1983.

———. *La société de cour*. Paris: Calmann-Lévy, 1969.

Force, Pierre. "Doute métaphysique et vérité romanesque dans *La Princesse de Clèves*." *Romanic Review* 83.2 (1992): 161–76.

Forestier, Georges. "Mme de Chartres, personnage-clé dans *La Princesse de Clèves*." *Les lettres romanes* 34 (1980): 67–76.

Francillon, Roger. *L'œuvre romanesque de Mme de Lafayette*. Paris: Corti, 1973.

François, Alexis. "De l'*Heptaméron* à *La Princesse de Clèves*." *Revue d'histoire littéraire de la France* 4 (1949): 305–21.

Furber, Donald, and Anne Callahan. *Erotic Love in Literature: From Medieval Legend to Romantic Illusion*. Troy: Whitson, 1982.

Furetière, Antoine. *Dictionnaire universel*. 1690. Paris: Robert, 1978.

Gaines, James F. "*Caractères*, Superstition, and Paradoxes in *Le misanthrope*." *Alteratives*. Ed. Warren Motte and Gerald Prince. Lexington: French Forum, 1992. 71–84.

Genette, Gérard. *Figures III*. Paris: Seuil, 1972.

———."Plausibility and Motivation." Lafayette, *Princess* [Norton ed.] 178–85.

———. "Vraisemblance et motivation." *Figures II*. Paris: Seuil, 1969. 71–99.

Girard, René. *Deceit, Desire, and the Novel: Self and Other in Literary Structure*. Trans. Yvonne Freccero. Baltimore: Johns Hopkins UP, 1972.

———. *Mensonge romantique et vérité romanesque*. Paris: Grasset, 1961.

Godenne, René. *Histoire de la nouvelle française au dix-septième siècle*. Geneva: Droz, 1970.

Goldman, Lucien. *Le dieu caché*. Paris: Gallimard, 1959.

Goldsmith, Elizabeth C. *Exclusive Conversations: The Art of Interaction in Seventeenth-Century France*. Philadelphia: U of Pennsylvania P, 1988.

Greenberg, Mitchell. *Subjectivity and Subjugation in Seventeenth-Century Drama and Prose: The Family Romance of French Classicism*. Cambridge: Cambridge UP, 1992.

Gregorio, Laurence. *Order in the Court: History and Society in* La Princesse de Clèves. Stanford: Stanford French and Italian Studies, 1986.

Guetti, Barbara Jones. " 'Travesty' and 'Usurpation' in Mme de Lafayette's Historical Fiction." *Yale French Studies* 69 (1985): 211–21.

Haase-Dubosc, Danielle. "La filiation maternelle et la femme-sujet au 17e siècle: Lecture plurielle de *La Princesse de Clèves*." *Romanic Review* 78.4 (1987): 432–60.

Haig, Stirling. *Mme de Lafayette*. New York: Twayne, 1970.

Harth, Erica. *Cartesian Women: Versions and Subversions of Rational Discourse in the Old Regime*. Ithaca: Cornell UP, 1992.

———. *Ideology and Culture in Seventeenth-Century France*. Ithaca: Cornell UP, 1983.

Henry, Patrick, ed. *An Inimitable Example: The Case for* The Princesse de Clèves. Washington: Catholic U of America P, 1992.

Hirsch, Marianne. "A Mother's Discourse: Incorporation and Repetition in *La Princesse de Clèves*." *Yale French Studies* 62 (1981): 67–87.

Horowitz, Louise K. *Love and Language*. Columbus: Ohio State UP, 1977.

————. "A Tale of Two Henry's, a Saga of Three Jacques's: *La Princesse de Clèves*." *Dalhousie French Studies* 26 (1994): 25–38.

Iser, Wolfgang. *The Act of Reading: A Theory of Aesthetic Response*. Baltimore: Johns Hopkins UP, 1978.

Johnson, Barbara. "Gender and Poetry: Charles Baudelaire and Marceline Desbordes-Valmore." *Displacements: Women, Tradition, Literatures in French*. Ed. Joan DeJean and Nancy K. Miller. Baltimore: Johns Hopkins UP, 1991. 163–81.

Judovitz, Dalia. "The Aesthetics of Implausibility: *La Princesse de Clèves*." *Modern Language Notes* 99 (1984): 1037–56.

Kamuf, Peggy. *Fictions of Feminine Desire*. Lincoln: U of Nebraska P, 1982.

————. "A Mother's Will: *The Princess of Clèves*." Kamuf, *Fictions* 67–96. Rpt. in Lafayette, *Princess* [Norton ed.] 206–30.

Kaps, Helen Karen. *Moral Perspective in* La Princesse de Clèves. Eugene: U Oregon Books, 1968.

Kaufer, David, and Kathleen Carley. *Communication at a Distance: The Influence of Print on Sociocultural Organization and Change*. Hillsdale: Erlbaum, 1993.

Koppisch, Michael S. "The Dynamics of Jealousy in the Work of Lafayette." *MLN* 94 (1979): 757–73.

Kritzman, Lawrence D. "Verba Erotica: Marguerite de Navarre and the Rhetoric of Silence." *The Rhetoric of Sexuality and the Literature of the French Renaissance*. Cambridge: Cambridge UP, 1991. 45–56.

Kuizenga, Donna. *Narrative Strategies in* La Princesse de Clèves. French Forum Monographs. Lexington: French Forum, 1976.

————. "*The Princesse de Clèves*: An Inimitable Model?" Henry 71–83.

Kusch, Manfred. "Narrative Technique and Cognitive Modes in *La Princesse de Clèves*." *Symposium* 30 (1976): 308–24.

La Bruyére, Jean de. *Les caractères*. Paris: Garnier-Flammarion, 1965.

Lafayette, Marie-Madeleine Pioche de la Vergne. *Correspondance*. Ed. André Beaunier. 2 vols. Paris: Gallimard, 1942.

————. *Histoire de Madame Henriette d'Angleterre*. Ed. Claudine Herrman. Paris: Femmes, 1979.

————. *Œuvres complètes*. Ed. Roger Duchêne. Paris: Bourin, 1990.

————. *Œuvres complètes de Mesdames de La Fayette, de Tencin et de Fontaines*. Ed. M. Auger. 4 vols. Paris: Lepetit, 1820.

————. *Œuvres de Madame de Lafayette*. Paris: Garnier, "Bibliothèque amusante," 1864.

————. *La Princesse de Clèves*. Ed. Antoine Adam. Paris: Garnier, 1966.

————. *La Princesse de Clèves*. Ed. Jean Mesnard. Paris: Garnier, 1996.

————. *The Princesse de Clèves*. Trans. Robin Buss. London: Penguin, 1992.

————. *The Princesse de Clèves*. Trans. Terence Cave. Oxford: Oxford UP, 1992.

————. *The Princess of Clèves*. Trans. Walter J. Cobb. New York: NAL, 1989.

————. *The Princess of Clèves*. Trans. John D. Lyons. New York: Norton, 1994.

————. *The Princess of Clèves*. Trans. Nancy Mitford. New York: Penguin, 1978.

————. *The Princess of Clèves*. Trans. Thomas Sergeant Perry. 2 vols. Boston: Little, 1891.

————. *Zaïde, Histoire espagnole*. Paris: Nizet, 1982.

Laugaa, Maurice. *Lectures de Madame de Lafayette*. Paris: Colin, 1971.

Leggewie, Robert, ed. *Anthologie de la littérature française*. 3rd ed. New York: Oxford UP, 1990.

Lever, Maurice. *Le roman français au dix-septième siècle*. Paris: PUF, 1983.

Lewis, W. H. *The Splendid Century*. New York: Morrow-Quill, 1978.

Lotringer, Sylvère. "La structuration romanesque." *Critique* 26 (1970): 498–529.

Lougee, Carolyn C. *Le Paradis des Femmes: Women, Salons, and Social Stratification in Seventeenth-Century France*. Princeton: Princeton UP, 1976.

Lyons, John D. *Exemplum: The Rhetoric of Example in Early Modern France and Italy*. Princeton: Princeton UP, 1989.

————. "Narration, Interpretation and Paradox: *La Princesse de Clèves*." *Romanic Review* 72 (1981): 383–400.

Lyons, John D., and Mary B. McKinley, eds. *Critical Tales: Studies of the* Heptaméron *and Early Modern Culture*. Philadelphia: U of Pennsylvania P, 1993.

Maclean, Ian. *Woman Triumphant: Feminism in French Literature, 1610–1652*. Oxford: Clarendon, 1977.

MacKinnon, Catharine A. *Only Words*. Cambridge: Harvard UP, 1993.

Madame de Lafayette, La Princesse de Montpensier, La Princesse de Clèves. *Littératures classiques* supp. Paris: Aux Amateurs de Livres, 1989.

Malandain, Pierre. "L'écriture de l'histoire dans *La Princesse de Clèves*." *Littérature* 36 (1979): 19–36.

————. *Madame de Lafayette:* La Princesse de Clèves. Paris: PUF, 1985.

Marin, Louis. *Le portrait du roi*. Paris: Minuit, 1981.

Marion, Marcel. *Dictionnaire des institutions de la France: XVIIe–XVIIIe siècles*. Paris: Picard, 1989.

May, Georges. *Le dilemme du roman au XVIIIe siècle*. Paris: PUF, 1963; New Haven: Yale UP, 1963.

McKinley, Mary B. "Telling Secrets: Sacramental Confession and Narrative Authority in the *Heptaméron*." Lyons and McKinley 146–71.

Merlin, Hélène. *Public et littérature en France au XVIIe siècle*. Paris: Belles Lettres, 1994.

Miller, Nancy K. "Emphasis Added: Plots and Plausibilities in Women's Fiction." *PMLA* 96 (1981): 36–48.

————. *Subject to Change: Reading Feminist Writing*. New York: Columbia UP, 1988.

Molière. *Les précieuses ridicules. Œuvres complètes*. Paris: Gallimard, 1971. 1: 247–87.

Mueller, Marlies. *Les idées politiques dans le roman héroïque de 1630 à 1670*. Harvard Studies in Romance Languages 40. Lexington: French Forum for the Department of Romance Langs. and Lits. of Harvard U, 1984.

Mulvey, Laura. "Visual Pleasure and Narrative Cinema." *Screen* 16.3 (1975): 6–18.

Navarre, Marguerite de. *The Heptameron*. Trans. P. A. Chilton. New York: Penguin, 1984.

———. *L'heptaméron*. Ed. Michel François. Paris: Classiques Garnier, 1967.

———. *L'heptaméron*. Ed. Simone de Reyff. Paris: Garnier-Flammarion, 1982.

Nelli, René. *L'érotique des troubadours*. Toulouse: Privat, 1963.

Niderst, Alain. La Princesse de Clèves: *Le roman paradoxal*. Paris: Larousse, 1973.

Painter, Sidney. *French Chivalry*. Ithaca: Great Seal–Cornell UP, 1961.

Pardailé-Galabrun, Annik. *The Birth of Intimacy: Privacy and Domestic Life in Early Modern Paris*. Trans. Jocelyn Phelps. Philadelphia: U of Pennsylvania P, 1991.

Pascal, Blaise. *Œuvres complètes*. Ed. Louis Lafuma. Paris: Seuil, 1963.

———. *Pensées*. Trans. A. J. Krailsheimer. Harmondsworth, Eng.: Penguin, 1966.

Paulsen, Michael G. *A Critical Analysis of de La Fayette's* La Princesse de Clèves *as a Royal Exemplary Novel: Kings, Queens, and Splendor*. Lewiston: Mellen, 1991.

Picard, Roger. *Les salons littéraires et la société française, 1610–1789*. New York: Brentano's, 1943.

Pingaud, Bernard. *Mme de Lafayette par elle-même*. Paris: Seuil, 1959. Rpt. as *Mme de Lafayette*. Paris: Seuil, 1978.

Princess Palatine [Elizabeth Charlotte, duchesse d'Orléans]. *Letters from Liselotte*. Trans. and ed. Maria Kroll. New York: McCall, 1970.

Roiphe, Katie. *The Morning After: Sex, Fear, and Feminism on Campus*. Boston: Little, Brown, 1993.

Rougemont, Denis de. *Love in the Western World*. New York: Schocken, 1990.

Rousset, Jean. *Forme et signification*. Paris: Corti, 1962.

Sarlet, Claudette. "A propos de Zaïde: Corps romanesque et corps social." *Rivista di letterature moderne e comparate* 39 (1986): 191–211.

Sartori, Eva Martin, and Dorothy Wynne Zimmerman, eds. *French Women Writers: A Bio-bibliographical Source Book*. Westport: Greenwood, 1991.

Schor, Naomi. "The Portrait of a Gentleman: Representing Men in (French) Women's Writing." *Misogyny, Misandry, and Misanthropy*. Ed. R. Howard Bloch and Frances Ferguson. Berkeley: U of California P, 1989. 113–33.

Scott, J. W. " 'Digressions' of *The Princesse de Clèves*." *French Studies* 11 (1957): 315–22.

———. *Madame de Lafayette:* La Princesse de Clèves. London: Grant, 1983.

Scudéry, Georges de. *Almahide ou L'esclave reine*. Paris: Courbé, 1660.

Scudéry, Madeleine de. *Clélie, Histoire romaine*. Paris: Courbé, 1654.

Sedgwick, Eve Kosofsky. *Between Men: English Literature and Male Homosocial Desire*. New York: Columbia UP, 1985.

Showalter, English. *The Evolution of the French Novel, 1641–1782*. Princeton: Princeton UP, 1972.

Stanton, Domna. *The Aristocrat as Art: A Study of the* Honnête Homme *and the Dandy in Seventeenth- and Nineteenth-Century French Literature*. New York: Columbia UP, 1980.

————. "The Ideal of *Repos* in Seventeenth-Century French Literature." *L'Esprit Créateur* 15.1–2 (1975): 79–104.

Stone, Harriet. *The Classical Model: Literature and Knowledge in Seventeenth-Century France*. Ithaca: Cornell UP, 1996.

————. "Exemplary Teaching in *La Princesse de Clèves*." *French Review* 62 (1988): 248–58.

Sweetser, Marie-Odile. "In Search of Selfhood: The Itinerary of the Princesse de Clèves." Henry 209–24.

————. "*La Princesse de Clèves* et son unité." *PMLA* 87 (1972): 483–91.

Thornton, Peter. *Seventeenth-Century Interior Decoration in England, France, and Holland*. New Haven: Yale UP, 1978.

Tiefenbrun, Susan W. "Big Women." *Romanic Review* 69.1–2 (1978): 34–47.

————. *A Structural Stylistic Analysis of* La Princesse de Clèves. The Hague: Mouton, 1976.

d'Urfé, Honoré. *L'Astrée*. Ed. Hughes Vaganay. Lyon: Masson, 1927.

Valincour, Jean Trousset de. "Letters to the Marquise ———— about *The Princess of Clèves*." Trans. John Lyons. Lafayette, *Princess* [Lyons] 123–36.

————. *Lettres à Madame la marquise de °°° sur le sujet de* La Princesse de Clèves. 1678. Ed. Jacques Chupeau. Tours: U de Tours, 1972.

Viala, Alain. *La naissance de l'écrivain*. Paris: Minuit, 1985.

Weinberg, Kurt. "The Lady and the Unicorn; or, M. de Nemours à Coulommiers: Enigma, Device, Blazon and Emblem in *La Princesse de Clèves*." *Euphorion* 71.4 (1977): 306–35.

Weinstein, Arnold. *Fictions of the Self: 1550–1800*. Princeton: Princeton UP, 1981.

Williams, Charles G. S. *Valincour: The Limits of* Honnêteté. Columbus: Ohio State UP, 1992.

Wimmers, Inge. *Poetics of Reading: Approaches to the Novel*. Princeton: Princeton UP, 1988.

Woodbridge, Kenneth. *Princely Gardens: The Origins and Development of the French Formal Style*. New York: Rizzoli, 1986.

INDEX